Charles Michel Alexandre de Brandt

Growth in the Knowledge of Our Lord

Meditations for every day: With appendix of additional subjects for each festival, day of retreat, etc., Volume 2

Charles Michel Alexandre de Brandt

Growth in the Knowledge of Our Lord
Meditations for every day: With appendix of additional subjects for each festival, day of retreat, etc., Volume 2

ISBN/EAN: 9783337256821

Printed in Europe, USA, Canada, Australia, Japan

"Growth in the knowledge of our Lord."

MEDITATIONS FOR EVERY DAY OF THE YEAR,

EXCLUSIVE OF THOSE FOR EACH FESTIVAL, DAY OF RETREAT, ETC.

Adapted from the French Original

OF THE

ABBÉ DE BRANDT,

BY A "DAUGHTER OF THE CROSS".

VOLUME II.

LONDON:
BURNS AND OATES.
1882.

Nihil obstat.

LAURENTIUS JOHNSON,
Censor Deputatus.

Imprimatur.

HENRICUS EDUARDUS,
Card. Archiep. Westmonast.

Die 21 Sept., 1882.

CONTENTS.

PRAYERS.

Our Father, Who art in Heaven; hallowed be Thy Name; Thy kingdom come; Thy Will be done on earth, as it is in Heaven. Give us this day our daily bread; and forgive us our trespasses, as we forgive them that trespass against us; and lead us not into temptation; but deliver us from evil. Amen.

Hail Mary, full of grace, the Lord is with thee, blessed art thou amongst women, and blessed is the Fruit of thy womb, Jesus. Holy Mary, Mother of God, pray for us sinners; now, and at the hour of our death. Amen.

Soul of Christ, sanctify me;
Body of Christ, save me;
Blood of Christ, inebriate me;
Water from the Side of Christ, wash me;
Passion of Christ, strengthen me;
O Good Jesus, hear me;
Within Thy Wounds hide me;
Suffer me not to be separated from Thee;
From the malignant enemy, defend me;

In the hour of my death, call me; and bid me come to Thee, that with Thy Angels and Saints I may praise Thee, for all eternity. Amen.

O God, Who didst teach the hearts of the faithful by the light of the Holy Spirit, grant that we may, by the gifts of the same Spirit, be always truly wise, and ever rejoice in His consolation. Through Jesus Christ our Lord. Amen.

Take, O Lord, and receive my memory, my understanding, my whole will: all that I have, all that I am, I give to Thee; to be made use of, according to Thy good pleasure. Give me only Thy love and Thy grace: with these I am rich enough.

O Jesus, living in Mary, come Thou and live in my soul;—by Thy Spirit of Holiness,—in the fulness of Thy Strength,—in the perfection of Thy Virtues,—in the power of Thy Truth,—and by communicating to me Thy mysterious Graces. Deliver me from all the enemies of my salvation; and govern me by Thy Spirit, to the glory of Thy Father. Amen.

O Loving Jesus! open Thy Sacred Heart to me, show me Its charms, unite me to It for ever: may every breath I draw, every beating of my heart, be so many proofs of my love; and remind Thee, that I belong entirely to Thee, O Lord. Receive graciously, O my God, the small amount of good I am able to do each day; so that I may bless Thee in this life, and praise Thee for all eternity. Amen.

O God, Who by the Immaculate Conception of the Blessed Virgin, didst prepare a fit habitation for Thy Son, we beseech Thee, that as by the foreseen Death of her same Son, Thou didst preserve her pure from all spot, so Thou wilt likewise grant, that by her intercession we may be made free from sin, and attain unto Thee. Through Jesus Christ our Lord. Amen.

We fly to thy patronage, O holy Mother of God; despise not our petitions in our necessities, but deliver us always from all dangers, O glorious and blessed Virgin.

MEDITATIONS.

Ninth of February.

The return of Jesus to Nazareth.

Jesus went down with them, and came to Nazareth: and was subject to them.—S. Luke ii.

I. Prelude.

Let us represent to ourselves the little House at Nazareth; —the small, poorly furnished rooms, and particularly the workshop, where Jesus laboured as a carpenter.

II. Prelude.

O Jesus, Model of true submission, give us a better understanding of Thy obedience, and grace to conform ours to Thine.

I. Point.

The obedience of Jesus should be the constant theme of our admiration.

He was subject to them. And then the holy Gospel is silent until thirty years of Jesus' Life have passed away!—

But these few words say very much : let us try to understand thoroughly the important lesson they convey. The Son of God came down from Heaven to procure the redemption of mankind ; to enlighten the world, and to instruct us concerning the way of salvation ; and yet He, the Second person of the Undivided Trinity, spent thirty years of His Life on earth in a state of absolute submission to Mary and to Joseph. What could be more incomprehensible ? He was subject to them ; He accomplished their will, as if it were of the first importance to do so ; as if He had no higher work to perform, than that of aiding Saint Joseph in carpentering,—and in attentively and lovingly assisting His Holy Mother in her homely duties : by His forethought anticipating their desires, and by His promptitude proving the willing readiness of His obedience. Our Saviour—to Whom each moment was precious—Who could do such mighty works—passed nearly all His Lifetime under the control of a poor artisan. What could He have done more astonishing to human reason ?—more instructive for us ?—more fitting to make us grasp the true idea of obedience ?—Do we love obedience as He did ?—Do we prefer it above all things ?—in order to practice it, do we give up our own gratification—pleasure—desires ? Let us entreat our Divine Master to make us real lovers of His spirit of obedience ; so shall we practice it as He did.

II. Point.

The obedience of Jesus should constantly be the object of our imitation.

It was the pride of man which our Lord came to condemn by His Example, even more than by His Words. Each of His steps leaves behind it, as it were, the impress of obedience, which we discover the more clearly, the more closely we follow Him. If we think of Him in the Home of His Childhood—of His Youth—and of the part He took in all the labour of the house, from His early years until He left its roof to fulfil His public Ministry, we may well ask ourselves, where our spirit of submission is? Does obedience demand of us that we should toil as Jesus toiled?—that we should perform lowly functions as Jesus did?—that we should serve those who may be, in some ways, inferior to us, as Jesus served Mary and Joseph?—If so, do we rejoice that we are permitted to share in the honour attached to submissiveness by God Himself?—The Great—the Wise—the All-powerful Creator served—obeyed His own creatures, and that in little ways;—for there was nothing great to be done in the carpenter's work-shop at Nazareth. Ought not this consideration to humble our proud wills? and cause it to be our delight, our nourishment, to do the Will of the Heavenly Father, manifested to us by those who are in authority over us?

Colloquy.

This lesson must needs be very necessary for me, O my Saviour, since Thou dost enforce it by Thy own example during the space of thirty years.—I humble myself at Thy Feet; and acknowledge all the imperfections of my obedience. I will endeavour to subject myself more entirely to Thy Will.—Make my heart like unto Thine, that it may esteem, love and practice this virtue of obedience,—indispensable in a Religious.

Resolution.

To obey my Heavenly Father, in the manner in which Jesus did so—at Nazareth.

THOUGHT FOR THE DAY.

My meat is to do the Will of Him that sent Me.

PRAYER.

Our Father, and Hail Mary.

Tenth of February.

The obedience of Jesus.

He was subject to them.—S. LUKE II.

I. PRELUDE.

Let us again picture to ourselves the little House at Nazareth;—the small, scantily furnished rooms;—and the carpenter's shop, in which Jesus worked.

II. PRELUDE.

Make us thoroughly to comprehend, O Saviour, the advantages and the merit of the excellent virtue of submissiveness; so that we may adopt it, as our own, more perfectly.

I. POINT.

Obedience is a sure and easy means of arriving at religious perfection.

Jesus, our Divine Saviour, would not have recommended so strongly, by His words and actions, the love of submission had He not known how manifold are the advantages which this ensures to such as exercise themselves in it.—The first of these advantages is—perfect security.—One who acts only by obedience is safe from illusion; God so loves this spirit of subjection that He will Himself take care to watch over every step of the child of obedience, directing each one towards the goal of eternal happiness.—Another advantage is this; that we shall avoid the sinfulness of self-will, of presumption, and of despair, if we place ourselves in the hands of those who receive their commission from God to guide others. The implacable enemy of our salvation hates nothing more than to see us thus awakened to the perception of his wiles; and escaping them by means of obediently following the counsel of our spiritual directors or superiors; and what satan hates most, must be that which is the very opposite to the sin to which he tempted our first parents. Obedience undoes his work. Saint Francis de Sales says: "Blessed are the obedient, because God never allows that they should go astray;—even if their rightly-appointed guides should err in their counsel, if there be no manifest sin, they do not err from the right path in obeying them; God may be in such a case trying and proving them; He knows how to bring good out of apparent evil".

II. Point.

The path of obedience is strewed thickly with merits.

God has prepared, for such as tread this path, rich rewards, both in time and eternity. Each step taken along its course, being the result of a supernatural motive, procures for the soul some further grace. Grace is the seed of glory; and that recompense which awaits the obedient is so great, that Saint Teresa (to whom our Lord made its measure known) remarks, "that she would not hesitate to endure all the torments of martyrdom, to obtain a single degree more of the special glory and happiness destined for the recompensing of the most ordinary actions—those most hidden—most insignificant—which had been ennobled by a lively motive of holy obedience." Reckon, if we can then, the the treasures of merit which are amassed in a single day by one who does nothing save by obedience, and whose every action, even the least, bears the impress of this excellent virtue. These riches are put in our way: let us accept the opportunities of winning them, with thankfulness.

Colloquy.

O Jesus, by the recollection of Thy Life at Nazareth, make me to understand the excellence of an entire submission of my own will:—increase in me the esteem and love of this virtue of obedience. May I make it the motive of all I do, so that I may act and speak in accordance with its promptings; thus pleasing Thee, and rendering myself worthy of an eternal reward.

Resolution.

To fulfil all my duties in the spirit of obedience.

Thought for the Day.

He was subject to them.

Prayer.

Take, O Lord, and receive.

Eleventh of February.

As Jesus advanced in age, His wisdom increased.

And Jesus advanced in wisdom and age, and grace with God and men.—S. Luke ii.

I. Prelude.

Let us look within the Home of the Holy Family.

II. Prelude.

Grant, O Saviour, that like Thee, we may increase in true wisdom, and be strengthened in grace, before God and man.

I. Point.

We should, each day, grow in holiness.

In saying that Jesus advanced in wisdom and in grace, as well as in age, the Holy Ghost would have us to understand that the Son of God manifested progressively that fulness of grace and of wisdom which He, in fact, possessed from the first moment of His Incarnation. From this we may learn that we must not stop in the path of perfection, but *he that is holy, let him be sanctified still.*—And where are we? Our progress in the ways of God,—the sanctity required by our profession,—is it as *a shining light, going forwards and increasing, even to the perfect day?* Are we becoming more disengaged from the ideas, the customs, the allurements of the world? Have we lately acquired a greater love of God? more fervour?—more sincerity?—more self-forgetfulness? As we advance in years is there more solidity and generosity in the virtues we practise? Let us make a serious examen of conscience on this subject of spiritual progress; for we ought to be very sure that (after the example of Jesus) we are advancing every day in grace and perfection.—Should there not be a perceptible difference between those who have just begun to tread in the path of religious perfection, and such as have long since made profession of serving God within the cloister?—Let none think they can stand still;—if we would not retrograde we must advance.

II. Point.

We ought to grow each day in virtue—before God, and before men.

We must increase in grace and in wisdom before God, that is to say, we are not to rest contented with an outward appearance of sanctity: God, Who trieth the hearts, can only be glorified by solid virtue.—Words—appearance—a certain exterior reserve may deceive man, but not God, Who sees if the thoughts are holy,—if the desires, the sentiments of the heart are pure and upright. We should be growing in grace day by day, so that we may approach more closely—as closely as possible—to the perfection of God Himself. *Be you therefore perfect, as also your Heavenly Father is perfect.*—We should also advance in virtue before men, because it is one of our chief duties to edify others. Even the world, all perverse as it is, expects to find an increasing holiness in those who make profession of religion; and amongst such as do, like ourselves, openly make this profession, what sincerity of desire should there not be, *to let the light of our good example so shine before men that they may glorify our Father, Who is in Heaven.* The cause that often so little progress is made, and perfection so seldom attained is this: almost always the dictates of nature and human reasoning are listened to and followed; and we will be guided so little, or not at all, by the Holy Spirit, Whose office it is to enlighten the understanding and to direct the will. However well human reason and good sense may help us to form a right judgment, they are powerless in themselves (if unaccompanied by the sevenfold gifts of the Holy Ghost) to produce religious perfection. Let us then see if, before God, our progress in holiness is real; if our neighbour has cause to be edified more and more by our good example.

Colloquy.

O Saviour, Thou hast poured out upon me Thy benefits, and placed me by Thy mercy in such a condition of life that I may find opportunities of advancing each day in the way of perfection; and yet how little have I profited by these spiritual advantages.—What ought I not to do, to make reparation for all my ingratitude?—to cause Thee, O Jesus, to forget it? It seems to me that I am less ready to sacrifice myself, less fervent in my prayers, less zealous in the discharge of my duties than formerly.—I will keep within the little House at Nazareth, and there learn of Thee how to advance in wisdom and grace.

Resolution.

I will try to serve God with somewhat of my first fervour, —begging Him to renew it within me.

Thought for the Day.

Going forwards and increasing, even to perfect day.

Prayer.

Soul of Christ.

Twelfth of February.

Jesus leads a hidden life in Nazareth.

Jesus dwelt in a city called Nazareth: that it might be fulfilled which was said by the prophets: That he shall be called a Nazarite.—S. Matt. ii.

I. Prelude.

Let us make our meditation within the little Home of the Holy Family.

II. Prelude.

O Jesus, make our hearts conformable to thy Divine Heart by a preference for an ordinary manner of life;—and by the practice of hidden virtues.

I. Point.

Beneath the ordinary exterior life, led by our Lord for thirty years, His perfections are concealed.

In meditating again to-day on the conduct of Jesus at Nazareth, we see that nothing remarkable appeared in His words or His actions.—When the time should arrive for Him to speak and teach openly, He would do so; but until then He would share the quiet, ordinary life of His Parents. He prayed—He worked with His Hands—He took His repasts—His rest, like other men; but in all this He was most pleasing in the Sight of the Celestial Father, because He did in the most perfect manner the most ordinary duties of life.—And this is what God wills:—in this consists that real excellence which God approves,—and the perfection of every condition, whether high or low.—He who does what God asks of Him, and does it well, the same is already perfect.—How important is it for us to take hold of this lesson: and to remember that we can acquire perfection, if we will only take pains to do well all—even the least duties of our calling, to do them out of love for God and with a view to please Him alone. We should ask Him (Who only can do this) to make us understand the excellence of a simple ordinary life; this being the shortest and easiest road to holiness and true happiness.

II. Point.

We should imitate the life Jesus led when He was at home in Nazareth.

Jesus, buried in retirement, spending His days in prayer and other daily duties, regulating His actions by the law of obedience, condemns the conduct of those who imagine that they should seek for sanctity outside the ordinary duties of their vocation. We find that some disturb good order by thinking that they ought to work when it is the hour for prayer; or they wish to pray when it is the time for repose; but this is not to act as Jesus acted. He did all things at the right time, and in the most perfect manner. Can we not in spirit dwell with Jesus, Mary and Joseph? so that we may the better observe the influence that the Presence of Jesus should have over all our actions, our words, our senses?—There would then be no want of regularity,—no ostentation,—no pretention,—no negligence,—no hasty words,—no discontent,—no love of ease,—nothing unmannerly.—We can still watch His actions.—Their one aim was to glorify unceasingly His Father in Heaven, and to procure the salvation of men.—To repair the Divine glory, which had been outraged by sin, and to augment the treasure of grace He was preparing for us, He multiplied His acts of virtue, even in the smallest details of His Life. He was always intimately united to God the Father; doing all things for love of Him, and in conformity with His holy Will.

Colloquy.

O my Jesus, how different is my daily life from what Thine was at Nazareth; and yet if I only studied it more diligently, more constantly, might I not make my actions a reflection of Thine own? O give me grace to keep near to Thyself, when engaged in the ordinary duties of my every-day life, so that they too may merit the approval of God, and be by Him rewarded. O Mary, O Joseph, witnessess of the effects of the hidden life of Jesus, ask of Him, for me, the grace to copy it better.

Resolution.

To avoid all that may draw attention to myself.

Thought for the Day.

And the world knew Him not.

Prayer.

O Jesus, living in Mary.

Thirteenth of February.

The Holy Family.

They had but one heart and one soul.—ACTS IV.

I. PRELUDE.

Let us enter silently into the quiet House at Nazareth, there to contemplate that which is taking place. We see Jesus, Mary and Joseph.

II. PRELUDE.

In contemplating the Holy Family—perfect model of a religious household—let us observe all that may speak to us of the holy life of each member of it.

I. POINT.

The spirit of unity existing in the Holy Family.

What beautiful harmony we find in the family life of Jesus, Mary and Joseph.—Three hearts—so pure—so holy—were united in loving,—adoring,—serving God perfectly. We first contemplate Jesus :—His bearing was noble and condescending,—His aspect kind,—His demeanour sedate,—His words were full of humility and peaceableness,—He was continually attentive to do the will of His Parents ; His whole Exterior forms a picture which we, as religious persons, should love to gaze upon. On the holy Face of Jesus there was never the least trace of anxiety nor trouble. It was a true index of that calmness and recollection which had such absolute possession of His Soul. Whether He spoke—whether He kept silence—at all times—He was gentle, kind, and thoughtful for others. How edifying and pleasant would it be to live in our company, if we, each one of us, resembled Jesus; then we should draw souls to God, —we should rejoice the hearts of those with whom we come into contact.—And if we now turn our attention to Mary and Joseph. In her features we see pourtrayed the most angelic qualities of heart and mind. In Saint Joseph we observe a quiet cheerfulness, and assiduity in his work; both of them live in the most intimate union with Jesus. The slightest cloud of misunderstanding never appeared to disturb the tranquillity of their lowly dwelling, there were no vexations,—no indiscreet words. Full of pure love, Jesus, Mary and Joseph formed a trinity on earth, which imaged forth the Holy Undivided Trinity of Heaven.

II. POINT.

The spirit of love which influenced the Holy Family.

Let us further meditate upon the admirable regularity and tender charity which reigned in the house of Joseph, to whom Jesus and Mary were subject, as being the head of this saintly household. What respect is paid to him; what deference!—and then what mutual care the one for the other, and sincere cordiality. We may readily imagine how the wishes and needs of one another were discovered—anticipated—and provided for; their charity being ingenious and active, and exercised with equal warmth of affection and calm unobtrusiveness. Jesus loved His Mother, and the venerable Joseph:—the holy patriarch and Mary loved Jesus:—and with what a pure unselfish love!—So should it be in a religious community; and so would it be, if through sentiments of respect and charity *we were subject, one to another, in the fear of Christ.* There should exist no other rivalry than that of being the most thoughtful for others,—the most unobtrusive,—the most gentle,—the most humble. If, as in the Holy Family, delicacy of feeling, and mildness of manner constituted the charm of our house,—if piety formed its riches, and the good pleasure of God its happiness,—if it were only so, we should find reigning amongst us, that gentle peace—that divine unity—that religious calm, which are infallible signs of the Presence of Jesus. Does He live amongst us?

Colloquy.

O noble and holy Family, I could not grow weary of admiring thy perfections, so attractive do I find them! I see before me the perfect model of community-life. Discover to me and to all around me, more and more, the beauty—the holiness—the advantages—the excellence of this life; that we may strive to revive amongst ourselves the sublime virtues which grew so luxuriantly in the abode of Jesus, Mary and Joseph.

Resolution.

I will make it my delight to serve and please all with whom I live, imitating the social virtues of the Holy Family.

Thought for the Day.

They had but one heart and one soul.

Prayer.

O Jesus, living in Mary.

Fourteenth of February.

The Baptism of Jesus Christ.

Jesus came from Nazareth of Galilee, and was baptised by John in the Jordan.—S. Mark i.

I. Prelude.

Let us go in spirit to the banks of the River Jordan; and there see Jesus amongst the crowds of people who came thither to receive baptism at the hands of Saint John.

II. Prelude.

O Divine Saviour, Who didst thus place Thyself amongst sinners, to teach us not to seek for any distinction, grant that the knowledge of our unworthiness, and of our misery may humble us deeply; and make us to seek rather to be considered as the last and the least of all.

I. Point.

Jesus begins His Public Life by practising humility.

Jesus leaves His home.—After having there practised, during the space of thirty years, all the virtues he proposed to teach openly during the remaining three years of His Life, He wills at length, according to the designs of the Heavenly Father, to begin His important Mission, and to appear for the first time in public. By what act does the Divine Saviour enter upon this new career, which is set before Him? He goes from the holy companionship of

Mary to take His place amongst sinners, and mingling in the crowd that surrounds Saint John, He asks of him the baptism of repentance. What an act of humility on the part of the Saint of saints!—He Who came to destroy sin, appeared to take upon Him the form of a sinner: He consented to pass for such. Until now, He had been concealed from the world; He begins to make Himself known to it, but under the guise of a penitent. How then will He be recognised as the Messias?—the Son of God?—the Saviour?—Truly the thoughts of God are different from those of men.—Jesus abases Himself;—He seeks not His own glory;—therefore His Father is waiting only for the right moment, to proclaim that He is His Own Beloved Son. Let us take care to profit by the first lesson Jesus gives us in His public Life; and to learn from Him the true means of drawing down upon us God's notice and approval. Yes! if we humble ourselves, and have no fear of appearing insignificant, full of defects, God—Who loves the humble, will bless us and our works.

II. Point,

We ought to begin, and maintain in ourselves, the spiritual life, by the exercise of humility.

If Jesus, the very Essence of sanctity, has willed for our instruction to prelude His evangelical career by a long period of abnegation; if the first step He took in that career was an act of profound humility, what humiliations should not they impose on themselves who aspire to the perfection of a religious life? These humiliations may lower us in the esteem of the world, and make us little in the eyes of men, but they raise us in the esteem of God. He looks down with pleasure on the true disciples of His Divine Son,—in being which our real glory consists. On occasions when we may prove our humility, we should consider that if men despise, censure, or ridicule us, before God we are exalted by the very means which lower us in their sight.—Jesus Christ Himself takes delight in seeing us wear His livery; the Angels envy us this honour. The victory the Saviour gained over the devil and the world, is the victory of humility over pride; and it is only with the same weapons that we can likewise triumph. If the Son of God, having taken the likeness of man, judged it therefore necessary to perform an act of open penance, in order *to fulfil all justice*, what does not this same justice demand of those who should participate in the holiness of the Saviour, and yet are sullied by many sins, and subject to many defects. It little becomes us to seek to pass for saints, when the Saint of saints willed to appear as a sinner.

Colloquy.

O my Saviour, how does Thy example confound my pretensions! When I see Thee humbly coming to ask for Baptism, amongst those who stood in actual need of it, placing Thyself in the throng with the guilty, I am ashamed of my unjustly claiming respect and esteem. I take pains to hide my weakness, and cover my failings with excuses. I understand how the sight of the sanctity and self-abasement united in Thy Divine Person, must have well pleased Thy Heavenly Father. Oh! that I might learn to please God in the same way that Jesus did.

Resolution.

I will keep before my mind the thought of my unworthiness.

THOUGHT FOR THE DAY.

Lamb of God, Who takest away the sins of the world, have mercy on me.

PRAYER.

Our Father, and Hail Mary.

Fifteenth of February.

Jesus,—the Beloved Son of the Father.

Thou art My Beloved Son, in Whom I am well pleased.—S. MATT. III.

I. PRELUDE.

Let us see Jesus, coming to be baptised: And the heavens opening. The Holy Ghost descends in a bodily shape, as a dove, upon Him; we hear a Voice, saying: *This is my Beloved Son, in Whom I am well pleased.*

II. PRELUDE.

O Adorable Jesus, Who didst manifest Thyself at length to the world, discover Thyself to us also; and grant that we may attach ourselves to Thee as the only object worthy of our affections.

I. POINT.

Jesus, the Beloved Son of the Father, is given to us.

God, the Father, in proclaiming Jesus as the Object of

His divine complacency, willed to call the attention of all the world to His Son, that He might be glorified. In the carrying out of this purpose, the proclamation is also made that *God is Charity; and hath so loved the world, as to give His Only Begotten Son.* It was not an Angel—not a Prince of His royal Court, whom He sent to instruct and to save us; from Heaven He speaks to earth and tells the inhabitants thereof that *He Who now cometh up out of the water*, is the God-Man, in Whom He is well pleased. Had we been present at that wondrous scene, what would have been our feelings? Should we not have poured forth our love and veneration at His Sacred Feet, and have protested that we would follow Him even unto death? Then let us do so now;—and whilst we are engaged in showing Him, Whom God has sent, every mark of reverence and affection, let us, in Him and through Him, praise and thank His Father and ours, for thus openly declaring that the Divine Nature and human nature are united in our Lord Jesus Christ.

II. Point.

Jesus, the Well-beloved Son of God, is worthy of all our love.

Who is more worthy to fill our hearts than Jesus? One with the Father, He possesses all the perfections of the Divinity, the fulness of these dwell within Him *Who is beautiful above the sons of men: grace is poured abroad in His Lips.* In His Sacred Person He was gentle, sedate, dignified. Now in Heaven His glorified Humanity is the admiration, the delight of those who encircle Him. And He loves us with an eternal charity; unchangeable as Himself. He came to earth to instruct us, to point out to us the way which conducts to endless happiness, and to merit this, for us, by His Death. During His public Life, He proved Himself to be the Good Master, and at the same time the Perfect Example. Our poor hearts, even at the best, are so incapable of loving Him as He deserves, but could we not love Him better if we got clear of the miserable slavery of self-love? We should then serve Him purely for love of Himself; and with the simple desire of pleasing Him alone. The consideration of His poor, laborious Life,—the persecutions and sorrowful Death He endured, should surely dispose our hearts to entertain a greater devotion towards Him, Who is the Well-beloved Son of the Eternal King.

Colloquy.

O my God, how good Thou art to have given Thy Divine Son, not only to live on earth as my Example, and to die on the Cross as my Saviour, but also to be the Lover of my soul, my Celestial Bridegroom. All praise, all glory be to Thee, O Lord! Make me to appreciate more and more the happiness of belonging to Jesus, may I love Him better and imitate His virtues more perfectly.

Resolution.

To strive to love Jesus more myself, and to win for Him the love of others.

Thought for the Day.

This is My Beloved Son, in Whom I am well pleased.

Prayer.

Our Father, and Hail Mary.

Sixteenth of February.

Jesus retires into the desert. He is tempted by the devil.

Jesus returned from the Jordan; and was led by the Spirit into the desert, for the space of forty days.—S. Luke iv.

I. Prelude.

Let us go into the desert with our Lord. He is about to lay the foundations of the penitential life, which should always accompany the apostolic life.

II. Prelude.

O Divine Master, grant that we may learn from Thee how to prepare aright for the performing of our works of charity; and how to resist the enemies of our salvation.

I. Point.

It was in retreat, and by prayer and mortification that Jesus made His preparation for His evangelical labours.

Our Divine Lord had no need at all to prepare for His public Life; but He desired to make it clear to those whom He would hereafter associate with Himself in the important work of saving souls, that they must qualify themselves for their mission. That was why, following the movements of the Holy Ghost, Jesus retired into the desert; and during forty days and forty nights remained in perfect solitude, and discoursed in prayer, with His Father, on that most momentous subject—the redemption of the world. To His continual prayer He added austere penance. These are the duties

He has traced out for apostolic men,—for all who work for Him. In the exercises of retreat, in the time of preparation for active labours, or renewal of the forces of our souls, we see how necessary it is to be penetrated with the spirit of our Lord; and the thought of what the loss must be to such as badly employ these seasons of retirement, is brought home to each one, who has enjoyed the privilege of following Jesus into the desert. Have we spent such seasons near Him in recollection and fervour? laying in a store of grace to help us to persevere amidst all the difficulties and temptations we may be called upon to encounter for Jesus' sake.

II. Point.

Our Saviour, in permitting the devil to tempt Him, proves that He compassionates our weakness, and would have us compassionate that of others.

Jesus Christ, having clothed Himself with our feeble degraded nature, willed to submit Himself to all its miseries, —sin only exempted. He, full of pity, knew how much temptation afflicts souls that fear to offend God; He subjected Himself to it, to show that neither sanctity of life, nor the solitude of the desert can shelter us from the attacks of the enemy of our salvation:—hence, when tried by them, we should be neither troubled nor discouraged, but have recourse to the Victor over Satan, with entire confidence. He would teach us also that no temptation can sully the soul that resists it;—it left Him untroubled, notwithstanding the artifices of the evil one; on the contrary the soul becomes by this means strengthened in virtue. That we may understand how needless are our alarms, even should the temptations be most painful, Jesus permitted the devil to approach, to handle His Sacred Body, and to transport It from one place to another. The consideration of Jesus in the desert, led there by the Spirit to be tempted, affords us much valuable instruction. By putting it into practice we shall render ourselves strong in His strength; and, in meeting temptation, know how to turn to His Sacred Heart for shelter and safety.

Colloquy.

I adore Thee, O Jesus, Source of all holiness and strength. I thank Thee for having condescended to subject Thyself to my weakness, so as to inspire me with courage to overcome it. Remembering the numberless combats, the continual warfare, in which Thy faithful servants—Thy best friends have been engaged, I will, instead of being discomfited by temptation, make it a subject of joy. In coming off victorious over my enemy, may I trust in Thy strength alone for the future, whilst I thank Thee for having upheld me by Thy grace; without which I should utterly fall.

Resolution.

I will watch against the attacks of my spiritual foe, and pray to be delivered out of temptation.

Thought for the Day.

Jesus was led by the Spirit into the desert to be tempted.

Prayer.

Our Father, and Hail Mary.

Seventeenth of February.

Jesus—the Lamb of God.

The next day John saw J*esus coming to him, and he saith: Behold the Lamb of God; behold Him Who taketh away the sins of the world.*—S. John i.

I. Prelude.

We see how full of joy Saint John-the-Baptist was, when he perceived Jesus coming to him: he pointed Him out to all those who were standing by.

II. Prelude.

O Divine Lamb of God, the very sight of Whom rejoiced Thy holy Precursor, discover to our souls Thy infinite goodness, that they may be attached entirely to Thee.

I. Point.

Jesus is called the Lamb, on account of His gentleness.

Gentleness and meekness were among the chief traits, pointed out by the prophets, which should characterise the Messias. Thus Isaias saith: He shall not cry, neither shall His Voice be heard abroad: the bruised reed He shall not break, and the smoking flax He shall not quench. How fully was the prophecy accomplished; for Jesus went about doing good,—preferring mercy to judgment,—practising patience and goodness towards sinners, whose conversion He desired. He was justly likened to a Lamb by reason of His innocence—His docility—His obedience. The Lamb of infinite value, unspotted and undefiled, sent on earth to be sacrificed, that by His Precious Blood men might be washed from their sins; sent to offer them a remedy for all their ills, and to procure for them an abundance of that good which is eternal. It was at the sight of this inexhaustible Source of all spiritual riches that Saint John rejoiced:—it was a renewal of that joy which he had experienced before his birth.—He loses no time in making Him known, directly he finds himself in the Presence of his Lord. Do we feel the same joy when we see Him before us, under the Veil of the Most Blessed Sacrament? With what love and respect ought we to hear the words of the Priest: *Behold the Lamb of God, Who taketh away the sins of the world.* Does His Presence fill us with the desire to make Him known to others, and cause us to pray for the extension of the knowledge of His Love in their hearts?

II. Point.

They who labour for the salvation of souls should win them to God by gentleness and goodness.

Let us consider how greatly gentleness and kindness assist, by their power and attractiveness, to gain hearts. Scarcely had Saint John announced Jesus as *the Lamb of God, Who taketh away the sins of the world*, when two of his own disciples leave him to follow the Lamb withersoever He should lead them. The very Title He bore captivated their hearts; a sacred attraction drew them after Him; they wished to know Him, and to enjoy His society. The effects of the gentle goodness which characterised our Lord, were extraordinary; often He, Who was holiness itself, was surrounded by sinners, whom He received with friendliness and instructed with simple kindness. It is not science, nor eloquence, nor talent, nor other human means, which render us fitting instruments to procure the salvation of souls;—but sanctity of life—a union with God—manifested by our charity, patience, and gentleness. These form the shortest, the easiest road into hearts; how many we should gain for God, how much glory we should procure Him, if we resembled the Divine Lamb in His patience and meekness. Perhaps we displease Him by the discouraging hardness of our manner, or the severity of our words, of our rebukes: if it be so, let us watch over ourselves, and keeping in view the Lamb of God, do and speak as He would have done.

Colloquy.

Even in the presence of Thy cruel tormentors, O Jesus, *Thou wast as a Lamb before its shearers;* after dealing so gently with others Thou wast Thyself so cruelly treated; Thou wast the Lamb of God, Whose Sacrifice, as such, had to be consummated, and Thou didst not open Thy Mouth. Under whatever aspect I see Thee—whether attracting Thy disciples to follow Thee—giving proofs of Thy meekness in Thy dealings with the sinful, the afflicted—or suffering patiently as a Victim of expiation, I must yield to Thy gentle influence. *Lamb of God, Who takest away the sins of the world, grant me Thy peace.*

Resolution.

To sacrifice for Jesus' sake all that is opposed to gentleness and kindness.

Thought for the Day.

Behold Him Who taketh away the sins of the world.

Prayer.

O Loving Jesus.

Nineteenth of February.

Jesus casts out the profaners of the Temple.

Take these things hence, and make not the House of my Father a house of traffic.—S. JOHN II.

I. PRELUDE.

We see before us Jesus, Who embodied in Himself all gentleness and forbearance, driving out those from the Temple who were profaning it.

II. PRELUDE.

Thou wast, O Saviour, so zealous for the glory of Thy Father that Thou couldst not suffer the violation of the purity of His Temple: inspire us with a like zeal, with regard to Thy material Temples; and also to preserve the sanctity of our bodies, the living Temples in which Thou dost deign to dwell.

I. POINT.

God makes our heart His Sanctuary.

Our faith concerning the Presence of Jesus in our churches is firm and unchangeable, and we love to offer to our Divine Master, Who willingly dwells in them, our homage of adoration, gratitude and love. But are we always careful to prove our belief by a reverent behaviour before the Tabernacle, within which Jesus reposes? The sellers were in the outer courts only, of the Temple; and they were selling what would be offered in sacrifice therein, and yet our Lord shewed more severity in His zeal for His Father's glory on this occasion than perhaps on any other. Let us bear this in mind to increase and confirm in ourselves a sense of awe and reverence for the Majesty of God, Who would not have even the surroundings of His Temple used for ordinary purposes. Let us guard our Holy of holies, not only from profanity, but from the slightest mark of disrespect. Does our faith also often remind us that God lives also in us? in our bodies, and in our souls, which form a Sanctuary for the Divinity. *Know you not that you are the temple of God, and that the Spirit of God dwelleth in you?* says Saint Paul. One should often repeat to one's-self,—"I am the dwelling-place of God—He is within me—He takes pleasure in being there, and in being thus intimately united with me". With this thought ever before us, how can we remain cold and indifferent in the Presence of our Divine Guest? Should it not cause our hearts to rejoice unceasingly? to turn towards Him with loving attention? and to fear nothing so much as to lose Him?

II. Point.

How zealously we should preserve personal holiness.

The zeal of Thy House hath eaten Me up. If it would grieve us deeply to witness any profanation of the sacred vessels, any irreverences committed in our Churches,—if we are happy to see our Altars adorned with all that is most beautiful, in honour of Him Who dwelleth there, with what carefulness should we not avoid the smallest fault which could tarnish the sanctity of our bodies, those sacred tabernacles which God inhabits? *Glorify God and bear God in your body.* With what fervour ought we not to endeavour to embellish these living temples, and to adorn them with all those virtues, which may render them pleasing to Him? Let us drive away far from us, with the scourge of mortification, all sensuality, vanity, and avarice, the spirit of the world, and all that might profane or violate the abode of the Spirit of God.

Colloquy.

O my God, Thou dost make of me, unworthy as I am of this high honour, a temple in which Thou wilt dwell. How often should I recall this consoling thought, how much should I rejoice in the assurance that Thy Spirit is within me, and that I am not my own!—May I be more careful to adorn Thy sanctuary with these virtues in which Thou dost take delight, making in my heart a tabernacle for Thee, out of the pure gold of charity.

Resolution.

To avoid the least faults, because they tarnish the tabernacle of the Thrice-holy God.

Thought for the Day.

Know you not that you are the temple of God, and that the Spirit of God dwelleth in you?

Prayer.

O Jesus, living in Mary.

Twentieth of February.

Guidance of the Holy Spirit.

The Spirit breatheth where He will; and thou hearest His Voice, but thou knowest not whence He cometh, or whither He goeth.—As Moses lifted up the serpent in the desert, so must the Son of Man be lifted up; that whosoever believeth in Him, may not perish, but may have life everlasting.—ST. JOHN III.

I. PRELUDE.

Let us represent to ourselves that scene in our Lord's Life, when Nicodemus, a ruler of the Jews, comes into His Presence; and receives His instructions with respectful attention.

II. PRELUDE.

Grant, O Lord, that we may ever be obedient to the Voice of the Holy Spirit; so that we may merit to enjoy the precious advantages of a truly spiritual life.

I. POINT.

It is the Holy Ghost Who causes us to advance in the spiritual life.

After having revealed to Nicodemus the mystery of the new life received in Baptism, our Divine Lord continues His instruction, and unfolds further secrets of the spiritual life. We may listen also to these heavenly lessons, which are particularly addressed to those who are called to a higher degree of perfection. *The Spirit breatheth where He will; and thou hearest His Voice, but thou knowest not whence He cometh, or whither He goeth.* The Voice of the Spirit speaks the divine language of holy inspiration and of the attraction of grace. It cannot make itself heard in restless souls, nor by those who seldom or never look within; nor occupy themselves with the Divine Guest. He seeks a heart which is recollected, attentive, and desirous of knowing the good pleasure of God. —*Thou knowest not whence He cometh.* Often this Voice is recognised after a fervent Communion—a pious reading—an instruction attentively heard—a meditation well made;—but at other times His visit is quite sudden—unforeseen. It may be in the form of a striking example—an edifying word, which awakens in us holy thoughts, and as with a flash of light illuminates our understanding. *Thou knowest not whither He goeth.* An inspiration, faithfully followed, often opens the door to a sequence of graces, which render progress in goodness both easy and rapid. How watchful should we be over ourselves, how recollected, how attentive to the movements of the Holy Spirit! How prompt to correspond to them also! for the moments of His special visits are most precious, but often of short duration.

II. Point.

Jesus proceeds to speak to Nicodemus of the end for which He Himself came into the world.

After having spoken of the office of the Holy Spirit and the necessity of Baptism, our Lord alludes to His own Mission, and His Death upon the Tree. From the stream of grace imparted to us by the operation of the Holy Ghost in our souls, He leads the mind of His disciple up to its Source—the Cross:—on it He is to be lifted up, so that all men being drawn to Him, and *believing in Him, may not perish but have everlasting life.* Let us place ourselves at His Feet, as He continues His instruction, and meditate upon the way in which, after the children of Israel in the desert had offended God by their ingratitude, they were saved from the punishment of death, in looking at the brazen serpent which Moses set up for a sign: a figure of Jesus Crucified.—When we are suffering from the wounds inflicted by sin, from the effects of the corruption of nature, do we look up to the Cross, with faith in the merits of the Passion and Death of Him Who hung upon it, in the desert of the world? The redemption of mankind, by God the Son, and his sanctification by God the Holy Ghost, were the mysteries revealed to Nicodemus, who came to Jesus by night. He made known to him, that *light had come into the world* in Himself; and that it would be perpetuated by the Spirit of Truth, Who should enlighten the Church, and guide Her into all truth.

Colloquy.

I thank Thee, O God, that in Holy Baptism, I have been born again of water and of the Holy Ghost: may He enlighten me by His grace and guide me by His Holy inspirations, and teach me all truth. I thank Thee that Thou, O Father, didst send Thy Only-Begotten Son into the world; may I keep near His Cross, and looking continually up to Him, be saved from the punishment I deserve, being cleansed from my sins in His most Precious Blood.

Resolution.

To be faithful to good inspirations, out of love and gratitude towards God.

THOUGHT FOR THE DAY.

The Spirit breatheth where He will, and Thou hearest His Voice.

PRAYER.

Our Father, and Hail Mary.

Twenty-first of February.

Distinctive characteristics of true zeal.

JESUS and His disciples came into the land of Judea; and baptised: John also was baptising in the Jordan: His disciples came and said to him: Rabbi, He that was with thee beyond the Jordan, to Whom thou gavest testimony, behold He baptiseth, and all men come to Him: John said: He must increase, but I must decrease.—S. JOHN III.

I. PRELUDE.

We represent to ourselves the towns and villages of Judea; where the Divine Saviour caused His converts to be baptised, by the hands of His Disciples.

II. PRELUDE.

Give us grace, O Lord, to despise ourselves, and seek only the advancement of Thy glory in all things.

I. POINT.

True zeal, like that of Saint John-the-Baptist, should be pure, simple, and disinterested.

We perceive how the disciples of Saint John, jealous for the honour of their master, could not see without anxiety that Jesus also was giving Baptism, and drawing to Himself the respect and confidence of the people. This natural feeling is but too common in persons, whose zeal is not yet sufficiently free from all selfishness; they do not relish the good that is done by others,—it even irritates them, and at times, under some specious pretext, they go so far as to oppose it.—All this arises from secret pride, which makes one believe that one is seeking only God's glory; and all the while there is only self-seeking, and self-glorification. Why, for instance, is it that those whom we succeed in some employment—some charge, have, nearly always, as we imagine, left fallow the ground they should have cultivated with care? Why do the good works of such an one, or the pious undertaking of another, appear, in our eyes, to be presumptuous or imprudent? Is it not because our zeal does not resemble Saint John's? is it not yet pure—simple—disinterested. If we were faithful friends of the Bridegroom, we should rejoice with unfeigned joy whenever, and by whomsoever His glory is advanced; instead of being envious of the success others procure Him, we should be truly glad. Let the means, and the instruments made use of, be what they may, it should delight our hearts to know that His power on the earth is on the increase. Is there not work enough in the wide field of this world for all? is there not in it variety enough, so that every capacity may find scope for its zeal and energy?

II. Point.

The way to render our zeal productive of good results.

Jesus must increase in us, and self must decrease. If we

would be successful in labours undertaken for God's glory and the salvation of souls, we must free ourselves from natural inclinations, and be filled with the spirit of God.—We are leaning perhaps on our own resources—our diligence—our constancy—and not on God's help alone: we feel pained if surpassed by others, or if our endeavours fail: if such be the case, our labour will be in vain in His Sight, Who weigheth our motives. God leaves such workers to work alone; how can they do any real good? But if, on the contrary, we mistrust our own powers, and depend solely on Divine assistance,—if we deny our natural tendencies so far as to be ready to suffer any humiliation, and to accept any sacrifice which may promote the honour and glory of God, keeping back no share of these for ourselves, then the empire Jesus has over our hearts is increasing. We shall be powerfully aided by His grace, and our labours will be productive of abundant fruits of salvation.

Colloquy.

My God, it is assuredly a proof of true zeal, and of being a faithful friend of the Bridegroom, to abase one's self as did Saint John-the-Baptist; so that the honour of Him, Who should be preferred before himself, might be upheld. I desire, after this example, to attribute to myself no good that I may do, but refer it to the Divine Author of all good: —so may Jesus Christ increase in me, whilst I grow in the knowledge of His love.

Resolution.

I will mistrust myself; and never say anything to depreciate the meritorious actions of others.

THOUGHT FOR THE DAY.

He must increase, and I must decrease.

PRAYER.

Our Father, and Hail Mary.

Twenty-second of February.

Conversion of the Samaritan Woman.

JESUS came to a city of Samaria, called Sichar. Now Jacob's well was there. JESUS therefore being wearied with His journey, sat down on the well: There cometh a woman of Samaria to draw water: JESUS saith to her: Give Me to drink.—S. JOHN IV.

I. PRELUDE.

We see our Saviour Jesus sitting by the well, patiently waiting for the woman whom He desired to convert.

II. PRELUDE.

O Loving Jesus, grant that, while considering the goodness with which Thou dost draw souls unto Thee, by the power of Thy preventing grace, our hearts may be replenished with love and thankfulness.

I. POINT.

The wisdom with which Jesus procures our salvation.

After many times soliciting a soul to turn to God, Jesus

waiteth still that He may have mercy, as He waited on that day, when He was wearied, for the Samaritan woman. It was not by chance that He found Himself by the well-side, when she came to draw water:—divine wisdom knows how to combine circumstances that they may issue in the conversion of souls. Can we not recall the multitude of ways that Jesus employed to attract us to His service? a certain concurrence of events brought about—in a manner which appeared quite natural—supernatural consequences: they had been planned by Providence, so as gradually to break the ties which bound us to the world; or the chains with which sin had enslaved us. Can we sufficiently admire the infinite wisdom and goodness of God in our regard? The thought of His patience, the memory of His forbearance, should awaken in our hearts such loving thankfulness, that we might spend our lives in giving Him fresh proofs of our gratitude.

II. POINT.

To effect the conversion of a soul, Jesus often asks of it a little kindness—a small act of charity; and then repays it largely.

In converting the woman of Samaria, Jesus began by asking her to give Him a little water. Thus it is that He draws a soul out of a state of sin or tepidity, by causing it to see in what way it can render God a little service. Each one of us knows what act of charity, of sacrifice, or of humility He requires of us. He tells us by some passing event, perhaps by a striking coincidence—by good counsel—or by an interior Voice. Happy are they who imitate the Samaritan woman: she at once appreciated the excellence of the gift Jesus bestowed on her in reward for her act of charity towards Himself: we see her yielding to His gracious importunity and receiving with eagerness the living water which flows so plentifully from His Sacred Heart. Ah! if we too knew the gift of God!—how much more earnestly should we pray that the fountain of water might in us *spring up into life everlasting*, so that we might never again thirst after any vanity or pleasure of the world; never go back into it, to draw consolation or natural satisfaction.

Colloquy.

O my Saviour, how marvellous are the effects of Thy grace in those souls that are sincere and teachable. Not only was the Samaritan woman converted, during Thy short visit, O Jesus, to Sichar, but many in the city owned Thee as the Saviour of the world;—while Thy chosen people the Jews, after Thy three years' ministry amongst them, remained in their state of wilful blindness. Seeing how much more difficult it is to rekindle the love of God in a soul which has been once enlightened, and has afterwards become cold and indifferent, I pray that I may never fall away from Thee, my Jesus, but, while doing little things for love of Thee, trust that Thou wilt give me largely of the living water of Thy grace.

Resolution.

To be attentive to give to Jesus whatever He asks of me,—opening my heart to receive the gift of God.

Thought for the Day.

Lord, give me this water, that I may not thirst.

Prayer.

Soul of Christ.

Twenty-third of February.

The Living Water is the Gift of God.

Jesus said to the Samaritan woman: If thou didst know the gift of God, and Who is He that saith to thee, Give Me to drink; thou perhaps wouldst have asked of Him, and He would have given thee living water.—S. John iv.

I. Prelude.

We represent to ourselves Jesus still sitting on the well; by the benevolence of His words disposing the heart of the woman of Samaria to true conversion.

II. Prelude.

Grant, O Jesus, that in meditating upon the secret manner in which Thou dost convey grace to the soul, we may learn the value of Thy gifts, and how to appreciate them better.

I. Point.

How precious are the gifts of grace!

God dispenses to His creatures the blessings of this life with excessive liberality; daily bread—health—honour—riches;—they are participated in by the faithful and by the unfaithful; *Our Father, Who is in Heaven, maketh His sun to rise upon the good and bad, and raineth upon the just and unjust.* These latter have often indeed the larger share, because God esteems worldly advantages too little to allow them to be dearly bought.—But with regard to supernatural blessings—the enlightenment of the soul—the inspirations which make us desire to belong entirely to God, and attract us powerfully to the practice of those virtues which are God-like,—these good things are so esteemed by our Heavenly Father, that the Blood of His Beloved Son was the price paid to obtain them for us. Therefore they may not be thrown away;—through the Church they are granted to His children, being multiplied and increased in those privileged souls, who by their faithful use of these highest, spiritual blessings, will turn them to account for Heaven. To all such as He would make partakers of them, Jesus says, *If thou didst know the gift of God?* if thou didst but fully comprehend its value? Let us beseech Him to discover it to us, to make us understand, at the same time, that the gift of God is not bestowed on account of our own merits, but is the fruit of the infinite merits of the Death of our Saviour. Appreciating it more and more, may it become to us so precious, that abandoning all else, sacrificing all else, we may be intent only on making a right use of that which God has given us; and remember that *to whomsoever much is given, of him much shall be required.*

II. POINT.

How desirable are the gifts of grace!

He would have given thee living water. Why does Jesus thus speak of the gift of God, under the similitude of flowing water? Doubtless to make us understand the numerous effects produced by it. As water is indispensable in many ways—under the ordinary exterior circumstances of life—so is the gift of grace necessary for our spiritual needs.—Water cleanses that which is soiled; so grace purifies from sin, and effaces its stains. Water refreshes the plants, and fertilizes the earth; so grace causes good desires to spring up, and renders our good-will vigorous and productive. How precious are the living waters of grace! how great the happiness of being able constantly to draw them in abundance from their very Source; that sacred and mysterious Source—the Heart of Jesus! Every day, every hour He is waiting by the well for us, to ask of us some act of love, and in return to give us *the water of life, gratis.*

Colloquy.

How immense is Thy charity, O Jesus! how can I show Thee that I am grateful for all the ineffable gifts Thou didst bring from Heaven?—the gift of Thy Divinity, of Thy Merits, of Thy Life in the mystery of the Incarnation;—the gift of Thyself in the Holy Eucharist;—the gift of my vocation, to which Thou hast united so many graces, so many benefits. Deign yet to add to all these the gift of perseverance in Thy service; and grant that my fidelity may become perfect, and be accompanied by a great love for Thee, my Saviour.

Resolution.

To think often during the day of the gifts our Lord has bestowed on me, and to see how I am making use of them.

Thought for the Day.

If thou didst know the gift of God.

Prayer.

Take, O Lord, and receive.

Twenty-fourth of February.

Feast of Saint Matthias.

See page 235.

Twenty-fifth of February.

The Will of God was the nourishment of Jesus.

In the meantime the Disciples prayed Him, saying : Rabbi, eat : But He saith to them : I have meat to eat which you know not : My meat is to do the Will of Him that sent Me, that I may perfect His work.—S. JOHN IV.

I. PRELUDE.

We see Jesus resting still by Jacob's well, when the Disciples returned from Sichar, where they had been to buy food.

II. PRELUDE.

O Adorable Son of God, reveal to us the secret of that loving obedience, which was Thy nourishment, and which should also be ours, since we ought to imitate Thee in all things.

I. POINT.

The Will of God the Father is the sustenance of God the Son.

My meat is to do the Will of Him that sent Me, that I may perfect His work. Jesus having come from Heaven to accomplish His Father's Will, consecrates Himself to this noble function with so much love, that He becomes wholly absorbed in it, and forgets to take the nourishment ordinarily necessary to support life. In the temple, He had already declared: *I must be about My Father's business.* To-day He goes still further, assuring His Disciples, when they persuaded Him to repair His exhausted strength, after His fatiguing journey and the labours of His ministry, that in fulfilling His Father's Will, He found His powers renewed. Thus does He teach us that in working for our own sanctification, or that of others, we should, through the accomplishing of God's designs, find strength and courage to support us in all we have to do. To perform the good pleasure of our Heavenly Father should be our meat and drink. Has this sentiment, spoken from out the depths of the Heart of Jesus, passed into our own? have divine love and zeal for souls the mastery over our self-love? does God's Will sustain us in our warfare against all that obstructs the path to perfection?

II. Point.

This spiritual nourishment is so little relished, even by those who ought to depend on it entirely.

How rare it is to find real imitators of our Divine Master, even amongst such as know full well that obedience essentially constitutes the religious life. Many indeed like to do the Will of God, when it is not contrary to theirs, or does not impose on them sacrifices too painful to nature; but this is a sure sign that they have not for the Divine Will a special preference to their own. They choose, on the contrary, to do that which flatters self-love, and satisfies their desires and inclinations : and yet, if we hope to keep up the life of our soul with any other nourishment than that which supported our Lord, we shall find our strength utterly failing, sooner or later. Since Jesus, Who was holiness itself, depended on the Will of His Father, and was obedient to it in the smallest particular, during His whole Lifetime, should not we, who are so weak, so unreliable, seek to derive all our force from it? and make it the motive of our every action?

Colloquy.

I adore Thee, O Most Obedient Son of Mary, and I thank Thee for the sublime lesson afforded me by the respect and love Thou didst manifest for the Will of Thy Heavenly Father. Grant me grace to love His Will, and to prefer it before all selfish considerations. And should it even subject me to painful trials, may I accomplish it courageously, and like Thee, glorify God by my dependence on Him.

Resolution.

To do all my actions in the intention of accomplishing the Will of God.

Thought for the Day.

My meat is to do the Will of My Father.

Prayer.

Take, O Lord, and receive.

Twenty-sixth of February.

The value of a good thought.

Thy thoughts shall be directed.—PROV. XVI.

I. PRELUDE.

Let us imagine the effect the words of Jesus had on the woman of Samaria, and how they inspired her with good thoughts.

II. PRELUDE.

Give us, O Lord, the spirit of attention to the holy thoughts inspired by Thy words and Thy example, and may we act upon them, so that we lose not their grace.

I. POINT.

How highly we should value holy thoughts.

To estimate fully the excellence of a good thought, we must be convinced that it is sent from God: it is a present coming from His beneficence, and which surpasses all the powers of human intellectual resources. The heart of man is like a sea, over which the winds pass, from various quarters. The spirit of the world—of the evil one—and of the flesh, blow across it; and cause vain, sensual or malicious thoughts to arise on its surface. The Spirit of God alone, by the favouring breeze of His inspirations, can conduct us into the port of eternal blessedness. It is the Holy Spirit Who is the Author of those movements towards good which we feel at a time perhaps when we least expect it:—they are a divine favour. When the Samaritan woman left Sichar on her errand—to draw water, she was thinking neither of her salvation, nor of the happiness awaiting her; but her God was thinking of her, her meeting with her Saviour was not by chance. Thus also when some circumstance awakens an idea in our minds which may have a good tendency,—when the example of those more pious, more modest, more virtuous than ourselves, arouses a desire to imitate them,—when our heart is touched by an exhortation—a warning, God is thinking of us, our Saviour is waiting for us, and His Holy Spirit offers us the gift of a good thought; to draw us on to greater fidelity—to greater perfection.—Who can tell the results, the eternal results, of one holy thought?

II. Point.

What God's designs are in giving us holy thoughts.

The Son of God in coming into the world, willed to sanctify His elect, and through them to procure the greater glory of His Father. To execute a project so worthy of His wisdom, He employs good thoughts to enlighten our understanding and to excite our will. These good thoughts fill our hearts with feelings of admiration, of love, and of gratitude towards our Lord. They discover to us where we are in the wrong, and the means to be taken to free ourselves from our evil passions. God sends holy thoughts to our aid when evil thoughts arise, so that they may displace them; and filling the mind, leave no room for the suggestions of the spirit of darkness,—the spirit of the world,—or the spirit of self—of nature. How much should we esteem even a single good thought; such thoughts come not from ourselves, we could not form one. What can we do but own our dependence on the mercy of God, and by making good use of His holy inspirations, open the way for others, which

He will send us undoubtedly and in larger measure; thereby to sanctify our hearts and minds more and more.

COLLOQUY.

O God, Thou dost fill the minds of Thy children with good thoughts, and their hearts with holy sentiments. Understanding their value and their blessed effects, may I learn to appreciate them better, and never reject one; for I know not what loss I may thereby bring upon myself, by such indifference. I beseech Thee not to leave me to my own thoughts and imaginations, but visit me with thy loving inspirations, and by them teach me what I ought to do.

RESOLUTION.

Thankfully to receive the good thoughts which come to me, and to respond most joyfully to all holy suggestions.

THOUGHT FOR THE DAY.

Speak, Lord, for thy servant heareth.

PRAYER.

Soul of Christ.

Twenty-seventh of February.

Jesus preaches the Gospel.

From that time JESUS *began to preach: and His fame went abroad.*—S. MATTHEW IV.

I. PRELUDE.

Let us represent to ourselves the Divine Saviour, in the midst of the people He was instructing. The noble majesty of His Person, united to the gentleness of His manner drew multitudes after Him, and won their hearts.

II. Prelude.

Grant, O Jesus, that in listening to Thy divine teaching, we may learn how we too may be animated by Thy words and example, in our daily life.

I. Point.

Jesus, the Wisdom of the Father, instructed men, for three years, in His own Person.

In having God for our Master—the Eternal Wisdom for our Teacher—have we ever considered thoroughly the honour conferred on us? The Light of light came in Person to dispel our darkness; to make us understand our divine origin, our sublime destinies, and the way which leads to the heights of everlasting glory. The mercy of God and the greatness of the soul of man are put before us in the strongest light, by Him who is Light. It is most instructive to reflect upon the Mission of the Incarnate Wisdom of the Father. He journeyed from place to place, visiting the towns and villages of the Holy Land, to teach the way of salvation. Wishing to regenerate mankind, and to make of them a holy people, He gave them a holy doctrine, which gathered up the teaching of the Old Law into one great precept,—that of divine love: a doctrine which should comprise all true religion, with its externals, its maxims, and its reality. Let us listen to what the Adorable Master tells us, as repeated by His Beloved Apostle:—*If you continue in My words, you shall be My disciples indeed.* Jesus on earth instructs us still.

II. POINT.

Since His Ascension Jesus continues His teaching by His Spirit, as He promised.

The zeal of our Lord was full of power and ardour: He would have enkindled in every part of the world the celestial fire He came to bring on the earth; but His zeal was regulated by the Heavenly Father's Will; therefore He remained in the land of His Birth. He did great wonders and performed astonishing miracles; and yet He said, that His disciples should do greater works than He had done. Jesus Himself prepared the way by His teaching for the coming of the Paraclete: the Apostles and those who were formed in His school, and under His own Eyes, could not be perfectly prepared for their mission, and to preach the Gospel with success until after the Descent of the Holy Spirit—*Who proceedeth from the Father and the Son*—Jesus therefore promised to send Him, to teach them all truth.—Our Saviour taught orally when He was on earth,—founded the Church,—laid down His law of Love,—and showed the way to Heaven through suffering, by the example of His Passion and Death.—Since the Day of Pentecost, He teaches us by His Spirit, which descends into our souls, to inspire, to enlighten, to guide, to strengthen, and to instruct us in the Will of God.

COLLOQUY.

O Holy Spirit, Who didst animate our Adorable Master in the work of His ministry amongst men, come Thou and give me grace to obey His law of love.—Make known to me that which He asks of me, in proof of my love for him; and strengthen me to overcome all obstacles that might prevent my following Thy holy inspirations. O Jesus, Thou didst say that *our Father in Heaven would give the Good Spirit to them that ask Him.* Thanks be to Thee, O God. I adore Thee, O Holy and Undivided Trinity.

THOUGHT FOR THE DAY.

If you love Me, keep My commandments.

RESOLUTION.

To persevere in the doctrine taught by Jesus Christ, and to follow the inspirations of the Holy Ghost.

PRAYER.

Our Father, and Hail Mary.

Twenty-eighth of February.

The marriage in Cana of Galilee.

Fill the water-pots with water, and they filled them up to the brim: and JESUS said to them:—Draw out now, and carry to the chief steward of the feast.—S. JOHN II. 7.

I. PRELUDE.

We see Jesus and Mary honouring with their presence the Marriage-Feast in Cana.

II. PRELUDE.

O good Mother, who hast such power over the Heart of Thy Divine Son; ask of Him to change our hearts, which are so cold and indifferent, into hearts full of love for Him and for thee.

I. Point.

The marvellous effects of grace.

If our loving Saviour, touched by the anxiety of the bridegroom when the wine failed, performed at the request of His Mother, a miracle to calm this natural solicitude, with what merciful goodness will He not listen to the requests which this same tender Mother daily addresses to Him on our behalf? How many graces have we not obtained through her intercession? Have we not found, by happy experience, that whereas we, at one time, served God through fear, we now serve Him with love and joy? The miracle is reproduced—the water is changed into wine; that celestial wine which so inebriates the soul, that it can only think of God, see God, and live for God. According to St. Bernard, the soul thus filled with divine love, feels no longer any grief, wearies not in any labour, and suffers contempt without knowing it. The Divine Spirit of our Lord, in thus taking possession of the soul, causes the effects of human passion to disappear, and renders His union with it entire, by communicating to it all that is of truest virtue; not permitting the higher life of the soul to be troubled or displaced by the lower,—the superior by the inferior. Thus it enjoys perfect tranquillity, a constant, unalterable joy; it yields to no fear, for it reposes in God; so that nothing can alarm it, or affect its peace and happiness. Even in this life such a soul enjoys a perpetual feast, being fed with spiritual meat and drink, of which the world knows nothing: for they consist of those unspeakable consolations, which, even they who taste of them, cannot describe. But it is most certain, that one word from Jesus, a look even, is sufficient to produce a change in our hearts yet more marvellous than that which was affected within the water-pots of stone, at the marriage-feast.

II. Point.

Jesus, the Celestial Bridegroom of our souls, gives not the best wine at the beginning of the spiritual banquet.

Jesus, at the marriage in Cana, favoured the guests with the performance of His first miracle;—what privileges has He not in store for those, His chosen ones, who partake of the Banquet He Himself spreads for them. At this spiritual marriage-feast, the guests drink of that cup wherein has been poured *the wine which maketh virgins*; partaking of that sacred chalice, with delight they quench their thirst for God. They receive its mystic contents—the Precious Blood of Him Who espouses them to Himself; and Who thus communicates to them His Life. This is a miracle of miracles; through it our Lord consecrates—makes divine even—the celestial marriage He contracts with His faithful ones. This is the foretaste of the Marriage Banquet of the Lamb; where the happy guests will be, not only in the Presence, but in the enjoyment and actual possession of the Heavenly Spouse; they will be replenished with happiness, the happiness of God Himself. Then shall we drink of the best wine reserved for the unending marriage-Feast; then will be the hour of recompense for those *who are come out of great tribulations*, having shared in the sufferings and humiliations of Jesus.

Colloquy.

O Mary, my dear Mother, thou lovest with a special love those who have consecrated themselves to be the Spouses of Thy Adorable Son; make me, through Thy protecting care, to become more faithful to the special graces granted to me, that I may win the loving regard of the Divine Heart of Jesus; and participate in the Eternal Banquet, where the sacred union will be consummated which I have here contracted with Him.

Resolution.

I ask of Jesus, through Mary, the grace most necessary to enable me to pass this day holily.

Thought for the Day.

Whatever He shall say to you, do ye.

Prayer.

Soul of Christ.

Ash Wednesday.

Duties of the Holy Season of Lent.

Lay up to yourselves treasure in Heaven.—S. Matt. vi.

I. Prelude.

Let us represent to ourselves Jesus in the desert, praying and fasting;—thus giving us an example of most austere penance.

II. Prelude.

We are to-day reminded, by the Church, of death: let us obtain from Thee, O Lord, the spirit of penance, so that we may, during this season of Lent, seek to become better prepared for the hour of death.

I. Point.

The thought of death disposes us to apply ourselves to the exercise of penance.

Remember, O man, that thou art dust; and into dust shalt thou return.—The ashes, and the words of the Priest, as he puts them upon us, forcibly recall the meanness of our origin, the condemnation to death under which we lie, and the obligation imposed upon us to do penance. Children of Adam, guilty as he, we ought indeed to humble ourselves when we carry on our foreheads the symbol of death; and with broken hearts should we repent of the sins of which death is the punishment. The marking with ashes preaches a mute but eloquent sermon; from which we learn that our bodies, although so much cared for, and cherished perhaps, are nothing but the dust of the earth, and after death will become the food of worms, will undergo corruption, and return to dust again. The ceremony of to-day teaches us also that by the fire of divine love we should reduce to ashes our evil habits—our unruly passions—our bad inclinations,—so that, during this holy season, they may, by a process of annihilation, be consumed and destroyed. We should understand from it also, that our sorrow for sin should be so great, our contrition so sincere, that our souls be bowed down to the dust before God.

II. Point.

Lent is the fitting time for laying up heavenly treasure.

Let us consider of how great value are the good works, and the acts of penance, in which the faithful occupy themselves during this holy season; they are treasures which we may lay up in Heaven: even in this life they will be a cause of unspeakable joy, and in the future life they will form *an eternal weight of glory.* The very least of these good works is of infinite value, provided that it be sanctified by the merits of Jesus. They should indeed be practised at all times; but Lent is a season of special grace, to such as spend it in prayer and fasting, with Jesus in the desert,—in learning better how to withstand the assaults of the devil,—in meditating on the Passion,—in performing acts of penance,—in mourning, with our holy Mother the Church, for our own sins and the sins of all Her children. *If we are converted to the Lord our God with all our hearts in fasting and weeping and mourning, will He not return, and forgive, and leave a blessing behind him?* How important is it then, for our growth in holiness, to enter into the spirit of the Church. —There are certain good works, in doing which all can now resolve to pass these days of Lent;—the practice of stricter silence, deeper recollection, a more entire mortification of our senses:—and going on further still, we should strive to subjugate our passions, repress our too natural desires, cut down our self-love. Have we not enough to do, if we would keep such *a fast as the Lord hath chosen?*

Colloquy.

O my Saviour, Thou Who wast perfectly innocent, didst set me an example of penance, that I, who am so guilty, might follow it and atone for my offences and many failures in my duty towards God. By bodily mortification, may I expiate the sins whereby my members have been instruments of iniquity; and by tears of contrition may I wash out the stains which sin has left upon my soul. Since Thou, O Jesus, hast shown me that exterior acts of penance must be accompanied by a truly penitential spirit, I wish, during this Lent, to reduce to nothing, by true mortification, all that I feel to be displeasing to Thee. Give me grace to accomplish my sincere desire.

Resolution.

During this holy time of Lent, I will practise each day some acts of penance.

Thought for the Day.

Remember, O man, that thou art dust, and into dust shalt thou return.

Prayer.

Our Father, and Hail Mary.

Thursday after Ash Wednesday.

Jesus weeping over Jerusalem.

We go up to Jerusalem, and all things shall be accomplished which were written by the prophets concerning the Son of God.—St. Luke xviii.

I. Prelude.

Let us represent to ourselves Jesus, surrounded by His Disciples, directing His course towards Jerusalem, which is to be the scene of His Passion and Death.

II. Prelude.

O Saviour, grant that entering into the spirit of those Mysteries of Thy Passion which we contemplate especially at this time, we may profit by the graces Thou dost now offer us, and love Thee more for all Thou hast suffered for love of us.

I. Point.

The mercy and compassion Jesus evinced towards Jerusalem.

We see our Adorable Saviour on the road which leads to that ungrateful city, that had so often witnessed the miracles of Jesus; and which was now about to put the finishing stroke to its crimes, by crucifying the Lord of glory.—The compassionate Heart of Jesus was more occupied with the thought of the misfortunes about to overtake the guilty city, than with the consideration of the sufferings He was so soon to endure: He wept over it, saying: *If thou, Jerusalem, hadst known the things that are to thy peace:*—if even, in this day, which is still given thee, thou wouldst turn thine eyes towards Him Who bringeth salvation! But no! a deluge of destruction shall sweep over thee; only a few more years, and the hour of thy fearful overthrow will arrive.—We feel moved at hearing our Lord thus sorrowing over the doom of this favoured place; and at the sight of the chastisement reserved, by divine justice, for it; but to-day let us rather dwell on the thought, that over all rebellious souls, which have been once favoured by God, as was Jerusalem, Jesus wept.—Has He had cause to shed tears on our account? If we imitate the ingratitude of the insensate people of that city, shall we not share in its unhappy ruin? Nothing arouses the wrath of God more sensibly than an abuse of His gifts and of His mercy. Let us look into ourselves, and strive to profit more by the numberless favours we have received in Religion, and the mercy again offered us in the meditation of the Sufferings of Jesus.

II. Point.

The spiritual penalties inflicted on the faithless soul.

Jesus in the picture He draws of the temporal evils about to be accomplished with regard to the perfidious Jerusalem, traces out also the spiritual evils which a soul may well dread, that obstinately continues to live according to the dictates of the inclinations of nature, and consequently in resistance to grace. For the days shall come upon it, when its enemies, that is, bad habits and propensities, shall cast a trench about it, and compass it round; so that neither grace, nor the Bread of Life, can reach it. Overpowered by the weight of iniquity, the spiritual edifice will be overturned, *there shall not be left a stone upon a stone, because it has not known the time of its visitation.* Where God no longer dwells, disorder is complete. Is it probable that such may be the fate reserved for us, on account of our ingratitude, and daily want of fidelity? Have we not cause at least to weep because of the little fruit we gather from all those abundant graces with which we are visited every day?—Ought we not to weep on account of our resistance?—our little love?—Ought we not to weep for the suffering we have caused Jesus? Should we not profit by this time of our visitation, when by contemplating these sufferings, our spiritual edifice may be fortified, and we may be strengthened, by this means, in grace?

Colloquy.

Adorable Saviour, Willing Victim for the sins of the world, how worthy art Thou of my gratitude! In going towards Jerusalem, Thou didst appear forgetful of the conspiracy which would be in a few days formed against Thy Life; Thou wast absorbed in thought—thinking of those whose salvation Thou didst desire;—and the sight of the multitudes who would withstand Thy love, caused Thee to weep. Grant that I may not be of their number,—that I may not be so unhappy as to render ineffectual, in my own regard, the Mysteries of salvation.

Resolution.

To avoid the doom of faithless souls, I will renew my fervour, and acquit myself better of the duties of my calling; and particularly of that one which I have neglected the most.

THOUGHT FOR THE DAY.

Now is the acceptable time; now is the day of Salvation.

PRAYER.

Our Father, and Hail Mary.

Friday after Ash Wednesday.

The sentiments with which we should meditate on the Passion.

I have a Baptism wherewith I am to be baptised: and how am I straightened until it be accomplished.—ST. LUKE XII.

I. PRELUDE.

Let us penetrate into the Sacred Heart of Jesus, and see how greatly He longs to finish the work of our salvation.

II. PRELUDE.

Divine Saviour, give us, we beseech Thee, such right sentiments in the contemplation of the Mystery of Thy sufferings, that we may draw therefrom much fruit; and increase in Thy love.

I. POINT.

In order to profit by the Mysteries of Thy Passion, we must meditate upon them fervently.

Our spiritual needs are so great, that we ought daily to

ascend the Hill of Calvary, to place ourselves at the foot of the Cross, and make known to Jesus, Who is there charged with all our iniquities, the necessities and the infirmities of our souls. From the Cross He speaks to us and says;—My Wounds are channels through which the waters of life flow forth abundantly: come then to Me: however great your misery, still greater is the desire I have to release you from it.—Let us eagerly accept the invitation of Jesus, Who will distribute the riches of His grace according to the measure of our desires. As we hear our Lord calling us to His Feet, to stay near Him in His Sufferings, let us be amongst the first in hastening to take our place by the side of Mary; and remain beneath the shadow of the Cross, in contemplation with her.—Jesus continues speaking to our hearts:—It is on the Tree of the Cross that I have yielded up My Life, to redeem you; I have there espoused you, My faithful ones, and given you pledges of My fidelity. On It, I have enriched you with My favours, and raised you to the exalted condition of being Mine, by applying to you the merits of My Passion and my Death.

II. Point.

In order to profit by the Mysteries of the Suffering of Jesus, we must meditate upon them in a spirit of faith.

Faith is indispensable, if we would penetrate into the Mystery of the Cross; without it our minds could never receive the light which shines forth from the Wounds of Jesus, and our hearts would be unmoved by the recollection of His Sorrows. Faith represents Jesus Christ to us, as actually suffering before our eyes; for although the events we consider are past, yet ever to the present belongs the application of the merits, of which He alone is the unfailing Source. Faith helps each one to comtemplate the Lamb of God sacrificed for him, as if he were alone in the world; and each may, by Faith, gather the Fruits of the Tree of Life, in as great abundance, as if Jesus had died for him only.—"Jesus was crucified for me; for me He shed all His Blood."—Lastly, Faith gives us an entrance into the Heart of Jesus, therein to discover the excess of love with which He suffered for us; and we are led, at least in desire, to feel the torments of the Passion, as if we had undergone them ourselves. We may take, by the hands of faith, the Crown of Thorns, and pressing it around our head, consider what it is in us which has crowned Him thus:—we may taste the bitterness of the gall which they put to His Lips, and feel the points of the Nails which pierced His Hands and Feet, and the keenness of the Lance with which His Heart was riven. Thus, in some degree, let us enter by Faith into the Mystery of Calvary.

COLLOQUY.

O Jesus, my Saviour, what ardent charity do I find in Thy Heart, which moved Thee thus to suffer for me; and in my own—what coldness, what indifference! Give me, I beseech Thee, so clear a view of the Cross and of Thyself as Thou didst hang upon It, that I may find there, at Thy Feet, those spiritual riches of which I long to be more fully a partaker.

RESOLUTION.

To excite in my mind lively sentiments of faith, in contemplating the sufferings of Jesus; and through them to unite myself to Him.

THOUGHT FOR THE DAY.

He loved me, and delivered Himself for me.

PRAYER.

Soul of Christ.

Saturday after Ash Wednesday.

The sentiments with which we should meditate upon the Passion.

He went forth to that place which is called Calvary.— S. JOHN XIX.

I. PRELUDE.

Let us go up to Calvary, and again witness the sufferings of Jesus, as those witnessed them who were actually present.

II. PRELUDE.

O Jesus Crucified, grant us grace, while considering this painful Mystery, to discover more clearly in Thee the Sovereign Majesty of God, and thereby to be filled with feelings of deepest veneration.

I. POINT.

All, in connection with this Mystery, commands our reverence and respect.

Nothing makes the infinite majesty of God appear more evident, than the satisfaction He derived from His Adorable Son—the King of kings—when He was, as it were, lost in an abyss of sorrow and contempt. On the other hand, nothing is more calculated to confound our pride, and to make us really humble, than this thought:—I am the cause of the torments, and of the death of my Saviour;—it is I who made Him suffer and die.—When we own this—(and are we not forced to own it?) ought we not to be covered with shame? Do we not then see the enormity of our sins, and our powerlessness to expiate them? O divine justice, how rigorous thou art! O human weakness, how extreme! Where, O Saviour, can our pride hide itself? it has rendered us so guilty—so feeble—so utterly dependent on Thy mercy. How can we dare to appear before Thee, O Lord Jesus, when we remember that we have caused Thee such anguish of soul and body? How can we repair the wrongs done Thee, Thou Who wast so scorned for love of us? how can we bear to think that we have reduced Thee to such a woful condition? But in the place which is called Calvary, *the Lord waiteth that He may have mercy on us.*

II. Point.

The Passion of Jesus should make us forget the things of this world.

We, who belong in an especial way to Jesus Crucified, whom He deigns to call His Spouses, in penetrating this Mystery of suffering, should understand that we must not live any longer to ourselves, but for Him alone; so that we may think only of Him, occupy ourselves only for Him; and, forgetful of self and of all creatures, love Him and none other. If we find that, after having followed in His Footsteps, only part of the way to Calvary, we have gone back and abandoned Him, let us now redouble our efforts to regain what we have lost, and beg our Lord to pardon us; and tell Him that we will not again forsake Him. Henceforth may the entrance to our hearts be open only to Him; for as He hangs upon the Cross does He not say to His faithful ones: *put me as a Seal upon thy heart?* In forgetting all but Jesus, we in fact imitate Him, Who forgot Himself to think of us. It behoves us then to forget our own interests, and all vain and earthly things, and to beg of our Lord to impress on our mind and memory the marks of His Sacred Wounds.

Colloquy.

O Sovereign Lord of Heaven and earth, Thou hast willed to suffer and to die for me: how can I ever sufficiently acknowledge my wretchedness—my unworthiness—and my thanklessness?—When shall I learn to despise the consolations and the joys of this world? When shall I forget all created things in a really eager search after those things which may promote Thy honour and glory, and which are eternal?—Give me grace often to call to mind the meekness with which the King of kings bore His humiliations; and thus to teach me humility, and how to bear suffering for His Sake.

Resolution.

Gladly to suffer, with the Hill of Calvary before my eyes.

Thought for the Day.

We account them blessed who have endured.

Prayer.

Take, O Lord, and receive.

First Week in Lent.—Sunday.

We should meditate on the Mysteries of the Passion with sentiments of love and admiration.

God forbid that I should glory, save in the Cross of our Lord JESUS CHRIST *; by Whom the world is crucified to me, and I to the world.*—GAL. VI.

I. PRELUDE.

We represent to ourselves Jesus suffering:—in the Garden of Olives,—bound to the Pillar,—nailed to the Cross.

II. PRELUDE.

Grant, O Jesus, that in considering the awful wonders of those hours of suffering, our love may be inflamed more and more, and bring forth the fruits of generosity and devotedness.

1. POINT.

The first effect of this contemplation should be to produce in our souls a grateful love towards our Lord Jesus Christ.

Although Jesus possesses such an infinity of perfections, nothing can form a more powerful—a sweeter attraction than His Sacred Wounds :—*From the Tree He reigns* over our hearts. Indeed, one glance at our God dying for us, ought to produce within us lively gratitude and ardent love for Him, the Saviour. A Saint has said : " They who wish to grow in virtue and increase in grace, should meditate on Jesus suffering—and that continually."—And how often have we heard it repeated that one tear shed at the remembrance of the Passion of Jesus Christ, is worth more than a pilgrimage to Jerusalem; or a year's fasting on bread and water? If He had been pleased to save us by the ministry of an Angel, we should have been constrained to love God above all, but our salvation was so dear to Him, that He would not confide the procuring of it to another. He took our iniquities on Himself. O Jesus, the most beautiful, the most lovable of all the children of men, art Thou not the Son of God? art Thou not our King, our Sovereign Lord, our All? and are not we Thy subjects?—but often, alas! ungrateful, rebellious ones. Yet Thou hast spoken of us to Thy Father, Thou didst offer to die in our stead, to preserve us from endless perdition. O Love of our Saviour! if thou dost not penetrate into our hearts, they cannot be hearts, but stones harder than adamant.

II. Point.

At the sight of Jesus Crucified, the faithful soul is filled with astonishment.

What could be more astonishing than the sight of our God dying on the Cross?—Who could be so insensible as to fail to admire the excess of love, which obliged him to die for those who put Him to death? and the patience with which He underwent such dreadful torments, at the hands of His creatures? And why this love—this patience in the Martyr of martyrs? He was suffering to save us from everlasting suffering.—The work of Creation, the effecting of Miracles, the Resurrection of our Lord are wonderful indeed, still they are in accordance with the grandeur of the Creator, but the Passion and Dying of Him *by Whom all things were made, and without Whom was made nothing that was made,* this it is which awakens the loving, adoring wonder of the faithful soul. O God, what art Thou and what are we? The Creator dies for the creature, the Master for the slave! O incomprehensible Greatness, in what depths of humility dost Thou hide Thyself!—Truly no mind can understand, no tongue can express the impenetrability of Thy secrets, the profundity of thy purposes, the capacity of Thy love!

COLLOQUY.

Is it not impossible, O Good Jesus, that I can doubt Thy love as I see Thee on the Cross? how is it then that I can ever refuse Thee mine? O Lord, I desire to love Thee as I ought,—Thou art my Strength, my Refuge, my Deliverer, my Jesus.

THOUGHT FOR THE DAY.

O Love, Thou art unknown!—O Love, Thou art not loved!

PRAYER.

Take, O Lord, and receive.

First Week in Lent.—Monday.

The Meditation of the Passion ought to produce in us sentiments of compassion and compunction.

Peter lifted up His voice and said: Let all the House of Israel know most certainly, that God hath made both Lord and Christ, this same JESUS, *Whom you have crucified: Now when they had heard these things they had compunction in their heart, and said to Peter and to the rest of the Apostles: What shall we do? Peter said to them: Do penance.*—ACTS II.

I. Prelude.

Let us represent to ourselves Mount Calvary, and Jesus fastened to the Cross.

II. Prelude.

In seeing Thee suffer the torments of Thy Passion, O Adorable Victim, may we feel deep compassion for Thee, and have compunction in our hearts, at the sight of all the faults in ourselves which have caused Thy sufferings.

I. Point.

Jesus asks us to compassionate His sorrows.

Yes! this is what the Son of God asks of us, that we should feel compassion for Him in the hour of His dread suffering. He was lifted up on the summit of a hill, so that He might be seen of all; He cried with a loud voice just before His death, to be heard of all.—We see Him, we hear Him still.—Are our hearts so hard that we cannot compassionate Him? if so, let us picture to ourselves some of the instruments of the Passion. Let us look at the scourges which have torn His Flesh, the Thorns and the Nails which have pierced His Sacred Head and Hands and Feet. Let us turn our eyes on that Beautiful Face, now so disfigured and covered with mire and blood. Then may we also gaze within the Wounded Side, and entering His Divine Heart, lay our hearts therein. How intimate are the ties which unite us to this Adorable Saviour! He is our Elder Brother, He is the Bridegroom of our souls; and can we remain untouched by all that One, so dear, has undergone for our sakes? If such were the case, should we not be indeed unworthy of the application of the merits of His Precious Death?

II. Point.

The contemplation of the Wounds of Jesus Christ will produce in our hearts true contrition.

Should our hearts be hard as a rock, yet, if we meditate often upon the Passion of Jesus, it is impossible but that we should be moved to grief, and conceive an extreme horror of sin. If we contemplate Him in the hands of his murderers, and ask of the Prophet Isaias who has caused His Scourging—His Crucifixion—he replies: *The chastisement of our peace was upon Him, and the Lord hath laid on Him the iniquity of us all.* And if we turn to Jesus and ask Him, He shows us His Five Wounds and says:—My Child, My Spouse, you have treated me thus, notwithstanding the many and special claims I have on your love. Can we listen to this reply without feeling an intense sorrow for our sins? our many iniquities? With bitter regret for having caused the Death of our Saviour, should not we exclaim: "O divine Justice! it is we who have sinned; it is we who have merited the nails, the thorns, the cross:—take vengeance on us sinners, but spare our Lord."—Yet no! on Him the hand of justice falls, and His sacrifice of Himself wins our pardon. Miserable sinners that we are, He has given His Life for us. Knowing that our guilt has been the cause of all His torturing afflictions, and that it formed the spear which pierced His Side, what can we do but grieve over our own iniquities? and fearing henceforth to re-open His Wounds say with St. Catherine of Genoa: "O Love! no never, never any more sin".

Colloquy.

O my Good Jesus, my Suffering Jesus, wilt Thou not give

to my eyes a fountain of tears, so that I may weep for my sins, which have caused Thee so much sorrow, and broken Thy Heart? That I may compassionate Thy sufferings as I ought, may they often occupy my thoughts, and by the same means shall I learn to detest my past sins, and to be more watchful, and more distrustful of myself in future.

RESOLUTION.

To suffer voluntarily in mind and body, with the desire of being crucified with Jesus.

THOUGHT FOR THE DAY.

O Love! no never, never any more sin.

PRAYER.

Soul of Christ.

First Week in Lent.—Tuesday.

Effects of the Mystery of the Cross.

And I, if I be lifted up, will draw all things to Myself.— S. JOHN XII.

I. PRELUDE.

We see Jesus Christ upon the Cross, dying in our stead: His Arms are stretched out to receive all penitent souls.

II. PRELUDE.

Make us to understand the greatness of the benefit of our

redemption; that in us may be excited lively gratitude and unbounded confidence.

I. POINT.

We owe to our Lord Jesus eternal gratitude for the benefits of redemption.

Know ye what I have done for you? Jesus put this question to His Apostles after He had washed their feet.—Do you understand the charity, which has induced Me to humiliate Myself, in order to give you an example of that virtue, which you should exercise one towards another? From the height of Calvary our Saviour seems to say to each of us: *Know you what I have done for you?* Let us think about this until we know more thoroughly what He has done, in becoming our Surety.—He has paid our debts in His Own Person; and in making us partakers of His infinite merits, has put us in possession of the riches of Heaven. O Lord, how deeply we are indebted to Thee,—what eternal treasures are hidden within Thy Sacred Wounds! We should, of necessity, love Thee and praise Thee perpetually, did we know the price of that Blood which Thou hast shed, and the joys of that Kingdom It has purchased for us. Never should we cease to prove our gratitude by offering up acts of thanksgiving,—by doing our utmost to avoid whatever might displease our Dear Saviour,—and by consecrating each instant of our lives to His honour and glory.

II. POINT.

The Cross of Jesus is the hope of all true Christians.

We may put all our confidence in the Passion and Death of Jesus, because, however great our spiritual infirmities may be, however violent our temptations, however numerous our infidelities, we shall ever find in the Cross a powerful—a certain remedy. One single drop of the Precious Blood is capable of purifying a thousand worlds. We cannot doubt the efficacy of this Divine Remedy, since its virtue is sovereign: nor the sufficiency of our Ransom, since it possesses a value which is infinite. In the same way that streams throw themselves into the ocean and are lost in it, so our offences disappear in the ocean of divine love. When therefore we do fall into some fault, let us not lose courage, but rise promptly, and have recourse to the Sacred Wounds of Jesus. *He hath loved us, and washed us from our sins in His Own Blood.*—His love for us has carried Him thus far:—to cleanse us from our iniquities He has prepared a laver, from which His Precious Blood flows over upon us. What had He seen in us, that He should have been inspired with such love for us? His Blood has cried to Heaven and for what?—that of Abel cried for vengeance, that of Jesus for mercy. Why would He buy our love at a price so high? Because, thanks be to Him, *He hath first loved us*, as only God can love.

Colloquy.

O Jesus, speak to my heart, and make me turn with confidence to Thine. It is in Thy Blood, shed for my salvation, that I place all my hope: I have chosen the place of my rest within Thy Sacred Wounds. As I look upon Thee on the Cross, I shall find strength to subdue my passions, and infinite riches to pay the debt which I owe to divine justice.

Resolution.

Out of gratitude, I will suffer all the afflictions and trials

God may send me; often kissing my Crucifix with loving reverence, as if actually kissing the Feet of Jesus.

THOUGHT FOR THE DAY.

He hath loved us, and washed us from our sins in His own Blood.

PRAYER.

Soul of Christ.

First Week in Lent.—Wednesday.

Further effects of the Mystery of the Cross.

And I, if I be lifted up, will draw all things to Myself.—S. JOHN XII.

I. PRELUDE.

Let us place ourselves on Calvary, and hear our Lord—our Divine Example—as He hangs upon the Cross, inviting all men to imitate Him, and to unite themselves to Him in His Passion.

II. PRELUDE.

O Jesus, grant that we may enter with a loving spirit into the Mystery of the Cross, and endeavour to resemble Thee in Thy patient suffering.

I. POINT.

Jesus is our example in suffering.

The motives which should incline us to form a resemblance between ourselves and Jesus Crucified are most forcible, and if we should shun the Cross after having considered the Passion of our Lord, our cowardice would be inexcusable. Could we really say that we would not bear the Cross He lays upon us? or refuse to be fastened to it? after that He has marked out the royal road to Heaven by means of His Own. As true disciples of Jesus Christ, as Religious, let us wish for nothing so much as humiliation, poverty, or suffering, in some form or other. Yes! there is a Cross to be borne every day! a precious Cross—for Jesus has inlaid it with blood-red gems like His:—a glorious Cross—for Jesus conquered through His gloriously, and so may we:—a Cross to be greatly desired, for no satisfaction can equal that of sharing in the sufferings of Him we love. *My Father loveth me*, says our Divine Saviour; *because I lay down my Life that I may take it again: no man taketh it away from Me, but I lay it down of Myself, and I have power to lay it down: and I have power to take it up again.* We should be able to say that which our Lord here says of Himself; for God, in calling to the religious life, leaves the choice of accepting or not to those whom He calls.—They too have the power to make or withhold the sacrifice. And the sacrifice resembles that of Jesus Christ more or less, according to the sincerity and love with which it is accompanied; and the fidelity with which all the practices of perfection are embraced. The sacrifice is only real when it is voluntary, and, if need be, life-long.

II. Point.

Union with our Lord is produced by the imitation of Him—our Example—in suffering.

Christian souls, truly religious persons, who remain

attached to the Cross, become intimately united to Jesus; and lovingly considering Him to be their All, they repose their whole trust in Him.—That we should be united to Jesus—as Jesus is united to His Father—such was the high purpose regarding us, our Adorable Saviour had in view, in the midst of His Passion: He saw that through it we might attain to this degree of sanctity, that we might become partakers of the divine nature by means of this life of union. *I in them*, says our Lord to His Father, *and Thou in Me.* What an unspeakable honour to be associated with Him, being of one heart, of one mind together, in Jesus. What a present joy and happiness! what an assurance of future glory! Can we shrink from suffering, either voluntary or involuntary, if through it we may participate in the Passion of the Son of God and may be able to say that we are crucified with Him?

Colloquy.

O my Jesus, by Thy grace I understand what a happiness it is to be united to Thee, by a willing conformity to Thy sufferings: may I be ready to say that I gladly receive my Cross, however heavy or painful it may be. Only do Thou stay near me after having given it to me. Under this condition, I feel I can accept any trial, any affliction, since they will attach me to Thee inseparably;—and after being united to Thee here, by suffering, I shall be so eternally in Glory.

Resolution.

I will bear all trials after the example of Jesus, and in union with Him.

THOUGHT FOR THE DAY.

I—Jesus—in Thee: and Thou—O Father—in Me.

PRAYER.

Take, O Lord, and receive.

First Week in Lent.—Thursday.

The blessed results of meditation on the Passion.

I live, now not I, but Christ liveth in me.—GAL. II.

I. PRELUDE.

Let us remain faithfully at the foot of the Cross, and once again see our Saviour stretching out His Arms to receive us.

II. PRELUDE.

O Jesus, grant us grace to understand this great Mystery of Thy love for man: then shall our hearts rejoice unceasingly in Thee.

I. POINT.

The Wounds of Jesus console us.

Notwithstanding all that there is in the Mystery of the Cross to afflict our hearts, there is much also to console and rejoice them. The Wounds of our Saviour call upon us to rejoice on account of the goodness with which our sins are pardoned by Him,—the benefits which are bestowed on us, in time,—and those which are reserved for us in eternity. The tears we shed at the foot of the cross—at the sight of our sins—or at the thought of our long exile—or in contemplating the Death of our Lord—find not their source always in unmixed sorrow, but result also from that pure and solid consolation which the guilty experience when they are granted full remission of their offences: they are indeed tears of penitence, but also of gratitude and love. O Divine Redeemer, how great is Thy charity! Thou takest all the bitterness of the Passion for Thyself, and givest us the blessed fruits of it. We come to Thy Feet; our hearts are bowed down with grief, and Thou desirest to fill them with consolation,—reminding us, by Thy patient endurance, that our salvation depends on One Who is ready to extend His pardon to the most sinful. Do we not know that our eternal interests are in those Hands which were pierced during the uttering of that all-prevailing prayer, *Father, forgive them, for they know not what they do?*

II. Point.

The joy which accompanies this Mystery of the Cross, springs from contemplating the love of Jesus.

Penetrated with thankfulness at the sight of our Saviour's Crucifixion, we experience strongly the desire never to forget the liberality of His mercy; and the immensity of the love which incited God the Father to give to us a Saviour in the Adorable Person of His Son. It is this consideration which has kindled in the Saints such holy ardour. Oh! that we might with them but lose ourselves in Jesus Crucified; our hearts participating in the affections and sentiments of His Heart. *He loved me and delivered Himself for me*—yes! for me in particular—was the thought that drew forth the love of Saint Paul; and is not each one of us under as great an obligation to Jesus, as if there were no other person in the world? And who could express what that love must be, which the Saviour has for each? It far surpasses that of a son for his mother, or a holier and better love still, that of a mother for a son. It has been revealed that our Lord would have been ready to die as many times as there are souls in hell, if only it were possible for their sentence to be reversed. O Jesus, Who art much more lovable, so much more worthy of being loved than aught besides, why is it that men love Thee so little? Make them to know what Thou hast suffered for each one,—make them to love Thee.

Colloquy.

I thank Thee and I adore Thee, O my Crucified Jesus, for all that Thou hast done in order to save me, Thy unworthy child. Whilst I sorrow for my sins, which caused Thy cruel Passion, may I also have a lively sense of the gratitude I owe Thee; and feel that consolation which arises from the assurance that Thou didst deliver Thyself up to the Death of the Cross for love of me. Give me the grace of partaking in Thy infinite merits;—being crucified with Thee, may I be more closely united to Thee now—and eternally.

Resolution.

With loving devotion to Jesus on the Cross, often to press my Crucifix to my lips, thanking Him for all He has done for my salvation.

Thought for the Day.

I would know nothing, but Jesus Christ, and Him crucified.

Prayer.

Soul of Christ.

First Week in Lent.—Friday.

Jesus is sold by Judas to the chief priests.

What will you give me, and I will deliver Him unto you? —S. Matt. xxvi.

I. Prelude.

Let us sympathise with the afflicted Heart of Jesus, regarding the perfidy of His Disciple.

II. Prelude.

O Good Master, Whose merits are infinite, may we understand the value of the treasure we possess in Thee, and never sell Thy friendship for anything the world can offer us.

I. Point.

The chief-priests and ancients of the people consulted together, how they might take our Lord, and put Him to death.

Jesus, after having been with His Disciples as their Lord and Master, now wills to prepare to become the Victim offered for the guilty world. This is why He returns to Jerusalem, and whilst He projects the scheme of our redemption, the Jews are holding assemblies to combine, in their false wisdom, the most astute measures for apprehending Him, and putting Him to death. And still, are not the world and our depraved nature plotting constantly to cause Jesus to die out of hearts and lives? We have given ourselves to God,—are then our senses and unruly inclina tions in league with the enemies of Jesus? Let us take care not to resemble the treacherous Judas, and to be seduced by their importunate solicitations; but, on the contrary, may we preserve the life of Jesus in ourselves by an inviolable fidelity to His holy law, and a constant care to please Him in all things. We should hate all pharisaical wickedness, which by means of artifice and hypocrisy, effects its purpose. *For the wisdom of the flesh is death: but the wisdom of the spirit is life and peace.* Never shall we advance in virtue, if we do not walk in sincerity before God and man. One who acts out of human respect, to gain some selfish advantage, cannot be upright in reality; and it is much to be feared that scarcely any thought enters such a person's mind, which is quite free from deceit; the religious exterior of such a one is a perpetual falsehood. Give us, O Lord, sincerity of heart and purpose, and may we be guided at all times by Thy Holy Spirit.

II. Point.

What will you give me and I will deliver Him to you? They appointed him thirty pieces of silver.

Into what acts of injustice are not those persons led who, in their blindness, allow their own judgment and evil tendencies to master them. Like Judas they give away the precious treasure of God's grace—and even Jesus Himself—in exchange for the filthy lucre of a fleeting gratification, which will certainly one day be a cause of despair and endless misery. They resemble the Jews, who, far from appreciating the value of the saintly, perfect Life of the Messias Whom they would not recognise, sacrificed it to the satisfaction of their private judgment, and of their uncontrolled passions. That which was most holy, most precious appeared mean in their eyes:—humility—mortification—silence—poverty, these virtues were despised by them.—And are there not many who still traffic with the enemies of our Lord, and hand over to them that which is holy, for the base metal of human passion?—And this shameful traffic is carried on, perhaps, by such as have been taught in the school of Jesus; and whom He has once called to follow Him closely. So blinded are they, that they know not how they crucify the Son of God again; and think not that they again condemn the Lord of Glory to the punishment reserved for slaves! They dream not of the wrong they do to Thee, O Father, and Him Whom Thou hast sent; nor of the ills they draw down upon their community—their family—their habitation—their country: of the never-ending misery they are laying up for themselves. How touched with compassion should we be, when we see any one bartering away the Life of Jesus—their own salvation—for less even than thirty pieces of silver. For such Jesus prays, not only in the spoken words, *Father, forgive them, for they know not what they do,* but His Wounds cry out to God, and His sorrows plead for them as eloquently as His words.—It behoves us also to pray for their enlightenment; and for ourselves—that our Lord may blot out the remembrance of our own guilt—if we have ever sold Him into the hands of His enemies.

COLLOQUY.

My Beloved Redeemer, I desire to buy Thy love—Thy Self—by giving Thee my love and myself in exchange. O happy barter! I beg Thee, Jesus, that it may be effected, and that I may in some degree, make amends for the cruelty of Thy once chosen disciples, who deal treacherously against Thee. And for myself, do Thou keep me from ever again betraying Thee.

Resolution.

To-day I will often remind our Lord that I desire to be His faithful disciple, and friend.

Thought for the Day.

He that thinketh himself to stand, let him take heed lest he fall.

Prayer.

Take, O Lord, and receive.

First Week in Lent.—Saturday.

Agony of Jesus in the Garden of Olives.

Jesus saith to His Disciples: My Soul is sorrowful, even unto death; stay you here, and watch:—And when He was gone forward a little, He fell flat on the ground:—And He saith: Abba, Father, all things are possible to Thee, remove this chalice from Me; but not what I will, but what Thou wilt: There appeared to Him an Angel from Heaven strengthening Him: and being in an agony He prayed the longer: His sweat became as drops of blood, trickling down to the ground.—S. Mark xiv.—S. Luke xx.

I. Prelude.

Let us go to the Garden of Olives, and imagine that we are, by a particular privilege, permitted to remain with the three Disciples near Jesus, and to witness His Agony.

II. PRELUDE.

O Lord Jesus, give us grace to taste the bitterness of that grief in which Thy Holy Soul was steeped, so that we may sincerely repent of all those sins which caused Thy Agony.

I. POINT.

Why Jesus suffered such terrible mental auguish.

Let us contemplate our Saviour—prostrated—with His Face to the earth—as He thought of the great Mystery He was about to accomplish—He put before His mind the awful spectacle of the sins of all mankind;—at that moment He took upon Himself their dread weight. The Lamb of God, so essentially pure and holy, and having so supreme a horror of sin, saw Himself in the Presence of His Father, as if charged with the innumerable crimes which then covered the earth; and all those also which ever had been, or would be committed, from the beginning to the end of time. Was this all?—by no means.—Jesus must look upon another fearful certainty;—a great number of those for whom He was to suffer would obstinately refuse to profit by His Passion and Death.—And He knew beforehand what He would have to endure, before He might commend His Spirit into His Father's Hands. His Heart was pained unspeakably, fear and dread seized Him, the pangs of death were already present:—pale and trembling, Jesus—the Son of Mary—fell into a mortal agony. His sufferings were redoubled; beneath them He succumbed; and a sweat of blood poured forth from His body, and bedewed the ground.—How can we be insensible to Thy sufferings, and the griefs of Thy sacred Heart, O Saviour? Do not permit that we should remain so. Make the sorrows Thou didst endure for us to pass into our hearts, that by sharing them, we may in some degree assuage them.—Give us to understand what our sins have cost Thee, so that the thought of this may cause in us a keen sense of the affliction wherewith we have afflicted Thee; and that our tears may mingle with those precious blood-drops which fell upon the ground in Thy hour of agony.

II. Point.

The violence of the sorrow that sin occasioned in the Soul of Jesus.

Before withdrawing Himself from the company of the three Disciples, Jesus had announced to them that *His Soul was sorrowful even unto death;* and yet when He returned to them He found them asleep. Awaking them, He gently reproached them, addressing His words particularly to Saint Peter. *Could you not watch one hour? arise—pray—lest you enter into temptation.* Has not our Lord had cause many times to rebuke us, as He did His Disciples, for our insensibility regarding His sufferings, and the warnings He gives us?—Jesus returns to the place where he had just been praying; His Soul is stricken, but He is calm and submissive to His Father's Will. He repeats the same words: *If it be possible remove this chalice; but not what I will, but what Thou wilt.*—How heart-rending is it to hear our Lord, even a third time, renewing this entreaty!—His act of resignation is again made, and again the intensity of the Agony is evidenced by the Sweat of Blood. It is not, as yet, the brutal fury of the executioners which sprinkles with Blood the vestments of our Redeemer, but the violence of the anguish our sins caused Him.—Who does not weep? Who does not detest sin? Whose heart is not softened to compassion, as that moonlight scene rises up before their eyes? His Father sends an Angel to strengthen Him.—Can we too not console Him, by gathering round Him in His Agony? lessening the affliction, and alleviating the suffering of His Sacred Heart, by sharing in them.

COLLOQUY.

Loving Jesus, Sweet Saviour, to what an extremity do I see Thee reduced?—How fearful a thing must sin be, when its aspect, and the effects it produces, caused in Thee such terrible prostration. How can I ever again resolve to commit it? Do Thou Thyself fill me with a holy horror of sin, however light it may appear:—may I fear it more than death.

RESOLUTION.

I will carefully avoid the very least faults, and thus during this day prove my sympathy with my Saviour.

THOUGHT FOR THE DAY.

My Soul is sorrowful, even unto death.

PRAYER.

Soul of Christ.

Second Week in Lent.—Sunday.

During His Agony in the Garden of Olives Jesus is visited by an Angel.

And there appeared to Him an Angel from Heaven strengthening Him.—S. LUKE XXII.

I. Prelude.

Let us go again in spirit to the Garden of Olives, and keep near Jesus, Who when sorrowful there and in agony, was visited by an Angel.

II. Prelude.

O Jesus, may that holy sadness which filled Thy Soul, take possession of ours; so that, with Thee, we may deplore our sinfulness, and seeking support in our afflictions from God alone, by Him be powerfully succoured.

I. Point.

Jesus was sorrow-stricken at the sight of our spiritual degeneracy.

This was the principal cause of the affliction of the Heart of Jesus—the pitiable condition to which sin reduces our souls.—In witnessing His excessive grief, and the cruel agony under which His human nature sank, we are reminded of the words of Holy Scripture: *It is a fearful thing to fall into the Hands of the Living God.* If we would thoroughly understand what sin really is, and how God exerts against it His anger and His vengeance, we have but to contemplate the Sacred Victim Who offered Himself to His Father to expiate it. Who has ever heard of such an oblation? of such love? Not only would He fall under the wrath of God as the Victim of Atonement, but also obtain for us the merits of His suffering, and the grace of conversion. And all this—for us! yet we do not fear to offend God!—The failings and sins of infirmity into which even His elect would fall pierced His afflicted Heart;—how can it be that we, whose faithlessness He deplored, scarcely feel anything of the painful effects it had on the Soul of Jesus? Wounded to the quick when it is a question of some passing trouble or vexation of this life, we are indifferent to our spiritual defects, perhaps remain even self-pleased and joyous; not wishing to recognize the offences which render us displeasing in the sight of God. The state of a sick person is more dangerous when he ceases to feel the result of his disease. Enlighten us, O Saviour, with a ray of that clear light in which Thou didst see our spiritual maladies; and aided by Thy grace may we hasten to seek their cure.

II. POINT.

Jesus was strengthened by the appearing of a heavenly Messenger.

If we were plunged, as our Saviour was, into profound sorrow at the sight of our sins, if, following His example, we put in God all our trust, and had recourse to Him in persevering prayer, our Heavenly Father, Who is so full of compassion, would send to us also a consoling Angel. He would come and calm our minds, strengthen our will, and make us accept with resignation the chalice which God, in His love, has prepared for us. His presence would shed abroad in our souls the precious balm of true consolation, and inspire us with courage to endure that which is painful, in expiation of our many sins. This Messenger from Heaven may bear in his hands the cup of sorrow, but we need not shrink from accepting it. Assuring us that it is sent by our Living Father, he will prevail on us to drink it to the very dregs. In all our afflictions and trials, never may we doubt God's love, but following the example of Jesus, *pray the longer*. The perseverance and fervour of our prayers should be in proportion to the depth of our repentant sorrow, and our confidence in God.

Colloquy.

O Jesus, teach me to suffer, as Thou didst, with calmness and submission: teach me how to persevere in prayer, until my heart accepts with resignation all that it may please Thee to send me. Thou, Who art the strength of the weak, succour me according to my need;—send Thine Angel to arouse my failing courage, but, at the same time, may I also be prepared to serve Thee when Thou withholdest Thy consolation; saying under all circumstances, from the bottom of my heart: *My Father, Thy Will be done.*

Resolution.

In the hour of affliction and of combat I will keep near Jesus in the Garden of Olives, and imitate His perseverance in prayer.

Thought for the Day.

Father, not My will, but Thine be done.

Prayer.

O Jesus, living in Mary.

Second Week in Lent.—Monday.

Treachery, and subsequent despair of Judas.

Judas, one of the twelve, came, and with him a great multitude, with swords and clubs: And he gave them a sign, saying: Whomsoever I shall kiss, that is He, hold Him fast: And forthwith coming to Jesus, he said: Hail Rabbi: And he kissed Him: And Jesus said to him: Friend, whereto art Thou come.—S. Matt. xxvi.

I. Prelude.

Let us imagine to ourselves how silent was Gethsemani at that midnight hour, when the enemies of Jesus arrived.

II. Prelude.

Make us to understand, O Saviour of our souls, how guilty they are who abuse Thy grace by betraying Thee; and what a fearful punishment is reserved for such.

I. Point.

The malice with which Judas betrayed his Master.

Judas, the Disciple of our Lord, raised to the supreme dignity of the Apostolate, admitted to His friendship, and in proof of it sitting at table with his Master, allowed himself to be ruled by a vile passion, and became the guide of the enemies of Jesus in their search for Him. He had sold his Lord, and was guilty of the blackest treason; making use of the kiss of friendship as a sign to ensure His being delivered into the hands of the chief priests. Who would not tremble at the sight of such a downfall? Who would pride themselves on the favours they have received? Who would dare to rely upon the sanctity of their calling merely? Rather should we humble ourselves, when we see of what we too might be capable; and sound the depths of our hearts, to find out if there be lurking in them any secret passion, which may, sooner or later, urge us on into some act of treachery, against our Good Master. Are we so entirely faithful that we need not fear the reproaches of our Saviour: *My friend,* dost thou esteem me so little, that thou wouldst sell Me, at so low a price?—To satisfy some passion, for the sake of some human affection, wilt thou sacrifice thy Master?—*My friend, whereto art thou come?* Thou hast withdrawn thyself from Me, thou hast left My side to join thyself to the emissaries of the devil. Why hast thou abandoned thy heart to evil inclinations, which will prove thy ruin? Reflect—see what thou art doing. Whither is this refusal of My mercy leading thee: My grace is still offered thee: I would receive thee yet, if thou wouldst return to Me. *My friend, whereto art thou come?* What indeed will not Jesus do—that True Friend of our souls—*so that a sinner should not die, but that he should be converted from his evil ways and live?* and however far a wanderer might have strayed in the paths of iniquity, our Saviour would never reject one who begged His mercy and forgiveness.

II. Point.

Judas yielded to the temptation of despair, and hanged himself.

This traitorous Apostle had shut his ears to the gentle words which Jesus, wishing to touch his heart, had spoken: He had once again called him *His friend.* But Satan, having goaded him on to complete his crime, now filled his mind with despairing thoughts. Persuaded that his sin was unpardonable, he shortly after destroyed himself and sealed His eternal reprobation; *that he might go to his own place.* This temptation to despondency assails those who, after having like Judas, had special graces bestowed on them, become unfaithful.—Presuming on the goodness of God, and then finally abusing it, neither the doctrine of the Church, nor pious exhortations, nor charitable warnings are capable of touching them. The Voice of God, reminding them of His readiness to pardon, is not heeded. They refuse the life that is offered them if they would repent, and then everlasting death comes in the guise of despairing thoughts, by which the devil persuades them that their salvation is impossible, and so completes his triumph. How dangerous are such thoughts.—Let us fear and avoid all unfaithfulness; but if, forgetting the justice of God, we have the unhappiness to fall into any fault, never let us, forgetting the mercy of God, fall into despair.

Colloquy.

O my Saviour, never permit that whilst detesting Thy betrayal by Judas, I should repeat it in any degree, by an abuse of Thy grace; but grant that, making good use of the privileges with which Thou dost favour me, I may render myself worthy to dwell in Thy holy company, and to be admitted to familiar intercourse with Thee. May I often recall to mind the end for which Thou hast chosen me, so that I may become more faithful in Thy service; and if, in consequence of my great frailty, I ever offend Thee, may I at once seek Thee; and throwing myself into the arms of Thy mercy, receive from Thee the grace of forgiveness.

Resolution.

I will often have this thought before me:—why am I here? is it to live according to the spirit of the world? or to become a faithful friend of Jesus Christ?

Thought for the Day.

Friend, whereto art thou come hither?

Prayer.

Take, O Lord, and receive.

Second Week in Lent.—Tuesday.

The soldiers come to seize Jesus.

Jesus knowing all things that should come upon Him, went forth: and said to them: Whom seek ye? They answered Him, Jesus of Nazareth. Jesus saith to them: I am He.— They fell to the ground.—S. John xviii.

I. Prelude.

Let us in spirit return to Gethsemani, and attentively observe all that is there going on.

II. Prelude.

Divine Jesus, grant us to understand the sentiments which filled Thy Sacred Heart at the moment when Thou didst deliver Thyself, for us, into the hands of Thy enemies.

I. Point.

At the sight of His enemies, our Divine Saviour, instead of flying from them, went forth to meet them. He, Who had hidden Himself, when they wished to make Him a King, now gives His Sacred Person into their power, when they have determined to put Him to death. He asks in a tone of divine authority: *Whom seek ye?—Jesus of Nazareth.— I am He*, said the Almighty Son of God, and at His word, they fell backwards in terror. We should remark the forbearance of Jesus, Who having the power to overthrow His enemies, yet abandoned Himself willingly to suffering and to death; thus, by His conduct, explaining that He was ready to offer Himself as a Living Sacrifice for the honour of His Father, and the salvation of mankind. May we not derive courage, from the example of our Saviour, to be faithful when the Divine Will asks of us some great sacrifice. The words spoken by our Lord—*I am He*—have very different effects on the hearts of those who hear them: they produce alarm, as they are intended to do, in sinners; so that through fear of the just judgment of God, they may repent and be converted; whereas in those who rejoice at the sound of the Bridegroom's Voice, His words produce true peace and a sweet sense of His Presence. May He often say to us, *I am He*, causing us to recognise in Him our God—our Good Master—our Jesus;—and that He comes to save us, by offering us the merits of the Death He endured, to give us life.

II. Point.

The care Jesus takes of His Disciples.

Our Saviour exposes Himself to death for His Disciples: and forgetful of Himself, thinks only how to save them. *Let these go their way*, He said to the band of soldiers that followed Judas. During the outburst of the storm, He covered His own with the shield of His power, and sheltered them from danger. Happy are those who remain beneath His kind and almighty protection. What peace is theirs who say, when encompassed with enemies: *Thou art my protector, and my refuge: my God, in Him will I trust.* Let us go forward with Jesus, and in His strength meet our foes; perhaps in our works of charity we may have opportunities of closely imitating Him, by warding off from those who are weak in spirit, or discouraged, the attacks of the foe, in the form of alarm and disquietude. *Let these go their way,*—we may sacrifice ourselves for the good of others, suffer in their stead, and obtain for them a reprieve, during which they may gather up their strength, for any future assaults with which they may be tried. Our Lord's words affected the soldiers, insomuch that the Disciples were permitted to depart unmolested: they were not in that night courageous enough to share in the shame and contempt, still less in the sufferings of their Master; therefore He adds: *Let these go their way: that the word might be fulfilled which He said: Of them whom the Father hath given Me, I have not lost any one.*

Colloquy.

O Jesus, how continual is Thy goodness towards me!—Thou art day by day my Defender, and takest my part against those foes who would assault me, and lead me away captive. May I listen for Thy Voice, and take courage as I hear Thee say, *I am He,*—do Thou Thyself bind me by the necessities of Thy Sweet Will; and make me rejoice that Thou hast put upon me the yoke of holy obedience to my Rule of life.

Resolution.

To please Jesus and to honour His bonds, I will willingly submit to all that duty and my holy Rule demand of me.

Thought for the Day.

I am He, thy Saviour—thy Defender.

Prayer.

Our Father, and Hail Mary.

Second Week in Lent.—Wednesday.

Jesus is taken Prisoner in the Garden of Olives.

They laid hands on Him and held Him.—S. MARK XIV.

I. PRELUDE.

Let us remain beneath the olive-trees, whilst Jesus is being surrounded by the soldiers :—they dare to lay their sacrilegious hands on His Adorable Person, and to bind Him as a criminal.

II. PRELUDE.

O Jesus, as we think of the cords wherewith they bound Thee, may we be drawn more closely to Thee by the attractiveness of Thy charity which far exceeded in effect any bonds Thy enemies could make use of, to effect their purpose.

I. POINT.

Jesus is taken prisoner.

The Redeemer was the precious Treasure on which the perfidious Jews dared to lay their hands, not to enrich themselves, but to lose It for ever ; because they would not appreciate Its true value. They who had before honoured the typical Ark of God, and had not lost the remembrance of Oza's rashness and his punishment, now despised the Antitype, when He fell into their wicked hands. O Jesus—sacred Treasure—how greatly do we grieve to see Thee thus seized, and treated with such profanity. Again : Thou as the Good Shepherd, wast about to give Thy Life for Thy sheep.—We behold Thee exposed to the fury of the wolves, to save the flock. They turn upon Thee with savage cruelty; anon Thou wilt permit Thy Sacred Body to be torn and mangled, so that on Thyself their rage may be vented, and exhausted. And all this for us!—The weight of our sins bowed Jesus down with His Face to the earth in Gethsemani; —and near to the spot where the Sweat of Blood trickled to the ground, the Shepherd was seized;—and why? *Because we like sheep have gone astray, and every one hath turned aside into his own way: He was offered, because it was His own Will.* Have we returned to His Fold?

II. Point.

Jesus is bound as a robber—a criminal.

What do we next look upon? The Hands of the Son of God are tied with cords;—He is bound—fettered. And by whom? by men whom He came to deliver from the bondage of Satan. Angels of Heaven, ye behold in astonishment your Creator bound! And Jesus, why didst Thou permit this outrage? what hast Thou to do with the fetters of slaves and criminals, Who art the Saint of saints—the King of kings—the Lord of lords? Why didst Thou not break Thy bonds, and deliver Thyself from the torments and the death Thy creatures were preparing for Thee?—Jesus would have us to understand that it is not the cords nor chains that prevent His escape, but love alone holds Him captive, and leads Him to suffer and to die for us. Love forms the only chain which could fetter the God-Man. Without it His enemies could never have succeeded in making Him their Prisoner. How powerful is the love of our Saviour! Oh, that it might bind us also, and that, so closely to Him, that nothing might be able to sever the links of our love for Jesus. When shall we be able to love Him as we ought?

Colloquy.

O my Saviour, seeing the manner in which Thy enemies seized Thee, and bound Thee, I weep to think of the cruel part I had, in all these outrages committed against Thee. But then, O Lord, Thou didst will to be thus fettered, that the chains of my sins might be broken.—Thy love led Thee captive for my sake :—how can I ever thank Thee enough for the merits of Thy sufferings in Gethsemani !

Resolution.

To practice the patience and meekness of Jesus.

Thought for the Day.

He loved me and delivered Himself up for me.

Prayer.

Take, O Lord, and receive.

Second Week in Lent.—Thursday.

Jesus is led before Annas, and then before Caiphas.

The band and the tribune, and the servants of the Jews took JESUS, *and bound Him: and they led Him away.*— S. JOHN XVIII.

I. Prelude.

We represent to ourselves our Adorable Saviour in the hands of those who brought Him before the high priest.

II. Prelude.

Divine Spouse of our souls, Who to free us from our condition of bondage, didst will to be bound as a criminal, grant that we may love the sacred chains of Religion which unite us to Thee.

I. Point.

Jesus was bound to free us from bondage.

Besides the condition of slavery to sin, into which all mankind is liable to fall, but from which Jesus undertook to deliver us by carrying its chains, there is another state of bondage from which religious persons are liberated by the Divine Captive. Is it not by virtue of His bonds that we receive strength to break off worldly ties, and to free ourselves from the thraldom of the senses—natural inclinations—and human passions? And since none can be his own master, and must choose between God and mammon, our Lord, by the cords wherewith He was bound, would release us from the service of mammon, and obtain for us the true liberty of the servants of God. To some is communicated the peculiar attraction of the livery of Religion: they who wear it are the personal attendants on their Master, and are bound to render Him a service of love.—Such are called upon to embrace a life of happy servitude, and to bear the light chains of their vows of chastity, poverty, and obedience, in exchange for those of the world, which are heavy indeed. What a debt of gratitude do we not owe our Lord and Master, Who has merited for us the privilege of belonging to His household! Let us then in spirit approach the Divine Captive, and with tender respect kiss His chains, which secured our liberty; and esteem it a happiness to carry the easy yoke of His service.

II. Point.

The patient gentleness with which Jesus allowed Himself to be taken from one tribunal to another.

We see how the God-Man, as a Prisoner, was dragged from place to place, during the Hours of His Passion. From the Garden of Olives to the house of Annas,—from Annas to Caiphas,—then to the prison. From the prison He was led before the council,—then to Pilate; from Pilate to Herod;—again we see Him before the judgment-seat of Pilate, then in the adjoining hall to be scourged and derided; lastly, He was conducted up the Hill of Calvary, to consummate His Sacrifice upon the ignominious Cross. What an example of patience and submission! The Evangelists have not been able to express fully all that His persecutors made our Lord Jesus endure, but their simple recital of the Passion excites in our hearts compassion and wonder,—and which meditation calls forth with greater intensity. Truly His enemies *have done unto the Son of Man whatsoever they had a mind.* He was in the hands of those whose rage it is difficult to conceive; He was left to their fury, abandoned by His friend: *And there was none to comfort Him.* Jesus obeyed those who were intending to take His Life, and shall we then, who are His Spouses, find any difficulty in submitting ourselves to those who hold the place of God in our regard?

Colloquy.

How ashamed ought I to be, O my Saviour, if, after making profession to follow Thee and to imitate Thee, I act in contradiction to what I profess! United to Thee by the ties of obedience, may I be guided unresistingly by those to whom I owe it;—at all times, and in every place being happy and contented, knowing that where obedience leads, I shall always find Thee, and Thy example of patient submission.

Resolution.

To renew fervently my religious engagement to be patiently submissive under any circumstance, however painful.

Thought for the Day.

I am the Lord, thy Redeemer:—a Man of Sorrows.

Prayer.

Take, O Lord, and receive.

Second Week in Lent.—Friday.

The flight of the Apostles.

Then His Disciples leaving Him, all fled away.—S. Mark xiv.

I. Prelude.

Let us represent to ourselves Jesus, left alone by His Disciples in the hands of the soldiers; they having taken flight through fear.

II. Prelude.

Preserve us, O Lord, from our own weakness, and never permit that we forsake Thy cause, either through human respect, or self-love.

I. Point.

The flight of the Apostles afflicted the Heart of Jesus.

How much our Lord must have felt it, when all the other Disciples forsook Him, on the night that Judas betrayed their Master. For three years they had been admitted to the privilege of living with Him, and following Him wherever He went. He had, during all that time, lavished on them signal proofs of His love. A few hours only had elapsed since He had crowned these benefits by instituting for them the Holy Eucharist. Then, as a good Father, on the point of leaving His beloved children, He had been speaking to them out of the fulness of His Heart:—and now,—where are they? Jesus knew that they were too weak in faith and courage to stand by Him; but how their flight must have pained their Master!—It is meet that we should compassionate Him, and question ourselves as to whether we have not often renewed this injury done to His love. Have we not forgotten that Thou, O Jesus, hast placed us amongst Thy chosen friends, enlightened us with the pure rays of Thy teaching, and elected us to do the work of apostles. And yet, how often have we shrunk back from even appearing to belong to Thee? how often acted through human respect, and kept back from some outward acknowledgement of Thee, through cowardice. We have indeed reason to fall at Thy Feet and crave Thy pardon; and appealing to Thy Sacred Heart, ask the courage to be more faithful for the future.

II. Point.

This trial which Jesus had to endure, ought to teach us that we should be ready to suffer the loss of human sympathy and love.

After having seen the Son of God enduring with so much calmness and gentleness the forsaking of His Disciples, how can we complain of the inconstancy and forgetfulness of persons who may have been very dear to us? Shall we avenge the ingratitude of those from whom we perhaps justly expected a different return? If God subject us to such a trial as the loss of friendship, let us learn of Jesus how to bear it. He felt keenly the injury done to His watchful love for His Disciples, but as ever, patient and gentle, and with unchangeable charity, He went to meet death for those who seemed so little worthy of His affection for them. After His Resurrection He deigned to appear where they were assembled, to call them His Brethren, and to bestow on them new favours. We learn from our Saviour what our conduct should be towards those whom frailty, or cowardice, or inconsistency renders unstable in goodness, and apt to yield before difficulties.—We should say to ourselves,—"Jesus would in this case exhibit patience, calmness and forbearance: He would not weary of helping the weak, and of giving proofs of His goodness, so that He might win them by love." Let us do likewise.

Colloquy.

When I see how the Pillars of the Church were shaken by temptation, how can I presume to trust my own resolves? —How frail is man!—how small a thing may cause him to fall!—I indeed feel, O my Jesus, my own weakness, but I depend on Thy strength, to which at all times, I may have recourse. Thy love will support me; and give to me, as to the Apostles, courage to make amends for my past faults, and zeal for God, which shall yield neither to suffering nor to death.

RESOLUTION.

In temptation to unite myself more firmly to my Saviour, and from Him obtain the grace of an entire fidelity to His love.

THOUGHT FOR THE DAY.

I would rather die, O Good Master, than forsake Thee.

PRAYER.

O Jesus, living in Mary.

Third Saturday in Lent.

The Sufferings of Jesus in the Court of the High Priest.

The chief priests and the whole council sought false witness against JESUS, *that they might put Him to death.*—S. MATT. 26.

I. PRELUDE.

Let us go, in thought, into the hall where our Adorable Saviour is standing as a criminal before His iniquitous judges, who are resolved that He should die.

II. PRELUDE.

O Lamb of God, Who by Thy sufferings and Thy patience hast expiated our sins, grant that in meditating upon Thy virtues, we may learn how we ought to bear the trials of this life.

I. POINT.

The patience and meekness of Jesus, when standing before the chief priests.

Caiphas, the high priest, having heard no accusation brought against Jesus, yet desirous of finding Him guilty, interrogated Him upon the doctrine He had taught the people. The wise and dignified response made by our Lord, so worthy of the admiration of all upright minds, earned for Him a most cruel and shameful outrage, on the part of one of the servants of the house, *who gave Jesus a blow.* This excited the laughter of the assembly; but our Saviour received this deep humiliation with unalterable patience and meekness. Let us learn from our God how to receive with humility and gentleness even personal insult, if He permit that we should be tried in this manner. Jesus accepted the outrage upon His Adorable Person with calmness; making only this just remark: *If I have spoken evil, give testimony of the evil; but if well, why strikest Thou Me?* How useful is this example of forbearance to ourselves!—We should recall it to mind when there is a danger of our wishing another to incur some blame; or of our desiring an accusation to be brought against a particular person, through a feeling of revenge.—If again we are likely to fall into any fault arising from anger or quick susceptibility, then should we remember to look at the Adorable Face of our Dear Lord, in which shone forth the majesty of His Divinity, and the charm of His Sanctity, even when suffering the most unjust treatment.

II. POINT.

Jesus is left in the hands of the brutal soldiers, and insolent servants.

When Caiphas retired for the night, the menials and the soldiers gathered round, to make sport of the Divine Prisoner; they took a wicked pleasure in maltreating Him.—Who can say what He endured during those terrible hours of darkness? Then were the prophetic words of Isaias accomplished: *I have given My Body to the strikers, and My Cheeks to them that plucked them: I have not turned away My Face from them that rebuked Me, and spit upon Me.* Yes, that Holy Face was so bruised and disfigured that *in Him was no beauty, nor comeliness.* Nevertheless, during the time He was undergoing all these outrages, Jesus was perfectly silent, and maintained His dignity and calmness of demeanour, even when covered with blood and wounds. The contemplation of this part of the Passion has drawn many souls to a deeper love of our Saviour;—should it not affect our hearts in a like manner? and as, by faith, we see with what meekness and charity He received these humiliations, let us learn to suffer and to bear contempt as He did, and in union with Him.

COLLOQUY.

How ashamed I ought to feel, O Jesus, when I contemplate Thee in this pitiable state, surrounded by those insolent miscreants, yet preserving such entire patience and meekness; and then remember my own easily ruffled susceptibility, if despised or even slighted.—How striking a contrast! I, a sinner, have deserved everlasting contempt, and yet am so sensitive about the least injury; whilst Thou, Most Innocent Saviour, wast treated with fearful insults, and showedst no resentment. Well may I weep over my cowardice—pride—and little resemblance to Thyself.—Give me grace to become more like Thee,—my Example at all times.

RESOLUTION.

To suffer all humiliations for love of Jesus; and to stifle susceptibility directly I am aware of it.

THOUGHT FOR THE DAY.

He was bruised for our sins.

PRAYER.

Take, O Lord, and receive.

Third Week in Lent.—Sunday.

The fall of Saint Peter.

Peter followed JESUS *afar off, even to the court of the high-priest: And going in he sat with the servants, that he might see the end.*—S. MATTHEW XXVI.

I. PRELUDE.

We see Saint Peter following Jesus at a distance; and then entering the hall and sitting down beside the fire, amongst the servants of the chief-priest.

II. PRELUDE.

O Jesus, the Strength of the weak, grant that, distrusting ourselves, and confiding only in Thee, we may be preserved from the danger of offending Thee.

I. Point.

Peter followed Jesus at a distance.

The principal cause of the fall of Saint Peter was, without doubt, his presumption. Though warned by His Divine Master of his liability to fall into temptation, he presumed too far on the sensible affection he had for Him; and therefore feared no danger. Happier had it been for this favoured Apostle, had he mistrusted himself, and leaned more entirely on the strength he should have sought from Jesus. But he did not seek this strength, and therefore was quickly intimidated by the appearance of those who came to seize our Lord: not wishing to abandon Him wholly, he retired to a safe distance; and then, accompanied by another disciple, *followed Jesus afar off.* This was the cause of his cowardice, this was how he unarmed himself, forgetful of the warning he had received that a combat might be expected.—What are we without the divine assistance? The strongest, the most courageous may well tremble, with the history of Saint Peter's denial of His Beloved Master before us. *He that thinketh himself to stand, let him take heed lest he fall.* However great may be our love, we are not proof against inconstancy.—We cannot be surprised at our frequent falls, if we follow Jesus only at a distance, through presumption or cowardice.—Apart from him we necessarily become feeble, and tepid; and are in constant danger of slipping. We do well to-day to examine ourselves as to the cause of our falls, and if we find it to be our trusting too much in our own strength, we must promise our Divine Master not to lose sight of Him, but to remain faithfully at His side.

II. Point.

Peter exposes himself to further danger.

If one lose sight of Jesus, the fear of offending God becomes less. Thus it was with Saint Peter. No longer under the Eye of His Master, he actually went into the midst of his enemies, not to influence them in His favour, but only to see what was going on.—What an unfitting and dangerous position for this Disciple! That he yields is no longer any wonder. He disguises his feelings, puts on an appearance of unconcern;—he adds deceit to cowardice. Thus exposed to temptation, it comes to him from an unexpected quarter. A maid-servant remarked that she recognised him as a companion of Jesus.—What an honour for Saint Peter! Why does he not gladly accept it?—He cannot—he is overcome by fear: he dreads the thought of being also arrested and of sharing the fate of his Master:—the breath of a single word has scattered all his promises of fidelity. This is he, who a few short hours before had said to Jesus: *I will lay down my life for Thee: Yea, though I should die with Thee, I will not deny Thee.*—This instance of human frailty should put us more than ever on our guard against being self-reliant; and make us see more clearly the danger of being in the company of the enemies of God. We should rather seek the society of His most devoted friends—His faithful servants, so that by their good example we may learn lessons of true piety, and profit by the influence of their holiness.

COLLOQUY.

There is no sanctity which is firm enough to stand alone—to support itself. I perceive indeed that there is no solid virtue but that which has its foundation in the unfailing holiness of Jesus.—Do Thou, therefore, O Lord, let me depend on Thee alone for strength and support: however good my sentiments and intentions may seem to me to be,

I will not trust myself, but place my whole being in Thy Hands, and under the protection of Thy Presence lose my fear, and gain courage to meet the trials through which Thou dost ordain I should pass.

Resolution.

To keep near to Jesus—so that I may avoid all danger of offending Him.

Thought for the Day.

Lead us not into temptation.

Prayer.

Our Father, and Hail Mary.

Third Week in Lent.—Monday.

Repentance of Saint Peter.

The Lord turning looked on Peter: And Peter remembered the word of the Lord, as He had said: Before the cock crow, thou shalt deny Me thrice: and Peter going out, wept bitterly.—St. Luke xxii.

I. Prelude.

We may see Peter still amongst the servants of the chief-priest. Jesus has not forgotten him, in the midst of His sufferings.—He now turns round and looks at His Disciple, who has just disowned his Lord for the third time.

II. Prelude.

In our hearts, O Jesus, broken with sorrow for our sins and Thy sufferings, engrave ineffacably the remembrance of Thy mercy.

I. Point.

The denial of Saint Peter wounded the Heart of Jesus most deeply.

Peter, the chief amongst the Apostles, and elected by Jesus to become the Head of His Church, denied his Master, and declared, with an oath, that he did not know Him. Let us imagine, if we can, what our Lord must have felt, on hearing this; and at the same time let us turn our thoughts upon ourselves, and see if we have ever had the unhappiness of re-opening the wound caused by the unfaithfulness and inconstancy of him whom Jesus had called to so high a destiny. Have we ever been ashamed to own that Jesus is our Master?—that we have been in His company?—that He has called us to walk in the way of humiliation—of poverty—of self-abnegation?—to follow along the path of strict observance—of penance—of suffering, a path marked out by Himself for those who have received the vocation to the Religious Life? Have we been guilty of such base cowardice and ingratitude? Are we ready to endure any reproach, any contempt, rather than deny, by word or deed, that we know, and love, and obey Jesus?

II. Point.

A look from our Lord produced sincere repentance in Saint Peter.

The goodness of our Saviour towards His cowardly

Disciple strikes us forcibly. On several occasions He had shown him some special favour, and He might have expected from him some special demonstration of fidelity.—When our Lord predicted his fall, He warned him, so that he might be aware of his danger, and at least be prepared to turn to Him for help when the hour of trial should arrive. Well had it been for him, if, finding himself on the troubled sea of temptation, he had again cried out: *Lord save me.*—Now that he disowned Him in so culpable a manner, his Master might have crushed him by a glance; but when those words of lying and of cursing reached His Ear, He turned round and cast on Peter a look of pity, which touched his heart, and produced in it such genuine feelings of contrition, that the repentant Disciple wept bitterly. What happy effects did not that compassionating look secure to Saint Peter? Jesus will also regard us, and with equally beneficial results, if we speak to Him of our helplessness, our infidelities, and of our sorrow for them. A look from Jesus is as full of mercy as it is full of power. —O Saviour, look then upon all sinners that they may be converted;—look upon us who profess to be Thy disciples, and recal us to a sense of our duties and privileges as such. —If we fall, raise us up in pity, and grant us a true spirit of repentance: *Look upon us according to the multitude of Thy tender mercies.*

COLLOQUY.

O my Good Master, like Saint Peter, I have been ungrateful and unfaithful, and I have many times wronged Thy love; touched by the power and sweetness of Thy grace, I would also wash out from Thy remembrance all my ingratitude, by tears of contrition. Grant that I may never again be ashamed of Thee, nor disown my privileges as Thy disciple.

RESOLUTION.

Often to ask Jesus to endue me with a true spirit of compunction; so that, while lamenting my past sins, I may avoid repeating them.

THOUGHT FOR THE DAY.

The Lord turning, looked on Peter.

PRAYER.

Take, O Lord, and receive.

Third Week in Lent.—Tuesday.

Pilate acknowledges the innocence of Jesus.

When the morning was come, all the chief priests and ancients of the people took counsel against JESUS, that they might put Him to death: And they delivered Him to Pontius Pilate, the governor. . . . Pilate said: I am innocent of the blood of this Just Man.—S. MATT. XXVII.

I. PRELUDE.

Let us follow our Saviour as He passes through the city of Jerusalem. He is led as a criminal before Pilate.

II. PRELUDE.

Give us grace, O Jesus, to understand from Thy own

conduct before Pilate, that we may confidingly leave the issue of all events in God's Hands.

I. Point.

Pilate questions Jesus concerning His Kingdom.

Amongst the false and extravagant imputations of blame whereby the enemies of our Saviour sought to obtain a confirmation of His guilt, there was one which particularly attracted the attention of Pilate. These accusers said: *This Man forbids to give tribute to Cæsar, saying that He is Christ the King.* Therefore Pilate questioned Him at once on this point. *Art Thou*, he said, *the King of the Jews?*—Jesus, Who knew so perfectly well when to speak and when to keep silence, now replies with wonderful wisdom: *My Kingdom is not of this world: If My Kingdom were of this world, My servants would certainly strive that I should not be delivered to the Jews: but My Kingdom is not from hence.* Let us carefully meditate on this important truth, concerning the spiritual Kingdom of our Divine King. It is indeed not of this world—but it was begun here, and then raised above the world. Jesus reigns, in eternity, over those hearts and minds which tend upwards, *and seek the things that are above.* He is occupied, not in visibly governing a temporary empire, but in enlightening souls by His Divine power of illuminating grace, and enkindling in hearts the sacred fire of love:—by these means he reigns, and prepares us to reign with Him in Heaven. His subjects, His servants, as He said to Pilate, are not of this world. They are in it, but not of it:—not being attached to it, they do not follow its maxims; the Object of their faith and their hope is the Eternal Good; acknowledging Him for their King, they love, listen to, and obey Him. O Blessed Kingdom!—O happy subjects of such a King! To serve Him, is it not to reign? May we find it so, by happy experience.

II. Point.

Pilate bears witness to the innocence of Jesus.

I find no cause in Him. We may not suppose that calumny causes innocence to lose anything of its purity. It is a ray of clear light, which shines through the blackest slander; a light which God makes to shine for His glory and that of His faithful ones, at the moment and in the way He has purposed. Thus, notwithstanding the hatred and malice with which the enemies of Jesus strove to prejudice the governor against Him, His innocence is acknowledged by Pilate.—Why then should we grow disquieted if we are slandered, or if contempt be shown towards us? is it not enough to have God for a Witness of our innocence? it suffices for Him to know what we really are. Let the world talk; we have only to take one precaution, which is, to give no ground for scandal. *I find no cause in Him,* was the the verdict of Pilate:—his wife besought him to do nothing against Jesus:—Judas had already accused himself of having betrayed innocent blood.—Like our Lord, let us only seek to please God, and to be guiltless in His Sight. If we too can say:—I seek not my own glory but that of God alone, we may rest assured that He will do us justice, and watch over our best interests.

Colloquy.

O Spotless Lamb, the silence and the composure Thou didst maintain when they so falsely accused Thee, condemns my frequent agitation and disquietude, and inspires me with an ardent desire to imitate Thy example. Besides, ought not

I, who am guilty, willingly to accept contempt and ignominy to satisfy the justice of God?—this is what I purpose doing, in order to render honour and glory to Thy perfect innocence, and to atone for my faults.

Resolution.

To preserve peace of mind, and keep silence when unjustly accused;—never justifying myself, except when the honour and glory of God necessitates my doing so.

Thought for the Day.

My Kingdom is not of this world.

Prayer.

O Jesus, living in Mary.

Third Week in Lent.—Wednesday.

Jesus is derided in Herod's Palace.

Herod questioned Jesus in many words: But He answered him nothing. And Herod, with his army, set Him at nought: and mocked Him, putting on Him a white garment: and sent Him back to Pilate.—S. Luke xxiii.

I. Prelude.

Let us accompany Jesus to the palace of Herod, and observe His conduct when set at nought and ridiculed.

II. Prelude.

Fill us, O Lord, with a great love of humility and silence, as practised by Thee when questioned by Herod.

I. Point.

Jesus answers nothing.

O mysterious silence! What wondrous secrecy is there in the wisdom of God! Jesus held His peace, because Herod was unworthy to hear Him speak. Amongst the children of the world, silence is regarded as a sign of a weak intellect: in the school of Jesus Christ it is often a mark of wisdom. The heart of a silent imitator of our Saviour becomes, by the intensified desire of holding intercourse with Him, a receptacle of heavenly graces. It would have been so easy for Jesus to have justified Himself; and by the wisdom of His words to have aroused the admiration of the court of Herod: but ever occupied with the thought of our salvation, He desired by an unspoken counsel to teach us how to keep silence, when silence is better than words. By the virtue of Thy silence, O Jesus, which Thou wouldst not break, in order to teach us a valuable lesson, give us a greater love for it. By means of it, may we draw God into the peaceful abode of our soul, and may it be a defence against the inroads of disquietude and anxiety. Give us, O Lord, the spirit of discernment, that we may know when to speak, and when to keep silence.

II. Point.

Herod, in mockery, had a white garment put on Jesus, before sending Him back to Pilate.

He was dumb as a lamb before His shearer: and He did

not open His Mouth. The proud spirit of the king and of his courtiers caused them to look with disdain upon the Meek and Holy Lamb of God standing silently before His persecutors, who treated Him as if He were demented.—This is the spirit of the world, that being a combination of the spirit of pride—which admires that only which has an appearance of pomp and greatness,—the spirit of trifling and of curiosity,—the spirit of irreverence—which despises grave and sacred things and turns them into derision, and a superficial spirit—which is far from appreciating true and solid virtue. Let us beware of this dangerous spirit of the world, and contemplate the gentle humility and modest silence of our Divine Saviour, throughout His trial.—After being clothed in a garment of ignominy, and treated as a foolish visionary, He was, in quitting the palace of Herod, assailed by the shouts and imprecations of the populace. He became indeed *the reproach of men, and the outcast of the people*: *All they that saw Him laughed Him to scorn.* May the remembrance of Thy humility, patience, and silence, O Jesus, be engraved in our hearts, and become the rule of our lives. May we desire to participate in Thy suffering and humiliation, so that we may more closely resemble Thee.

Colloquy.

O Supreme Wisdom, Thou didst consent to pass for One devoid of reason, and as such, was clothed in a garment of dishonour. Is it not right and just, that if I would walk in Thy Footsteps, as a true disciple, I should receive silently and willingly the reproaches and the disdain the world may cast upon me. Should I receive any humiliations, O Jesus, teach me how to bear them in silence, and to rejoice even at being despised, for Thy Sake.

RESOLUTION.

During the day, often to adore Jesus in His humiliation.

THOUGHT FOR THE DAY.

I was the reproach of men, and the outcast of the people.

PRAYER.

Soul of Christ.

Third Week in Lent.—Thursday.

Barabbas the Robber is preferred to the Son of God.

Pilate, calling together the chief priests, and the magistrates, and the people, said to them: You have presented unto me this Man as one that perverteth the people, and behold I, having examined Him before you, find no cause in this Man touching those things wherein you accuse Him: But you have a custom that I should release one unto you at the Pasch; will you therefore that I release unto you the King of the Jews? —Not this Man, but Barabbas.—S. LUKE XXIII., S. JOHN XVIII.

I. PRELUDE.

Let us remain in the Presence of Jesus, Who, with His Eyes cast down, and in the posture of a criminal, awaits His verdict.

II. PRELUDE.

Divine Lamb of God, Who art about to sacrifice Thyself

for love of us, grant that, understanding what we owe to Thy love, we may give the preference to Thee before all other things, with our whole heart and soul.

I. Point.

Jesus was compared to Barabbas.

Every kind of insult had already been levelled against our Lord: He had been calumniated,—had been struck,—had been spit upon,—degradingly bound and dragged through the streets like a vile malefactor: in the court of Herod He had been derided: and all this to work the cure of our pride.—What a terrible evil pride must be!—Now we see Jesus again, in Pilate's judgment-hall, where He was put in comparison with whom? With a wretched prisoner, who was loaded with crimes; a robber—a promoter of sedition—an assassin—whose freedom would again imperil public safety, and increase vice; —and yet, this is he whom they would choose to tolerate in their midst, rather than that the Holy One and the Just should be set at liberty. After this shall we presume to complain when we are little, and others greatly esteemed? when our talents, our services, are badly appreciated? when others are preferred before us?—The Jews preferred a murderer to the Author of Life.—Jesus, having been thus treated, how gladly should we imitate Him, and bear the little humiliations, pre-arranged for our good by Providence, with patience and meekness. *Learn of Me*, our Saviour seems to say, as He hears the cries of the multitude in favour of Barabbas, *because I am meek and humble of heart.*

II. Point.

Barabbas is still often preferred to Jesus.

How foolish is the world, how blind and unjust do the

passions of men render them! Do they not still prefer that which causes death, to that which brings life?—Life and death are put before us,—grace and nature,—good and evil, —Jesus and Barabbas.—Yet such is the blindness of the multitude, that a passing gratification is preferred to eternal delights,—vanity and transitory honours to immortal glory,—the perishable goods of this life to the unfailing riches of Heaven,—Satan to God.—But that which is still more deplorable, as it is still more surprising is, to find amongst those who are the most favoured by our Lord—amongst those even who have been called to the religious state, some who are also blinded in their preferences. For is not their own will often preferred to the holy Will of God? their inclinations to His good pleasure?—imperfection to perfection?—themselves to Jesus? O God, preserve us from making such a choice. Having once chosen Jesus instead of the world, may we never go back from our determination to lose all, rather than lose Him and His love. *Choose this day that which pleaseth you,—whom you would rather serve.*

Colloquy.

O Wisdom, O Incarnate Truth, Thou Who weighest all things in a just balance, grant me to know how to show my preference for Thee above all things created. Thou art my God, and therefore my All. Heaven without Thee would be nothing; without Thee what would the possession of the whole earth be worth? Thou alone, O Jesus, the Well-Beloved of my heart, sufficest me:—my choice is made for ever.

Resolution.

Often to do some act of love, to evince my preference of God's Will to my own.

THOUGHT FOR THE DAY.

Whom will you? Jesus or Barabbas.

PRAYER.

Take, O Lord, and receive.

Third Week in Lent.—Friday.

The Scourging of our Lord at the Pillar.

Pilate took JESUS and scourged Him.—S. JOHN XIX.

I. PRELUDE.

Let us enter the Prætorium, and see our Saviour already fastened to the Pillar, awaiting with perfect submission the cruel torment He is about to endure on account of our sins.

II. PRELUDE.

O Divine Jesus, what a profound mystery we now meditate! Give to us a right understanding of it, that we may gather therefrom courage to suffer for Thee.

I. POINT.

The submission of Jesus to His Father's Will.

The Lord hath laid on Him the iniquity of us all. In contemplating this terrible scene of the Flagellation, our attention should be arrested, not by the inhuman crowd who came for the gratifying of their barbarous love of cruelty, nor by the brutal men who were there to tear with their scourges the Sacred Flesh of the Saviour, but by that Adorable Victim, Who in expiation of our sins, acquiesced calmly in the judgment pronounced, that His Body should be thus tortured. We see Him standing there, no murmur escaping His Lips; His aspect betokening perfect resignation to the will of His Heavenly Father, to Whose decree He submitted with entire respect. O my Father—He seems to say—I am ready to receive these strokes of Thy Divine Justice. I give My Body into the hands of these men to be torn with scourges, but it is because Thou hast so ordained. How generous, how unparalleled is the loving obedience of Jesus! Are we submissive as He to the commands of God? do we accept afflictions with humility and courage for love of Him, and for our sanctification? Thy heroic virtues, O Saviour Jesus, should inspire us with an ardent desire of copying them—of being bound to the Pillar with Thee by the cords of love and obedience. Thus, by being united to Thee in suffering, may we receive strength from this mystical union, and accept with resignation whatever punishment Thy Justice may inflict.

II. Point.

Our sensuality has been the cause of the Scourging of Jesus.

We ourselves have inflicted on our Saviour this terrible punishment, by our sins of sensuality.—How can we be so insensible to the tortures He endured during the Flagellation as ever to allow our unmortified senses to have dominion over us? *They that are Christ's have crucified the flesh.* —Our Dear Lord is stripped of His garments, and His Pure and Sacred Body is beaten with whips and rods. His Precious Blood flows, and as the strokes are given with redoubled fury, the Flesh is torn away :—still the scourging continues, until some one standing near, believing that He will die too soon if it be continued, cuts the cords which bind Him, and Jesus falls, bathed in His own Blood. What a scene of heart-rending cruelty! In what detestation does God hold the sins which scourged His Son! How incomprehensible is His Charity! Let us look upon His Wounds as fountains, whence flow, continually, streams of grace. How thankless should we be if we wounded Him afresh by any unfaithfulness to that grace, which is all-sufficient to enable one to lead a life, not only of Christian mortification, but of angelic purity.

Colloquy.

My Saviour, grant that by the merits of Thy cruel Scourging, by the Wounds thereby inflicted on thy Sacred Body, I may be delivered from all tendencies to sensuality. For love of Thee may I hate all that caused Thee so much suffering, and keeping my senses under the control of Thy holy law, prove my gratitude to Thee for having called me to the practice of daily mortification, and of angelical purity.

Resolution.

For love of Jesus, and to resemble Him, I will mortify my senses, and practise some definite act of mortification every day.

Thought for the Day.

He was wounded for our iniquities; He was bruised for our sins.

Prayer.

Soul of Christ.

Third Week in Lent.—Saturday.

Jesus is stripped of His raiment,—clothed with purple, —and crowned with thorns.

The soldiers led Jesus into the court of the palace, and they call together the whole band: And they clothe Him with purple, and platting a crown of thorns, they put it upon Him.—S. Mark xv.

I. Prelude.

Let us follow Jesus into the court of the palace, which is to be the scene of His enthronment, as a mock king, in the midst of a ferocious multitude.

II. Prelude.

We beseech Thee, by Thy being despoiled of Thy garments, and by Thy humiliations, that we may find grace to put off the old man, and to live henceforth in accordance with Thy spirit of holiness.

I. Point.

Jesus, in being thus stripped of His raiment, teaches us that we should be despoiled of self. Scarcely had our Lord put on His raiment after the Flagellation, when they ruthlessly took it off again, using such violence that the painfulness of the open wounds was intensified, and the Blood poured forth anew. An old purple mantle had been found, which they put over our Lord's Shoulders: thus arrayed, He was mockingly saluted as the King of the Jews. Deeply should we compassionate this particular suffering, and dwell upon the lesson it imparts.—By the stripping off of His garment, Jesus desires to teach us how we too must be prepared to endure a real sense of pain if we would divest ourselves entirely of the old man: if we would tear off the evil propensities which cling so closely to us, if we would put away from us all mere human attachments.—To do this, will certainly cost us something; but let us cast a look on our suffering Lord, as the rough soldiers dragged off, from His Aching, Wounded Body the vesture dyed with His Blood,—and then compare, if we can, our pains with His!

II. Point.

Jesus, crowned with thorns, is our King.

This crowning with thorns was an unprecedented torment, reserved for the King of Martyrs. It was suggested by the title which He had had bestowed on Him—that of *King of the Jews.* Divine Providence would hide beneath the cruel circumstance of this coronation, the Mystery of the eternal Royalty of our Redeemer. Jesus is our King:—by creation He has a sovereign power over us; by conquest He has an undoubted right to our allegiance. He has delivered us from the slavery of sin and the tyranny of the prince of darkness, for us He was victorious (through His Cross and Passion) over Death and Hell: He is verily the King of the true Israel of God.—Has He not proved Himself to be the King of those soldiers of the Cross—the holy Martyrs—Confessors—and Virgins—who have been so powerfully attracted by the Mystery of His Sufferings, that they have been ready to brave any hardships, and meet death itself if they might but thereby manifest their loyalty? Has it not been love for their Sovereign in the day of His humiliation, which has rendered them so intrepid? so magnanimous?—And upon ourselves has it not had the effect of making us despise the world, with its allurements and vain pleasures? have we not freed ourselves from the empire of His enemies, and put ourselves under the regal sway of our Deliverer from them—our Divine King? Consecrated to Him, let us remain ever His faithful subjects, happy in our allegiance, now and for all eternity.

COLLOQUY.

Beneath the purple mantle of scorn, under the title of the King of the Jews, and crowned with thorns, I recognise Thee, O Sovereign Ruler of my heart. I fall down before Thee, and adore Thee with all the love and reverence Thy sufferings and Thy humiliations call forth. May no rival ever claim any part of my affections!—I lay them down at Thy Feet to-day.—As I see Thee derided by those who will not have Thee to reign over them, may I offer Thee the best consolation I can, by devoting myself more completely to Thy service?

RESOLUTION.

To sacrifice the inclination or defect of which Jesus has been asking me (for some time perhaps) to divest myself.

THOUGHT FOR THE DAY.

The Lord is our King,—He will save us.

PRAYER.

Take, O Lord, and receive.

Fourth Week in Lent.—Sunday.

Jesus is crowned in mockery, and saluted as the King of the Jews.

Platting a crown of thorns, they put it upon His Head, and a reed in His right Hand: And bowing the knee before Him, they mocked Him, saying: Hail, King of the Jews.— S. MATTHEW XXVII.

I. PRELUDE.

Let us again to-day enter the court, where Jesus is sitting, exposed to derision. His enemies continue to maltreat and to deride Him: we will pay Him our homage of praise and adoration.

II. PRELUDE.

O Divine King, as we contemplate Thee when Thou wast treated with scorn and saluted in mockery as a pretender, give unto us an increase of zeal for Thy glory,—and for our own perfection.

I. POINT.

The Son of God is mocked at by the impious soldiers.

After having arrayed our Much-loved King and Saviour in the purple mantle and crown of thorns, they placed a reed in His Hand, mockingly to suggest the idea that His Sceptre—His sway over others—was impotent; that He was powerless to command. To add to this indignity, they took again the reed from Him, and with it struck His Sacred Head, so that the cruel thorns were driven deeper into the temples, causing excruciating pain. And then they again dared to spit upon Him. As a crowning insult, before leading Him away to crucifixion, they bowed the knee, and wickedly pretended to adore Him, saying: *Hail, King of the Jews.* Little did they believe that He Who was now in their power, would one day appear *sitting on the right Hand of the power of God.* Thus was the Son of God treated by these barbarous soldiers.—They were His own creatures, who had so degraded themselves by their slavery to human passion, that no power could have restrained them, save the power of His grace which they had rejected. Their God—their Creator they utterly disowned. Which of us does not burn with a desire of making amends for such outrages, by rendering Him the true unfeigned homage of our hearts and lives?—by proving our gratitude for the power He has deigned to exert over us, either in keeping us from evil, or in bringing us to repentance. Did we take part in these acts of cruelty? Were we, by means of our iniquities, amongst those who insulted the King of the Jews? Have not our sins of hypocrisy often mantled the real state of our souls? Have not our sins of thought woven a crown of proud imaginations? And has not our bad example been the sceptre of misused power, we have laid down, perhaps, too late? Have we indeed put aside for ever the instruments which tortured our Saviour, and in a spirit of true contrition and of true humility, bowed the knee before Him, and owned Him as our King in the sight of His Church, and of the Angels?

II. Point.

Since the love of Jesus has induced Him to endure so many humiliations and sufferings, we ought to be entirely devoted to the promoting of His glory, and our own perfection.

It was not really necessary that our Lord should have endured such torments and such ignominy; but His love knew no bounds, and on our behalf He would acquire infinite merits. He would that *where sin had abounded, grace should much more abound.* He desired to encourage generous souls by becoming their Model and their Guide in the path of suffering and of humiliations. They are the most happy who profit the most by the favours their Divine Master has merited for them; and who, with generous fervour, are seeking to attain perfection for the sake of *the Author of their Salvation Who was Himself perfected by His Passion.* Only to think of doing just enough to be saved, would be a proof of great ingratitude.—We should be ready for every opportunity of immolating ourselves with regard to what is most dear to us; sparing ourselves neither trouble nor pain, where it is a question of sanctifying our hearts, that they may be more worthy of Him to Whom they justly belong. Holy practices of penance—humiliations—silence—self-abnegation—how highly should we value these :—by them we are rendered more conformable to Jesus; and witness for Him a more tender and perfect gratitude.

Colloquy.

What hast Thou not, O most Suffering Lord Jesus, a right to expect from one whom Thou hast called to follow closely after Thee in the path which is traced with Thy Blood? And should I not be guilty of ungratefulness, and unworthy of Thy favour, if I refused to do this? and chose to walk at ease along the world-beaten track, which leads to destruction, because it leads away from Thee? By the way Thou callest me will I go, until I reach the goal, and find Thee waiting to receive me into everlasting rest from toil, and strife, and weariness.—Grant, O Jesus, this my one desire—final perseverance in following Thee.

RESOLUTION.

In a spirit of gratitude to seek opportunities for self-sacrifice.

THOUGHT FOR THE DAY.

Hail! my Master and my King! I adore Thee with most profound reverence.

PRAYER.

O Jesus, living in Mary.

Fourth Week in Lent.—Monday.

Pilate, showing Jesus to the people, said: Behold the Man.

Pilate therefore went forth again, and saith to the people: Behold I bring Him forth unto you, that you may know that I find no cause in Him: JESUS therefore came forth, bearing the crown of thorns and the purple garment: And Pilate saith to them: Behold the Man: When the chief priests and the servants had seen Him, they cried out, saying: Crucify Him, Crucify Him.—S. JOHN XIX.

I. PRELUDE.

Let us represent to ourselves that part of Jerusalem where the palace of the Roman governor was situated. It was surrounded by a frenzied multitude gathered together, savagely to feast their eyes upon the humiliation and distress of Jesus.

II. Prelude.

Grant, O Divine Jesus, that in proportion as we meditate upon Thy Sacred Passion, love of Thee, hatred of sin, and contempt of self, may be increased in our hearts.

I. Point.

Behold the Man!

Upon whom else can our pitying eyes rest?—Jesus presents Himself to us, and His Heavenly Father seems to point Him out to our notice, and thus to speak to each:—Behold the Man! This is Jesus. Consider Him with sorrowful attention, His Sacred Body is all torn by the Scourging, His Head is pierced with the thorny Crown that encircles It, His Holy Face is bruised and covered with Blood, His Heart is overflowing with grief. This is the Man of Sorrows—the Saviour I have given Thee. The condition to which Thou dost see Him reduced makes thee shudder, but His love has not judged it to be too abject, therefore He descends to it. The greatness of the evil He has gone on earth to repair demands an extreme remedy. Behold the Man! He is the Mirror in which thou mayst see reflected My mercy—My justice—and the greatness of sin.—Understand then how much I love thee, and respond, by thy love, to the interest I feel for thee, and the designs I have purposed with regard to thee: In this Mirror behold (if thou canst) thy own humility, gentleness, charity, mortification and sanctity:—discover therein if thou hast already acquired any points of resemblance to the God-Man. In Him thou seest the life, the strength of mankind; and in His Heart are the sources of all grace—perfect love—and true holiness. Behold then thy Friend, thy Saviour, thy Refuge!—In such words God the Father appears to address us, as Jesus is led forth, and the governor shows Him to the multitude.—*Behold the Man!*

II. Point.

The reply made by the people.

Pilate imagined, no doubt, that the rage of the people against Jesus would be appeased, if they saw to what a state of suffering and exhaustion He was already reduced. Therefore, partly out of pity, partly out of contempt, he brings Him forward; and appeals to them on His behalf. But their cruelty is not yet satiated; and the whole multitude and the soldiers cry out: *Crucify Him, Crucify Him;* and when Pilate remonstrates, the Jews reply: *We have a law, and according to the law, He ought to die.* What law was it which demanded the Death of the Son of God? In reality it was the law of human passion, the law of the natural senses, the law of evil inclinations, which Jesus came to abrogate—to destroy—by the introduction of the law of the Gospel. The sight of Jesus, crowned with thorns—humiliated—covered with wounds—troubled the upholders of the law of sin. *Away with Him,—away with Him* from before our eyes! to see Him exasperates us, they say. According to our law He ought to die. Are there not still some who say: "We have a law—the law of our own will and judgment, our own pleasure and inclinations, our own ease and gratification; we prefer this law to that of the suffering Jesus, which is a law of self-sacrifice". It is well for those who call themselves the disciples of the Redeemer, to see by which law they are really governed. Is it certain that we never say in our hearts: *Away with Him?* Are we not governed by any law which might condemn our Lord again to crucifixion?

Colloquy.

I hear the words—*Behold the Man*, and looking up I see my Saviour, bearing the insignia of His Passion. What are my innermost feelings as I gaze upon that Human Form, in which *there is now no beauty, nor comeliness?* And yet what an irresistible power He exerts over true hearts, as the Man of Sorrows. As I hear the cry of: *Crucify Him, Crucify Him*, I pray for grace that I may never *crucify again the Son of God, and make Him a mockery.* Save me, O Jesus, by the power of Thy hour of weakness.

Resolution.

Often during the day to look at Jesus, *despised and the most abject of men:* and to practise some acts of mortification in union with His Sufferings.

Thought for the Day.

Ecce Homo. Behold the Man.

Prayer.

Take, O Lord, and receive.

Fourth Week in Lent.—Tuesday.

Jesus is condemned to death.

Pilate, taking water, washed his hands before the people, saying: I am innocent of the Blood of this Just Man: look you to it.—S. MATT. XXVII.

I. PRELUDE.

Let us represent to ourselves Pilate seated in the judgment-hall, delivering Jesus up to His enemies, notwithstanding the warning voice of conscience.

II. PRELUDE.

Enkindle more and more in our hearts, O Jesus, love for Thee; and inspire us with courage to die to ourselves, so that we may share in the merits of Thy Precious Death.

I. POINT.

We ought to fear imitating the injustice of Pilate.

Pilate had several times acknowledged and recognised the innocence of Jesus, but seeing that he could not gain over the Jews to his opinion, he caused water to be brought, and whilst washing his hands before the people, he said: *I am innocent of the Blood of this Just Man: look you to it.* What strange blindness on the part of this unjust judge! He is convinced of the innocence of our Lord; he feels that he ought to release Him as guiltless; but because he has not the courage to sacrifice his private interests to the cause of justice, he seeks to calm his perturbed conscience, and to justify himself by the practice of a ceremony in use amongst both Jews and Gentiles. He considered himself to be free from all blame, because he observed this ceremony in due form; and then proceeded to authorise a most cruel and revolting injustice. Unhappily Pilate has his imitators. How many wish to appear just in the eyes of men, and care little to be so really to the eyes of Him *Who trieth the hearts and reins.* Amongst religious persons are there not many who neglect the cultivation of true spirituality and devotion, and think much of the externals of piety? and whilst employing the best exterior means, neglect their true object? For example, they consider it an essential point to recite many prayers, to communicate often, to speak well about the things of God; but at the same time they neglect to mortify their senses, and their pride; they will not deprive themselves of anything they hold to be necessary for their comfort, nor submit to the restraints imposed by the rules of the Religious Life. It behoves us to examine seriously what is the nature of our piety, and without deceiving ourselves, to rectify what we find to be defective.

II. Point.

Pilate delivers Jesus into the hands of the Jews.

Let us consider what must have been the feelings which filled the Heart of Jesus as He listened to His sentence of death. Standing before that unjust judge, the crown of thorns around His Head, the purple mantle upon His Shoulders, He heard with imperturbable serenity and patience the final decision, by which He was condemned to die.—*Pilate gave sentence*, but it was the love of Jesus, and our sins which dictated it. We should dwell upon this thought: it will awaken the liveliest gratitude in our breasts; it will make us understand what claims this self-devotion on the part of our Saviour has upon us; and how right it is that we should do all, and suffer all, to requite, in some little degree, His unbounded love. How guilty should we be if we repaid such love with cowardly indifference, or cold insensibility: it would be to be feared that we should not profit by the merits with which Jesus desires to enrich us—infinite though they are. Rather let us, as we look upon the Adorable Victim Who goes to die for us, cast at His Feet all our pride; and embracing them with loving tenderness, learn how to humble ourselves;—for the Son of God, the Creator of heaven and earth, stands condemned to die the most shameful death of the Cross.

Colloquy.

O my Saviour, Who wast humble to excess, during Thy Passion, how can I ever rightly acknowledge the love that burned within Thy Sacred Heart for me? As I hear Thy sentence of death pronounced, may I pass sentence of death upon all that in myself may have caused Thee to die.—By Thy Passion, O Jesus, give me grace to die to myself.

Resolution.

In a spirit of self-sacrifice and thankfulness to crucify in myself all that is displeasing to Jesus.

Thought for the Day.

Shall I crucify my King?

Prayer.

Take, O Lord, and receive.

Fourth Week in Lent.—Wednesday.

Our Lord carrying His Cross.

They took off the purple from Him, and put His own garments on Him, and they led Him out to crucify Him.—S. Mark xv.

I. Prelude.

We imagine to ourselves the streets of Jerusalem, and the road to Calvary, which was steep and rugged.

II. Prelude.

Give me grace, O my Saviour, to enter with Thee, on the sacred way of the Cross, and to walk along it until my life shall end.

I. Point.

With what feelings does Jesus take up His Cross, that He might carry It to the summit of the Hill of Calvary?

At length the hour has arrived which has been so long anticipated; that hour for which He came into the world. The way to Calvary opens before Him: He sees in the distance the place where He will shed all His Blood, and render up His last sigh. The true Isaac now bears upon His Shoulders the Wood for the Sacrifice, and *takes His way to the place which God had commanded Him.* He is drinking to the very dregs the chalice of bitter woe, and yet His Thirst for sufferings devours Him more and more. Mysteries are being accomplished, the depths of which no created intelligence can ever sound.—Jesus endures a hidden strife, beyond all human comprehension.—God, Who proportions the trials He sends us to our weakness, used no such precaution with regard to His Own Beloved Son; He was borne down by the immense weight of His Father's wrath.—It needed all the strength of Jesus not to be utterly overpowered by that dread burden, and yet His strength was the strength of the God-Man. In taking up the Cross He lifted on to His Shoulders the sins of the world, from the first sin of Adam down to the sins we have to-day committed.—As the weight of the Cross bowed down His Sacred Body, so the weight of sin bowed down His Soul. *He hath borne the sins of many.*—With deep contrition let us mourn over the way in which we have deliberately added to that terrible load; and promise our Lord to suffer any pain or loss, rather than again increase its weight.

II. Point.

We must enter on the road towards Calvary with Jesus.

Both love and justice summon us to follow the All-holy Victim on His way to the place of Sacrifice.—His Sacred Heart is the loadstone which attracts hearts to Himself, even on the road to Calvary.—The way is traced by the Cross; it is sprinkled with the Precious Blood, which causes graces to fructify amongst the thorns, along the rough and stony path: there it is that virtues spring up and may be gathered, while vices are trodden under foot.—He who has found out this road has found out the sure way to Heaven; that of the Cross being the royal road our King has chosen, when going on His way to take possession of His Kingdom in the hearts of man. From the Tree He is to reign. *If I be lifted up from the earth I will draw all things to Myself.*

Have we good reason to believe that we are really mounting, day by day, the Hill of Calvary? are we carrying a true cross? and that willingly? are we treading down—overcoming our faults? are we increasing our store of virtues? are we advancing towards perfection?

Colloquy.

I render Thee, O Jesus, heartfelt thanks for having called me to follow in Thy Footsteps along the way of the Cross, since it leads to Life. Teach me to look out of myself, and to fix my eyes on Thee: let me take up the cross Thou designest for me—willingly—joyfully—heavy though it be. Thy own love prepared a Cross for Thee: my sincere desire is this—that I may be worthy to bear one, formed and laid upon me by Thy Fatherly Hand.

Resolution.

To look upon all my troubles and sufferings as sacred particles of the true Cross.

Thought for the Day.

He that taketh not up his Cross and followeth Me, is not worthy of Me.

Prayer.

Our Father, and Hail Mary.

Fourth Week in Lent.—Thursday.

Jesus meets His most holy Mother.

The Mother of Jesus met her Divine Son (according to a generally received tradition) at the end of a street in Jerusalem, which joined the road leading to Calvary.

I. Prelude.

Let us represent to ourselves the crowded streets, in which Mary met Jesus.

II. Prelude.

O God, we beseech Thee, give us grace to share alike in the sorrow and in the love of the Sacred Hearts of Jesus and Mary.

I. Point.

How sorrowful this meeting must have been to both the Mother and the Son.

Jesus left the Prætorium, and after descending its marble steps, took up His Cross. Mary saw this, and now advanced to meet Him, in order to accompany Him to Calvary.—Who can rightly measure her grief? such grief as no Mother had ever before, or has ever since endured: the sword of sorrow was entering her soul. And then, on the other hand, what anguish did not the Heart of Jesus, so tender and so loving, experience when He saw His holy Mother join herself to Him, to share in His ignominy and disgrace, and tread the way to Calvary by His Side. This meeting served to augment their mutual suffering: Mary was distressed in seeing Jesus suffer, and Jesus was afflicted at witnessing the grief of Mary; and by a communication of sorrow and of love, these two Hearts, so closely united to each other, endured a mysterious agony, in contemplating which, we lend our sympathy, and long to participate in it; but we can never fully fathom its depths. Every sentiment that was noble, generous, and tender with regard to each other's feelings, was aroused at that moment, as the Eye of Jesus met the saddened gaze of Mary. Can we be insensible to this touching scene, when we remember that it was on our account that this mystery of suffering was endured? For our salvation Jesus and Mary made such great sacrifices. What are we doing to prove our gratitude to them?

II. Point.

The example of Mary teaches us how to follow Jesus.

Called by our vocation to follow Jesus to Calvary, we may learn of Mary how to tread the way of sorrow—the pathway of tribulation. Our holy Mother walked close to Jesus, full of love, courage and submission to God's Will. —She united her sufferings to those of her Adorable Son; the sentiments of His Heart she made her own. It is in the same way that we should walk in the Footsteps of our Divine Master. We are by no means forbidden to feel the pain of sacrifice; nor the being afflicted, when God appears to deal severely with us; but what He expects of us is this, —that our will should be entirely submitted to His.—He further enjoins us to remain faithful to Him, notwithstanding all the difficulties from without, and repugnances from within, which may seem to obstruct our progress.—If zeal for the glory of God should make us desire opportunities of making sacrifices, we ought to love them also, simply out of charity towards poor sinners.—When we generously suffer the ills of this life, when we courageously submit to the hardships which our vocation—our duties impose on us, we make satisfaction (together with Jesus) for them, and appease the most just anger of God against ungrateful man. How pleasing to God is such charity; how richly will He recompense it hereafter, by causing us to share in the glory of His Son, having shared here in His tribulation. Our glory will be enhanced by finding ourselves surrounded in Heaven by those to whose eternal happiness we shall have contributed. O Mary, obtain for us a constancy like to thine; and a courage which no trial may be able to break down.

COLLOQUY.

Mary, Mother of Jesus, thou didst act so valiantly in accompanying thy Son to Calvary amid the execrations of the people; manifesting thereby the strength of thy love, and the union of thy suffering with His. Would that I had the courage to defy all that hinders me from following closely after Him,—human respect, the spirit of the world, repugnances, cowardice.—Show me how to surmount all these, and steadily to keep near thee, for thou art always near to thy Son.

RESOLUTION.

To bear with courage, in union with Jesus and Mary, all afflictions and trials which may come to me.

THOUGHT FOR THE DAY.

Heart of Mary, pierced with the sword of sorrow, pray for me.

PRAYER.

Soul of Christ.

Fourth Week in Lent.—Friday.

Simon of Cyrene assists Jesus to carry His Cross.

As they led JESUS away, they laid hold of one Simon of Cyrene, coming from the country; and they laid the Cross on him, to carry It after JESUS.—S. LUKE XXIII.

I. PRELUDE.

Let us represent to our minds Jesus just leaving the outskirts of the city, as He proceeds on His way, accompanied by Mary.

II. PRELUDE.

When we consider Thee, O Saviour, assisted by Simon in the carrying of Thy Cross, may we obtain grace to embrace with love the crosses Thou art pleased to send us, and to unite them with Thine.

I. POINT.

What was the intention of the Jews in obliging the Cyrenian to bear the Cross?

It was not out of pity that the murderers of our Lord lightened for Him the burden of the Cross: the sight of the condemned Jesus, all covered with Wounds, weighed down by sorrow, and enfeebled by all the torments He had undergone, made not the least impression on their obdurate hearts,—but they feared to see Him expire before the measure of their iniquity was filled up:—this it was which induced them to force Simon the Cyrenian to aid our

Saviour in bearing His Cross.—Jesus knew their motive; but always submissive, humble, obedient, and full of gentleness, He accepted this assistance, as promptly as He had taken its whole weight upon His Shoulders when He left the judgment-hall.—Yes! Jesus knew their motive, but He knew at the same time that the Father had pre-ordained that Simon should be instrumental in enabling Him to continue His course towards the place where He, at length, would be able to say: *It is consummated.*—That moment, decreed from all eternity, was not to be anticipated. Our Lord's failing Footsteps must be traced upon the hill-side, up to the very summit. Nothing happens without the permission of God; therefore the intentions of the wicked He can over-rule, and He can cause Simon to pass by at the right moment, coming out of the country, to effect His eternal purposes, and carry out His designs. How greatly should the consideration of this incident tend to increase our confidence in God!

II. POINT.

What was the intention of Jesus in permitting Simon to help Him?

Jesus, Victim most obedient, allowed His enemies to lead Him to execution, and permitted the full weight of an inexpressible grief to oppress Him; but He accepted this assistance on the part of Simon, firstly, to accomplish His Father's Will; and secondly, to give us an important instruction. This man, who was so privileged in having the happiness of helping Jesus to carry His Cross, represents those generous souls who have the courage to follow Jesus; and by bearing their own cross bravely, aid Him in carrying His. They are united to Him in suffering and in sorrow:

—it is as if a precious particle of His Cross were set as a priceless jewel in their every cross; and by an exchange, worthy of the liberality of the Sacred Heart, He recompenses their courage and generosity by a bestowal of all those graces He has merited for them on Calvary, even as He recompensed Simon for his services.—Sufferings become indeed most precious when viewed in the light of Faith. Have we well considered this, that the trials of this life are really a participation in the carrying of the true Cross?

Colloquy.

As I consider the Cyrenian helping Thee, O Jesus, to carry Thy Cross, feelings of regret arise within me that I have not assisted Thee, as I might have done, to bear it. Let me even now make amends for my discontent—my repining—my delays through cowardice—my actual refusals, when Thou Thyself hast invited me to take part with Simon in bearing a portion of the Cross:—some sacrifices—some affliction—some trial—some proof of Thy favour—of Thy love.

Resolution.

To keep near Jesus carrying His Cross; and to help Him to bear It by suffering patiently and voluntarily any trial He may ask me to endure for His Sake.

Thought for the Day.

In all things we suffer tribulation, but are not distressed.

Prayer.

Take, O Lord, and receive.

Fourth Week in Lent.—Saturday.

A pious woman, according to tradition, wiped the face of Jesus.

Perfect charity casteth out fear.—1 S. John iv.

I. Prelude.

Let us represent to ourselves the way by which our Saviour was led through the streets of Jerusalem, when passing on to Calvary.

II. Prelude.

O Jesus, give us strength to imitate the courage of the pious Veronica; and deign to engrave in our hearts Thy divine Likeness, as Thou didst imprint It on the veil she offered Thee.

I. Point.

Veronica gave Jesus a striking proof of her faith and charity.

Jesus, bearing His Cross, was passing painfully along, by the outskirts of Jerusalem, when a holy woman perceived Him, in the midst of His executioners, who were conducting Him to the place of crucifixion. On seeing our Lord's Face, covered with blood, and drops of sweat and dust,—His Head crowned with thorns, she was deeply moved to compassion. Making her way through the crowd, she came and fell on her knees before Jesus, and wiped with her veil that Holy Face, which was so sadly disfigured. How the example of this woman confounds our indifference to our Saviour's sufferings! How her love condemns our coldness, and her courage our cowardice! The activity of her faith covers us with confusion, when we compare it with the weakness and sterility of our own. She was almost a stranger to Jesus,—we are His familiar friends:—He had not asked her to do Him some service,—how often has He asked us?—Let us see Jesus in the poor—the afflicted—the sorrowful—and hasten to render them some act of charity, in memory of the sympathy and attention given to our Lord by Veronica, and of the miraculous manner in which He showed His appreciation of her charity.

II. Point.

Jesus recompensed the faith and charity of Veronica.

Our Saviour not only accepted the kindly office of this pious woman, not only did He permit her to wipe His Sacred Face, but on the veil with which she did so, she found the Features of It clearly delineated. How greatly must she have been consoled to find herself in possession of such a treasure! We may imagine the respect and love with which she carried the Divine Picture to her home, with what care she preserved it, and with what joy she showed it to the Apostles and Disciples after the Resurrection of Jesus Christ.—If, like her, we were courageous enough to brave the fear of men, to overcome the repugnances of our own nature, to rise above human respect; if we were full of ardent desire to procure the honour of Jesus, and to make amends for the outrages that He receives from sinners, then our Dear Lord would imprint His Divine Likeness on our hearts:—by this means we should become really like unto Him. This Likeness would betoken a most intimate union between Jesus—our Celestial Bridegroom—and us His Spouses, who should reflect in our lives His Image formed in us. Our hearts belong to Thee, O Lord, soften them, melt them in the furnace of Thy Love; and as we offer them to Thee, do Thou mould them as Thou wilt, and impress Thyself as a Seal upon them.

Colloquy.

O Jesus, my Well-Beloved, I feel that I could envy Veronica on account of the high favour Thou didst accord her; and as I think of her happiness in possessing the likeness of Thy Divine Features. And yet, I may, if I will, obtain from Thee a holier pledge of Thy abiding Presence with me. Make me, by a faithful correspondence to Thy grace, worthy to bear Thy Image more distinctly portrayed in my heart.

Resolution.

To recall the scene of Veronica's obtaining from Jesus His Divine Likeness, frequently during this day.

Thought for the Day.

My heart hath said to Thee: Thy Face, O Lord, will I seek.

Prayer.

Soul of Christ,

Passion Sunday.

Jesus addresses the Women of Jerusalem, who follow Him.

There followed a great multitude of people, and of women, who bewailed and lamented Him: But Jesus turning to them, said: Daughters of Jerusalem, weep not over Me, but weep for yourselves and for your children.—S. Luke xxiii.

I. Prelude.

We see Jesus on the way to Calvary, followed by some Jewish women, who wept at sight of the cruelty with which the soldiers were treating Him.

II. Prelude.

Adorable Jesus, discover to me what were Thy thoughts, when Thou didst address the women who wept on Thy account.

I. Point.

Jesus was more touched by the consideration of the evils the Jewish nation was drawing upon itself, than by that of the wrongs He had to endure.

It is in moments of overpowering affliction that the most magnanimous of men often become selfish; for an excess of suffering absorbs the soul, and keeps it so enfolded within itself, that any extraneous sorrow is scarcely perceived. But the Soul of Jesus Christ was raised far above this weakness; His Heart was so different from the hearts of other men.—Bent down by suffering, hardly able to support Himself beneath its weight, He saw the women of Jerusalem weeping over Him; and foreseeing the storm that was about to burst over that much favoured city, in punishment of the crime of Deicide which that same day was to witness, Jesus again experienced those sentiments of sorrowful regret that He had evinced in so marked a manner a few days before, when He had wept over Jerusalem, so soon to be laid waste, and that utterly. *Daughters of Jerusalem, weep not over Me:* My sufferings would become sweet and pleasant to Me, if the benefits of my Death might be applied for the saving of those who are about to shed My Blood: but they will not profit by its merits,—they will not do penance. Ah! weep then over them, over your country's ruin, and for your children, who will be witnesses of its impending desolation and destruction. O Heart of Jesus! how immense is Thy charity, which makes Thee forget Thy own sufferings, in thinking of the sufferings which Thy chosen people are bringing upon themselves. This thought gives us confidence in praying for the forgiveness of ourselves and others, *since Thou art not willing that any should perish.*

II. Point.

Jesus prefers tears of penitence to those of mere compassion.

We know that Jesus was not unmoved by the tears shed on His account, and He recompensed the pitying women by an outpouring of His grace; but at the same time He desired to make them understand that tears, to be availing, should produce lasting fruits of penance. Above all He wishes for their salvation, and the salvation of those who were dear to them.—From this we draw a valuable lesson for ourselves.—We recognise the goodness of our Saviour, Who places our spiritual advantage, our eternal happiness, far beyond every other consideration.—Our compassion, even for His own sufferings, must not be sterile; but should become meritorious, by causing us to shed tears of contrition on account of the share we have had in making Him endure so much. Our tears must be worthy to mingle with the drops of His Precious Blood; so forming a sovereign balm for the diseases of the soul. Let us then, in obedience to our Redeemer's injunction, weep holy tears of penitence for ourselves; and with tears of charity implore God's mercy on the souls of others. How insensible we are to the greatness of our spiritual needs! were we not so, we should *pour out our hearts like water before the Face of the Lord, and lift up our hands to Him* for ourselves and all His erring children.

Colloquy.

My Jesus, amongst those who accompanied Thee to Calvary, what a little number sympathised with Thee in Thy sufferings. May I be reckoned amongst Thy faithful companions, especially as Thou passest along the way of the Cross. Wherever Thou art, it is good for me also to be:—wherever Thou goest I shall be happy in following Thee. I will listen to Thy words as if addressed to myself:—Weep, My Daughter, not out of mere compassion, but weep and plead with God on account of thy own needs, and the needs of others; and sacrifice thyself entirely for the love and glory of the Heavenly Father.

Resolution.

To excite in myself, often during the day, true contrition for my sins.

THOUGHT FOR THE DAY.

Blessed are they that mourn, for they shall be comforted.

PRAYER.

Soul of Christ.

Passion Week.—Monday.

Jesus, arriving at the summit of the Hill of Calvary, was fastened to the Cross.

When they were come to the place which is called Calvary, they crucified Him there.—S. LUKE XXIII.

I. PRELUDE.

Let us represent to ourselves the top of the Hill of Calvary—and look at the rock which has been hollowed out to receive the foot of the Cross.

II. PRELUDE.

O Jesus, Victim of Love, unite us to Thy Sacrifice, and make us to share in those sentiments which animated Thy Sacred Heart in the hour of Thy Crucifixion.

I. POINT.

Jesus at length arrived at the place of Crucifixion.

Having reached the summit of the hill, on which was to

be consummated His Sacrifice, Jesus looked around Him. There lay the Cross,—the nails and the hammer were already in the hands of the executioners. What at this moment was it, that most afflicted the Heart of Jesus? Was it the sight of the preparations made for His Death? No! a thought more overwhelmingly painful than that completely occupied His thoughts, while awaiting the signal to place Himself on His Death-bed of the Cross. He saw that His Sacrifice would be unavailing in regard to an immense number of souls, who would refuse to profit by the grace of redemption. He looked all along the course of ages, and saw those, for whom He was about to die to save, and whom He loved better than His own Life, straying away from the path of salvation, to be lost in the abyss of eternal destruction. At this painful sight His remaining strength forsook Him, and He fell to the ground under the incomprehensible weight of a world's ingratitude. O Jesus, our Saviour, ought not an ardent zeal to be indeed enkindled within us for the salvation of souls, when we see to what an extent Thou hast loved each one that Thou hast called into existence? Ought we not gladly to accept any portion of the affliction Thou hadst to endure, and thus *to fill up those things that are wanting of the sufferings of Christ for His Body, which is the Church?*—Should we not *account them blessed who have endured?* and those who are still called upon to suffer?

II. Point.

Jesus was fastened to the Cross.

Jesus obeyed the order given that He should place Himself upon the Cross. He approached—then laid Himself upon it. Having presented His right Hand to the executioners, it was roughly seized, and with cruel blows the large nail was driven through it into the wood.—Notwithstanding the agony He endured, Jesus uttered not a word of complaint; only the sounds of the hammer were heard, and re-echoed in His Mother's heart. Jesus, the Adorable Son of Mary, Whose actions could never belie His gentleness and His love, presented His other Hand, which, being forcibly stretched upon the other arm of the Cross, was nailed in the same cruel manner as the first. Then the Sacred Feet were fastened with still more cruelty to the wood, already empurpled with the Precious Blood. They raised the Cross and with a terrible shock planted it in the hole, dug in the rock, to receive It. What did Mary feel as those dear Hands and Feet were further riven? when the soldiers, to fix the Cross firmly in Its place, furiously struck the wedges which were to secure it. Let us lift up our eyes, and look at our Saviour.—Has the Heavenly Father ever demanded of us an act of obedience so painful?—a sacrifice so hard?—a humiliation comparable to that which He asked of His Own Beloved Son? God grant that, at least, we may esteem ourselves happy, in some little degree to resemble Him on the Cross, and glory only in this: *that by Him the world is crucified to us, and we to the world.*

COLLOQUY.

O Love of my Saviour, who could ever understand thee fully? I am not able to prove my thankfulness for the favours I have received from thee, but at least, I will enter into the teaching of this wonderful Mystery and crucify my unruly inclinations:—accept the sacrifice of all my thoughts, words and works. O Precious Blood, which didst flow from the Wounds of my Saviour, flow into the wounds of my soul, and heal them by thy inherent virtue.

RESOLUTION.

To pass this day in much recollection, thinking of Jesus, and His perfect obedience.

THOUGHT FOR THE DAY.

They have dug My Hands and Feet: they have numbered all My Bones.

PRAYER.

Soul of Christ.

Passion Week.—Tuesday.

Jesus hangs on His Cross, between two robbers.

They crucified Him: and the robbers, one on the right hand, and the other on the left.—S. LUKE XXIII.

I. PRELUDE.

Let us again represent to ourselves the Hill of Calvary, and our Lord, immediately after the Crucifixion.

II. PRELUDE.

As we think of Thee, O Jesus, forsaken by almost all Thy friends, do Thou detach our hearts from all creatures, and attach them more entirely to Thyself, whose love alone suffices us.

I. Point.

The consideration of what Jesus had to endure, when abandoned on the Cross even by God, and the Holy Angels.

During the Agony in the Garden, a Messenger was sent from Heaven to strengthen our Lord; when on the Cross no such celestial Visitant brings help or consolation.—Holy Angels, are ye insensible to the Sorrows and Suffering of your King?—God the Father has also turned away His Face; He is hidden from the Saviour's Sight by the dark clouds of His just anger. Jesus Christ, having undertaken *to bear our sins in His Body upon the Tree*, must drink to the very dregs, without any diminution, the bitter chalice of God's wrath. The excess of His Suffering proves the excess of His charity towards mankind, and how unspeakably must His Sorrows have been aggravated when Heaven itself had closed its gates; and none passed through to bring a token of the Eternal Father's love. Are we not ready, after this, to bear, in union with Jesus, all privation of sensible consolation, all spiritual dryness, and the seeming rigour with which God treats us, from time to time? Are we not convinced that the supernatural death to self should precede the natural death of the body, if we would be partakers hereafter of the glory of Him *Who was perfected by His Passion?*

II. Point.

Jesus was abandoned by friends.

With the exception of His Blessed Mother, some few holy women, and the Apostle Saint John, there was not found a friend—a disciple near Jesus, to witness His last sufferings, or listen to His last words. Where were those who a few short hours before, owned Him as their Lord and Master? Where were the multitudes, who only six days since cried out: *Hosanna to the Son of David. Blessed be the King Who cometh in the Name of the Lord!* Where were all those whom He had loaded with benefits? Jesus was forsaken: left alone to the fury of His executioners, and the ignoble companionship of two robbers. O incomprehensible abandonment! O mystery of ingratitude! Shall we be also faithless, and forsake Jesus on the Cross? Shall we consent to let Him endure His Agony alone, without consoling Him by our love? without manifesting our willingness to share in His afflictions? O, our Well-Beloved! we will keep in the company of those few faithful ones who stood—as sad witnesses of Thy cruel torments and Death—beneath the Cross: in all our tribulations and trials, either of body or soul, there we shall be able to bear with resignation the additional grief of the loss of friends: —provided that we have Thee, O Jesus, entirely forsaken—alone—we can never be. How are we practising the virtue of detachment? If we are in any adversity, do we wish that it should occupy the time and attention of others? Are we apt to complain if we believe ourselves to be forgotten? Do we murmur against God's decrees if He takes away those who are dear to us? Are we fearful when He seems to leave us alone?

COLLOQUY.

I feel ashamed, O my Saviour, when I see Thee bearing, with such wonderful patience, Thy loneliness on the Cross. On condition that God might be thereby glorified and Thy children rescued from hell, Thou wast satisfied.—Thou didst forget Thyself in consenting to be abandoned by

Heaven and earth. Let me learn to forget myself, and freed from the yoke of self-love, to be in future entirely satisfied if the good pleasure of God be accomplished; counting myself happy to know His holy Will, so that I may more exactly fulfil it.

Resolution.

When abandoned by creatures I will keep near to Jesus, forsaken on the Cross.

Thought for the Day.

They have heard that I sigh, and there is none to comfort Me.

Prayer.

Soul of Christ.

Passion Week.—Wednesday.

The Title on the Cross.

Pilate wrote a title and he put it upon the Cross: And the writing was: Jesus of Nazareth, the King of the Jews.—S. John xix.

I. Prelude.

Let us go in spirit to Calvary, and ponder well the superscription which was written upon the Cross.

II. Prelude.

As we meditate upon the Title placed by Pilate over the Head of Jesus, may we obtain a renewal of grace and strength, to own Jesus for our King, and to fight manfully in His cause.

I. Point.

Jesus is our King.

The superscription which announced that our Lord was the King of the Jews, was written in three different languages.—Pilate was unwittingly an instrument in the Hands of Divine Providence: God had arranged this circumstance, in order to publish in the sight of all the assembled people, the fact that Jesus was a King. It was to be read, not only by the Hebrews, but also by the Greeks and Romans; the Gentile world was henceforth to know Him as the Ruler over all nations. Let us encircle, with deep respect, the mysterious Throne of the Divine Monarch, Who gives His Life for the salvation of all His subjects. Let us render Him profound adoration, and grateful love. Let us contemplate Him *upon the Tree, from which He reigns;* and bless Him for having, by means of its sacred wood, re-established His power, consolidated His kingdom, and secured to His people present peace and eternal wealth, happiness and life; while the Cross of humiliation becomes the Victor's trophy. Could one be so ungrateful, so much one's own enemy, as to seek to free one's self from Thy empire, O Lord, and to refuse to submit to Thy laws? We pray Thee rather to reign absolutely over us,—over our hearts and minds, our senses, our whole being.

II. Point.

An eternal truth is proclaimed by the Title on the Cross.

Jesus kept silence, with regard to His kingly character, after having answered the question of the Roman governor on this subject, and once declared that His Kingdom was not of this world. Little did Pilate imagine, as he wrote the Title to be placed on the Cross of Jesus, that he was lending his aid to make known the truth of God, to proclaim among the Gentiles: *the Lord reigneth.* How wonderfully, how mysteriously does God work out His designs! What food for thought may we not find in the reading of the superscription: *This is Jesus*—the despised Son of Mary—*the reproach of men and the outcast of the people:—He Who has humbled Himself, and become obedient unto death, even the death of the Cross.* All this is implied in those words, *Jesus of Nazareth.* But God has given Him *this Name to be above every Name,* and even on the Cross that name is to be honoured; there on It, it is declared to be His royal Title. The Heavenly Father has hidden His Face;—He does not, as by the River Jordan, or on Mount Thabor, speak from Heaven saying: *this is My Beloved Son,* but He causes Him to be acknowledged as a King—the Eternal King of His chosen people—His elect—the future denizens of the Holy City—the New Jerusalem. The enemies of Jesus said: *write not that He is our King: we will not have this Man to reign over us:* what do we His friends say?—are we His faithful subjects?

Colloquy.

O my Divine Lord, let me beseech of Thee to keep before the eyes of my soul that mysterious Title which was placed above Thy Sacred Head : far from saying in my heart that I will not own Thee for my King, let me daily praise and bless Thee, that from the Cross Thou makest me to feel the power Thou dost exert over me :—that power of suffering and of love, which has won me to be for ever Thy loyal subject.

Resolution.

To pray for the advancement of the Kingdom of Jesus Christ in the hearts of all men ; so that they may own no other sway.

Thought for the Day.

Thou art the Son of God : Thou art the King of Israel.

Prayer.

Take, O Lord, and receive.

Passion Week.—Thursday.

The soldiers divided the garments of Jesus between them.

The soldiers, when they had crucified Jesus, took His garments : and they made four parts, to every soldier a part. —S. John xix.

I. Prelude.

Let us notice, on the one hand, the complete spoliation to which Jesus was subjected ; and, on the other, the rapacity with which the executioners possessed themselves of His raiment.

II. Prelude.

Grant to us all, O Jesus, Thine own true spirit,—that of detachment from all created things.

I. Point.

The state of poverty in which Jesus willed to die, distinctly condemns our love of possessing.

Our Divine Saviour was born in poverty! His whole life was passed in the midst of privations of every kind; and He would die as He had lived, absolutely dispossessed of all things: to show us to what an extent He loved poverty, and despised earthly goods. Let us study the holy sentiments of His Divine Heart, and compare them with those which animate us. It was not only to sensible objects that the detachment practised by our Lord extended itself: He carried the exercise of it so far, as not to appropriate as His own, those gifts of nature and of grace, the full plentitude of which He, as Man, had received. Are we faithful to our engagement, as disciples of Jesus Christ, to love poverty? do we look upon all that we possess—talents—spiritual advantages—intellectual gifts, as really belonging to God and only lent to us, to be made use of for His glory? Or, like the soldiers, do we take the things that appertain to God, and call them ours? If tempted to do so, let us remember that Jesus from the Cross is looking at us. As Religious, do we practise detachment with regard to all earthly possessions? Do we allow ourselves to be despoiled of all things, without murmuring or complaining?

II. Point.

They are happy who appropriate nothing to themselves; in imitation of Jesus on the Cross.

Having nothing, yet possessing all things. The true sense of these words is so little understood, even by religious persons. They were put into practice most perfectly by our Saviour: He Who was Lord of Heaven and earth, died in utter destitution—both bodily and spiritual. Do we act in the spirit of the words—*Having nothing?* In serving God, do we not seek too much the consolations of piety?—Do we not appropriate to ourselves the good we do?—Is there not, too often, self-seeking in those actions, in which self should certainly find no place? *What have we, that we have not received,* either in the order of nature, or of grace? And again, have we not consecrated all these gifts to Him, Who first bestowed them upon us?—so that they are doubly His. What an injustice it must be in God's Sight, when we consider ourselves as the real proprietors of our goods, our talents, our powers of mind or body, our virtues: He has declared that He hates *robbery in a holocaust* offered to His Divine Majesty; which holocaust should be consumed entirely for His Glory. During these days of special grace, as we dwell particularly on the thought of the wonderfully perfect example, given us by our Saviour in His condition of *having nothing,* let us ask ourselves if we are in any way depriving God of what belongs solely to Him.

Colloquy.

I find in myself so much that is in opposition to the true spirit of self-abnegation and of holy poverty. How far, O my Jesus, my practice falls short of my promises, in this respect. I feel how poor in virtue and in merits I am, because I throw so much away on myself,—and give Thee nothing worthy of Thy acceptance.—How little treasure I am laying up for eternity! Help me by Thy Holy Spirit to begin again to exercise myself in the virtue of detachment, remembering that I am in no way my own.

Resolution.

I will immediately sacrifice to God, all to which I find myself to be over attached.

Thought for the Day.

They parted My garments among them; and upon My vesture they took lots.

Prayer.

Take, O Lord, and receive.

Passion Week.—Friday.

Mary at the Foot of the Cross.

Now there stood by the Cross of Jesus, His Mother.—S. John xix.

I. Prelude.

Let us place ourselves upon the summit of the Hill of Calvary, and see Mary standing near her Son.

II. Prelude.

O Mary, Queen of Martyrs, may our hearts, fully alive to the affliction which filled thy heart, sympathise with thee; and renounce all affection for sin which caused thee such bitter sorrow.

I. Point.

What the sorrows of Mary must have been in seeing her Divine Son suffer and die.

The most certain proof of our love towards Jesus Christ is to follow Him, as Mary did, to Calvary: those who are His most faithful friends approach the nearest to His Cross. Mary united herself perfectly to the Sacrifice of our Adorable Saviour, she stayed near to Him during the course of His Passion; she participated in all the sufferings and in all the sorrows of His Heart. She went up with Him to Golgotha, and there, *standing at the foot of the Altar of holocaust*, she was not only the witness of the immolation of her Son, but she voluntarily offered Him herself, in union with His own Will, to appease the justice of the Most High. —What Martyrdom can be compared to that of this tender Mother? Who can understand the bitterness of her grief? She feels every torment He endures,—she sees the Blood which flows from His Wounds,—not one of His sufferings escapes her notice;—all this makes on her heart so deep an impression, that she becomes the perfect resemblance of her Crucified Jesus. O incomprehensible sufferings of our dear Mother! may we be associated with her, in her martyrdom of love! Calvary—the place of meeting for the true Spouses of Jesus; the Cross—on which self is crucified; Death—to natural affections; such is the portion of those souls whom God calls to promote His glory in an especial manner; those whom He desires to raise to an eminent degree of sanctity, and whom He has destined to fill places of highest glory in His Kingdom. There on Calvary's summit, let us then desire to stay with Jesus and Mary.

II. Point.

The afflicted heart of the Mother of Jesus should often engage the thoughts of us her children.

What important and holy lessons does Mary offer us, as we contemplate her, enduring so much sorrow beneath the Cross! Great though her sorrow was, her resignation, and the peace of her soul were not diminished, and the Mother, whom the power of love nailed to the Cross with the same nails which fastened her Divine Son to It, was offered in Sacrifice, together with His Oblation of Himself, for the glory of God and the salvation of souls. If all Christians should endeavour to copy into their lives the virtues practised by the Mother of Dolours on the Hill of Calvary, this obligation is more strictly binding on those who bear the title of Children of Mary, and Spouses of Jesus Christ, —they should strive to resemble the One and the Other—Mary and Jesus. All the tribulations, permitted by God, and through which He calls us to pass, tend towards one end, that of uniting us to the suffering Life of Jesus, so that we may hereafter share in His glorious Life. We ought like Mary our Mother, to adore the Will of God in the afflictions He sends us, accepting them with calmness and patient resignation. Obtain for us, O Mary, grace to understand this deep lesson in spirituality; and understanding it, to practise it more perfectly.

Colloquy.

My dear Mother, how strong was the love with which Thou wast actuated, when Thou didst draw near to witness the Passion and Death of Thy Beloved Son: it may well be said that in thee, *love was stronger than death;* for without this perfection of divine charity, many a time thou must have succumbed beneath the weight of thy sorrow. Neither thy own sufferings, nor the fury of those who tormented and crucified Jesus—not even His Death—could lessen thy courage, nor interrupt the flow of thy soul's holy affections towards God. Teach me how to love generously, courageously; and in the hour of suffering, how to be less occupied with the evils that I endure, than in learning how to accomplish the good pleasure of God.

Resolution.

I will suffer with patient love, and in union with the Sacred Hearts of Jesus and Mary, all that I find painful to bear.

Thought for the Day.

Queen of Martyrs, who didst stand by the Cross, pray for me.

Prayer.

O Jesus, living in Mary.

Passion Week.—Saturday.

The Blasphemy of the Jews:—the Patience of Jesus.

They that passed by blasphemed Him, wagging their heads: saying: Vah, Thou that destroyest the Temple of God, and in three days dost rebuild it, save Thy own Self: if Thou be the Son of God, come down from the Cross: In like manner also the chief priests with the scribes and ancients mocking, said: He saved others, Himself He cannot save: if He be the King of Israel, let Him now come down from the Cross, and we will believe Him.—S. MATT. XXVII.

I. PRELUDE.

If, in spirit, we transport ourselves to Calvary, we shall see there a number of impious men, who are uttering blasphemies against Jesus.

II. PRELUDE.

Give us grace, O Crucified Saviour, to resemble Thee in that unalterable patience, of which Thou dost give us so perfect an example on the Cross.

I. POINT.

Jesus suffered with patience the injuries done to Him by the chief-priests and scribes, and ancients of the people.

When a malefactor is delivered up to be treated according to the rigour of the law, justice being satisfied, pity is felt for him:—but the hatred of the enemies of Jesus was insatiable, and seemed to increase at the sight of the torments He had to endure. These ruthless men were not ashamed to come to Calvary on purpose to insult Jesus in His agony and helplessness on the Cross. The chief-priests, forgetting the dignity of their office, and the respect they owed to themselves, mingled with the scoffing crowd, and vented their rage still further against its Victim; tauntingly saying: *If thou be the Son of God, come down from the Cross; and we will believe Thee.* Jesus however *held His peace*—He, Who could have at once destroyed these blasphemers and precipitated them into hell.—But He is silent; His forbearance and patience is inexhaustible; His Divine meekness disarms the wrath of God the father. In the Cross is nothing but mercy towards sinners; our Saviour will complete His Sacrifice perfectly, and become the Author of Salvation, so that all may be forgiven through the power of His Suffering. Let the thought of His patient forbearance under insult, draw forth our admiration, love and constancy.

II. Point.

We should imitate the patience we see exemplified in Jesus Christ.

Jesus wishes indeed to fill us with sentiments of love and gratitude, which are most justly due to Him; but above all, He desires that, with ardent zeal, we should endeavour to make our hearts conformable to His own. Let us beg of Him to produce in us therefore His divine patience; that precious virtue which is the gift of the Holy Spirit, and the practice of which fills the soul with suavity. Jesus accepted the outrages committed against Him, as a part of the punishment that He would suffer in our stead; and He accepted them with entire resignation. If we have so much difficulty in bearing the slightest affront—the least word of contradiction,—if we cannot endure the smallest humiliation, or suffering, it is because we are not sufficiently convinced of the necessity there is to imitate Jesus; and that, together with Him, we may make satisfaction for our sins, to the divine justice:—it is because we do not love our Saviour as we ought: for the flame of true love is fed by acts of self-sacrifice; it increases through suffering and is kept pure by means of affliction. The more we reflect on the calm endurance of Jesus, the better we understand the value of each act of patience which we practise; and we shall thus learn by degrees to suffer like Jesus, to be patient like Jesus, and to love as Jesus loved—sacrificing ourselves.

Colloquy.

Adorable Saviour, how far I am from resembling Thee: have pity on my weakness. I embrace the foot of the Cross, from which Thou dost instruct me so forcibly; I will remain beneath It, so that the abundant graces which flow from It may be shed forth upon my soul, and communicate to me strength to suffer for Thy Sake.

Resolution.

To bear with patience any words or actions on the part of others, which may wound my self-love.

Thought for the Day.

All they that saw Me, have laughed Me to scorn.

Prayer.

O Jesus, living in Mary.

Palm Sunday.

General considerations on the Crucifixion of our Lord.

And they watched Him.—S. MATT. XXVII.

I. PRELUDE.

Let us close our ears to the sound of other voices on the Hill of Calvary, and observe our Lord, listening to what He will say; and seeing in what we should imitate Him.

II. PRELUDE.

O Saviour of us Thy children, let us watch Thee, not as Thy enemies did, in scorn and hatred, but with love and reverence, as did Thy holy Mother, Saint John, Saint Mary Magdalene, and other pious women.

I. POINT.

Before the darkness came on, Mary and the few faithful followers of Jesus, watched Him.

We are looking up to the Face of God—our Saviour—our Master—our Example, Who is lifted up upon the Cross, as a spectacle to the world. He speaks but few words, but all the while He is teaching, with an eloquence which can never be rivalled, the sublimest truths of Christian doctrine. He tell us what we ought to hate—to love—to esteem—to practise. Truly spiritual persons, who meditate as they ought on the Mystery of scorn and torment which Jesus Christ endured, will conceive for sin, and all that leads to sin, a horror which it would be impossible to express. They will esteem the Cross only:—that is to say, the afflictions, and humiliations, of this life; understanding full well that it is by the Cross that Jesus has proved to us their necessity and efficacy. Do we understand this? Is it by means of them that we hope to become worthy to receive the benefit of His merits? The more we watch Jesus, the more He will become the Object of our hearts' deepest affections, the more generously shall we embrace the Cross, and practise meekness, courage, patience, and mortification.

II. Point.

By His grace Jesus merits for us every grace: we should be ever on the watch to receive them.

Around the Cross we find graces flowing in abundance; let us hasten to avail ourselves of them.—There are the graces of conversion; many of those who saw the Son of God die, *smote their breasts.* There are the graces of sanctification: the penitent robber was permitted to enter Paradise the very day of his death.—There are the graces of deliverance: the holy souls, detained as captives in limbo, were set at liberty.—There we find also the graces of perfection: at the foot of the Cross souls are enlightened and purified: hearts are enkindled with divine love. Saints are formed, by their rapid growth in holiness beneath its shadow. And we shall not look there in vain for the final grace of victory. From the Cross we shall have gained force to triumph over ourselves,—to free ourselves from our enemies—the world, the flesh, and the devil;—we shall have been strengthened in our resolutions unceasingly to watch Jesus on the Cross: so shall we undoubtedly win our last victory in the might of His power. *Death is swallowed up in Victory.*

Colloquy.

O my Jesus, Thou wast lifted up upon the Cross, that with the eye of faith I might be ever watching Thee: and, looking away from myself, learn how to resemble Thee.—Keep me ever by Thy Side, so that with the pious women who followed Thee to Calvary, I may compassionate Thy Suffering,—with Saint Mary Magdalene I may shed tears of penitence,—with Saint John I may have Mary for my Mother,—and with Mary herself I may love Thee only.

Resolution.

To go in spirit to Calvary, and there watch Jesus—and learn the science of the Cross.

Thought for the Day.

I will look towards the Lord God, my Saviour.

Prayer.

Take, O Lord, and receive.

Holy Week.—Monday.

Words of Jesus Christ spoken immediately after the Crucifixion.

Jesus said: Father, forgive them, for they know not what they do.—Jesus said to the robber: Amen I say to you, this day thou shalt be with Me in Paradise.—Jesus, seeing His Mother and the Disciple standing, whom He loved, saith to His Mother: Woman, behold Thy son: He saith to the Disciple: Behold thy Mother.—S. Luke xxiii., S. John xix.

I. Prelude.

Let us represent to ourselves Jesus on His Cross, between two robbers: His Eyes rest on His Mother and Saint John.

II. Prelude.

O Divine Saviour, grant that as we listen to the words spoken by Thee on the Cross, they may sink into our hearts, and be a source to us of perpetual consolation.

I. Point.

Jesus manifests His goodness and mercy towards the greatest of sinners.

Who can fail to be touched by the forgiving charity of the Heart of Jesus? He was the Object of the hatred, cruelty, and mockery of His murderers, as He was hanging upon the Cross; and yet He forgot His cruel suffering, He forgot the wicked malice of His enemies, and thought only of saving them, and of excusing their crime. He therefore addressed to God that prayer, which condemns for ever all hatred and all resentment: *Father forgive them, for they know not what they do.*—How often we should make this prayer our own, as we plead with God for sinners! In union with the pleading of Jesus, who can doubt its efficacy?—There was a robber hanging beside our Saviour, who, at first, joined in the reproaches uttered against Him, but hearing the prayer of Jesus for His enemies, and moved to compassion and repentance, he confessed his sins, and heard from the Lips of Jesus those words: *Amen I say to thee, this day thou shalt be with Me in Paradise.* His act of contrition, and prayer of confidence obtained the grace of absolution.—With regard to His murderers Jesus exercised, in His charity, the office of Redeemer and of Advocate; and proved, by His prayer, that no crime is too heinous, no ingratitude too enormous to be forgiven. His words to the penitent robber evince clearly that no act of real contrition can come too late for acceptance. Let none presume, for Jesus can only pray, and cannot forgive, where there is no repentance;—let none despair, for the robber was rescued at the eleventh hour, by means of his humble confession. *The Son of Man hath power on earth to forgive sins*, and exercising this power upon the Cross, He delegated it hereafter to His representatives, to the end of time. What lessons of charity and hope may we not draw from the two sentences spoken by our Lord, on behalf of sinners, in His dying moments!

II. Point.

Jesus gives Mary to us to be our Mother, and He gives us to her, as her children.

Here is a further manifestation of the tender solicitude of the Sacred Heart. Knowing that soon He was to die, Jesus lovingly regarded His Holy Mother. She, who had been watching that beloved Face so attentively, understood that He would speak to her. By His glance towards Saint John, He attracted her notice also to the Apostle, and then, in words of deep meaning addressed them both: *Woman, behold thy Son.—Son, behold thy Mother.*—Mary must have felt at that moment that she was indeed losing her own Dear Son, but she at once united her will to His; and while making the sacrifice demanded of her, she accepted us as her children in the person of Saint John; and engaged herself to fulfil towards us the duties of a good and loving Mother. Jesus, having all His Life been the one Object of Mary's tenderness and love, wished, before His Death, to enkindle in her heart a like tenderness and love for us, of whom He is the Elder Brother. What wonder then that love enkindled and directed at such a moment, under such circumstances, should have had most marvellous effects, and glorious results in the Christian world. What special graces have not we, each one of us, obtained through Mary? how many times, notwithstanding our numerous infidelities, have we felt the effects of her maternal solicitude? To us Jesus says: *Behold thy Mother*, once standing near my Cross, and now seated beside me in glory: look up to her, speak to her of all your needs,—your joys and sorrows,—your hopes and fears.—Eternal thanks and praises be unto Thee, O Jesus!—to thee, O Mary, our gratitude and love!

Colloquy.

O my Saviour, less occupied with Thine own sufferings than with the means of salvation Thou wouldst procure for us through their infinite merits, I thank Thee for the hope of pardon which Thy words on the Cross impart to my soul; and for the joy of sharing in the same love which Mary had for Thee. By that love, more entirely perfected in Heaven, receive her petitions on my behalf:—I know indeed that Thou canst not reject the intercession of Thy dear Mother.

RESOLUTION.

To recall those words of purest charity, of pardon, and of consolation uttered by Jesus on the Cross.

THOUGHT FOR THE DAY.

Lord, remember me in Thy Kingdom.

PRAYER.

Our Father, and Hail Mary.

Holy Week.—Tuesday.

Words of Jesus Christ on the Cross, spoken during the miraculous darkness.

When the sixth hour was come, there was darkness over the whole earth until the ninth hour: And at the ninth hour JESUS *cried with a loud voice, saying: Eloi, Eloi, lamma sabacthani? My God, My God, why hast Thou forsaken Me?—Afterwards* JESUS *knowing that all things were now accomplished, that the Scripture might be fulfilled, said: I thirst.*—S. MARK XV., S. JOHN XIX.

I. Prelude.

Let us represent to ourselves the Hill of Calvary covered with thick darkness, and the enemies of Jesus taking flight, being seized with alarm.

II. Prelude.

We will not leave Thee, O Saviour; but remain to hear and meditate upon those words of anguish which have merited for us so many graces; may we be content to suffer with Thee in desolation, and share Thy thirst for our sanctification.

I. Point.

The cause of the lamentation made by our Saviour, to His Divine Father.

The Holy Soul of Jesus Christ, plunged in profound desolation, was bearing the crushing weight of divine justice. The blindness of the Jewish nation, and the full knowledge of the loss of that multitude of souls who would not profit by His Death, were added to the many sufferings that afflicted Him. And then came the crowning sorrow! —the Heavenly Father hid His Face: this caused Him to utter the lamentation which indicated the torture He was enduring:—*My God, my God, why hast Thou forsaken Me?*— The answer we hear by the mouth of the Prophet: *He was as one struck by God, and afflicted: the Lord hath laid on Him the iniquity of us all.* Yes! we here see the effect of our innumerable infidelities.—Would we, after this, repeat one single fault deliberately, so as to renew the grief of soul our Lord endured?—In His giving Himself up to this deep sadness, we see another proof of His charity.—He would merit the consolations necessary for us in our hour of trial.—We feel instinctively that the abundant graces of which we have experienced the efficacy, under afflictions and desolation, are the precious fruits of that extreme anguish of soul Jesus suffered on the Cross. Who can sound the depths of divine justice ?—and divine love ?

II. Point.

Our Saviour thirsted for the salvation of souls.

The strength of Jesus was well nigh exhausted through loss of Blood, when He uttered the fifth Word from the Cross: *I thirst.*—It expresses how much He desired the salvation of all men :—He had for all an infinite love ; and because of this ardent longing that all should avail themselves of the merits of His Death, He cried out: *I thirst:* —I thirst for the salvation—I thirst for the sanctification of mankind. We can offer Thee some relief, O Sweet Jesus, by striving to become saints, and by corresponding to the graces of our holy vocation : by devoting ourselves to gain souls for Thee : by giving to weak and fainting souls *a cup of water because they belong to Thee*—have been redeemed by Thy Precious Blood. Thou canst find so few on whom to bestow the plenitude of Thy heavenly benedictions :—standing beneath Thy Cross to-day, we offer ourselves to suffer with Thee, so that being purified by tribulations, we may be deemed worthy to allay the thirst which consumed Thee.—*Lord, when did we see Thee thirsty, and gave Thee drink?* Thou knowest better than we.

Colloquy.

O Jesus, forsaken upon the Cross, grant that by the remembrance of the bitter lamentation poured forth from Thy anguish-stricken soul, I may be consoled in the midst of darkness and desolation. "Jesus suffered as I am suffering," let me say to myself:—And as Thou didst thirst for my sanctification, so may I thirst for Thee—for Thy love—for Thy presence—for Thy glory, and for the sanctification of souls. The more I love Thee, the more I feel the longing to love Thee better.

RESOLUTION.

So to act, that each thing I do may be an act of love.

THOUGHT FOR THE DAY.

Depart not from me;—my soul thirsteth after the strong, living God.

PRAYER.

Our Father, and Hail Mary.

Holy Week.—Wednesday.

The two last Words spoken by Jesus on the Cross.

JESUS said: It is consummated. And crying with a loud voice, He said: Father, into Thy Hands I commend My Spirit.—S. JOHN XIX., S. LUKE XXIII.

I. PRELUDE.

Let us remain near the Cross, to receive and meditate upon the last Words our Saviour spoke.

II. PRELUDE.

Grant, O Lord Jesus, that we may so well employ the time that remains for us on earth, that we may co-operate with Thee to accomplish the great work of our sanctification, and in dying, give up our souls with confidence into Thy Hands.

I. POINT.

As Jesus perfected the work of redeeming mankind, so we should strive to perfect the work of our sanctification.

Jesus, in finishing His earthly career, threw a glance backwards, over the thirty-three years of His Life—begun in the Stable of Bethlehem, and now ending upon the Cross of Calvary.—He saw that every moment had been faithfully employed in the accomplishing of His Father's Will:—He saw that all the prophecies concerning Himself had been verified in His Person:—that the foundations of His Religion had been laid.—He saw hell vanquished—mankind redeemed.—He saw the justice of His Father satisfied,—the Treasury of His merits replenished, whence His Church until the end of the world, should be enriched.—There was nothing more to retain Him on earth:—all was accomplished.—O Jesus, what should we render to Thee for all Thy benefits?—On the part of our Redeemer all has been perfected, but not on our part yet. He has done all that was necessary in order to communicate to us His infinite merits, but to fit ourselves to receive His graces we must co-operate with Him more entirely, and fulfil all the duties His law imposes upon us, according to our state of life. We must follow His example, and reduce to practice His divine lessons. We must worthily receive the Holy Sacraments, and correspond to His grace with ardent love and constant fidelity. And further we must, with Saint Paul, *fill up those things that are wanting of the sufferings of Christ for His Body, which is the Church.* Jesus will apply to us His merits, provided we really labour to make our sanctification perfect:—then at the hour of our death, we too shall be able to say: *It is consummated.*

II. Point.

In commending His Spirit into the Hands of His Father, Jesus exhibits a loving confidence, and merits for us a great grace.

My Father, into Thy Hands I commend My Spirit. By these words Jesus made a most perfect act of adoration, trustfulness, and love. He had just been suffering the terrible strokes of divine justice;—He had been forced to utter that cry of anguish, *My God, My God, why hast Thou forsaken Me?*—and yet His confidence, far from being diminished afforded Him sufficient strength to pronounce in a loud voice His dying words: *Father, into Thy Hands do I commend My Spirit,*—honouring the sweet Name of Father with a love made most pure in the crucible of affliction. In committing His own Soul into the Hands of God the Father, our Adorable Saviour would also present to Him the souls of all the elect. It was a petition to our Father that He would favourably receive our souls if, in quitting the world, they be united to Himself—passing away in His grace and His love, into the Hands of God. In the dying words of Jesus what a source of confidence do we find! what a powerful motive to unite ourselves closely to Him!—Grant then, O my God, that living in holiness as becomes the Spouses of Thy Divine Son, we may be enabled, in our last hour, to say, in union with Him: *Father, into Thy Hands do I commend My Spirit.*

Colloquy.

Redeemer of my soul, in proclaiming that all was accomplished which Thou didst come into the world to do, I may rest assured that there is no grace which is unattainable, if, by a faithful co-operation with Thy work of Redemption, I labour to perfect my own Sanctification, remembering that *it is God Who worketh in me, both to will, and to accomplish, according to His good Will.* With confidence therefore I cast myself at the foot of the Cross, and commend myself, as I listen to Thy last Words, O Jesus, into the Hands of our Father in Heaven.

Resolution.

To strive earnestly to finish the work which God has given me to do.

Thought for the Day.

Father, into Thy Hands do I commend My Spirit.

Prayer.

Our Father, and Hail Mary.

Holy Thursday.

See Page 244.

Good Friday.

Death of Jesus Christ.

And bowing His Head He gave up the Ghost.—S. John xix.

I. Prelude.

Let us represent to ourselves the Hill of Calvary still shrouded in darkness, the last moment of His suffering Life is over.—Jesus is dead.

II. Prelude.

O Saviour, grant that, entering by faith into the Mystery of Thy Death, we may understand that we should no longer live to ourselves.

I. Point.

Jesus dies.

Jesus, having cried out with a loud voice, gave up the Ghost. After suffering on the part of His enemies all that the most barbarous cruelty could invent, our Blessed Saviour completes His Sacrifice. The pallor of death steals over His agonised Features, His Eyes close, and He is dead. His Soul has passed to an unseen world.—Let us prostrate ourselves with Mary Magdalene at the Feet of Jesus, bathing them in tears of sorrow and contrition, while with broken hearts we mourn over the remembrance of our sins, which have crucified Him. Jesus is dead—He Who came to bring happiness to His people, to teach us the precepts of truth—and to redeem us from eternal death, by the

Sacrifice of His own Life. And we whom He came to save—each one of us—have put forth our hands to take the instruments of the Passion wherewith to wound Him and to crucify Him:—therefore Jesus is dead.—Let us contemplate the Victim of our sins, and behold the evil deed that we have perpetrated. Let us avow, with deep compunction, that we have been guilty of the Blood of our Saviour; and join with all nature in lamentation for the death of her Creator:—with the Centurion in acknowledging Him to be the Son of God:—with Mary, and the faithful Disciple in rendering our homage of sorrowing love, and of devotion to our Jesus, our Lord.

II. Point.

What we ought to do in acknowledgment of the love Jesus had for us, evidenced by His Death.

Since there can be no higher proof of love than that of giving one's life for a friend, Jesus could not have carried His love to a greater excess, than He did in dying for us. His Death was the price paid for our souls. We belong to Him, and no longer to ourselves,—nor to the world,—nor to any creature,—still less to His enemies: therefore for Him we must live, suffer and die. We cannot be insensible to the intense love which caused Him to immolate Himself for our salvation. O Crucified Jesus, engrave on our souls the Mystery of Thy Death, that we may never fall into the sin of ingratitude again. We will hide ourselves within Thy Precious Wounds. The lance has pierced Thy Side; let us take shelter within Thy Sacred Heart, and make It our beloved Retreat.—There, within the very Home of Divine Love, may our hearts learn how to love God perfectly, after the example of the Son of His Love.

Colloquy.

Holy Father, accept the Sacrifice that Thy Son has completed by expiring on the Cross, in order that He might reconcile me to Thyself. I render Thee thanks, O Just and Merciful Father, for having sent Thy Only-Begotten Son into the world to die, that I may live. Send me both light and grace, that I may study to know Jesus Crucified daily more and more; spending my life near His Cross, that thus the remembrance of His Passion and Death may never fade from my mind.

Resolution.

To unite to the Sacrifice of Jesus, and the Sorrows of Mary, all that I may find difficult to bear.

Thought for the Day.

It hath well pleased the Father, to reconcile all things unto Himself, making peace through the Blood of the Cross, the Cross of the Son of His love.

Prayer.

Soul of Christ.

Holy Saturday.

The Burial of our Lord.

Joseph of Arimathea (a disciple of JESUS*) besought Pilate that he might take away the Body of* JESUS*: And Pilate gave him leave: And Nicodemus also came, bringing a mixture of myrrh and aloes, about a hundred pound weight: They took the Body of* JESUS*, and bound It in linen cloths, with the spices: Now there was in the place where He was crucified, a garden; and in the garden a new Sepulchre,—there they laid* JESUS.—S. JOHN XIX.

I. PRELUDE.

Let us contemplate the Sacred Body of Jesus, as it is taken from the Cross and laid in the Sepulchre.

II. PRELUDE.

O Mary, our dear Mother, we draw near to thee, and watch thee performing the last sad offices for thy Dead Son—our Beloved Saviour.

I. POINT.

After the Deposition from the Cross, Jesus is placed in the arms of His Mother.

Let us consider with what respectful carefulness Joseph of Arimathea, Nicodemus, and Saint John detach Jesus from the Cross, and lay Him in His Mother's arms;—and the loving gentleness with which Mary receives His lifeless Form.

She gazes with all a mother's tender affection on that Beloved Face, and tears of woe betoken the sorrow of her heart. Mary Magdalene is prostrate at His Sacred Feet: let us weep with her, and kiss His Precious Wounds: they should be to us as fountains of charity and devotedness.—We look from Jesus to Mary, and again from the Mother to the Son.—Who can express her grief, as she sits on Mount Calvary, bearing on her knees His pale, disfigured Corpse? Hitherto Jesus has shared in her sorrows and sympathised in her sufferings; now she is alone—comfortless.—Our sins have caused this bitter separation; on our account she is desolate. Let us bewail our unfaithfulness; promising her, as we kneel beside her Son, that we will never more add to her grief; and let us ask her to obtain for us the grace of loving Jesus as she did.

II. Point.

The circumstances of the Burial of Jesus teach us how to dispose our hearts for Holy Communion.

As we see the Disciples of Jesus bearing His Holy Body from Calvary to the Garden, we feel inclined to envy them their high privilege.—Let us, as we follow them to the Sepulchre, and meditate upon that wonderful scene, thank God that we are so often permitted to carry His Son within our hearts, in which He places Himself in Holy Communion.—Why was Jesus laid in a new Sepulchre? Why were the sweet spices used? Apart from the consideration of the particular designs of God, Who willed that all the circumstances connected with our Saviour's Entombment should witness incontestably to His Resurrection, we may find most instructive and helpful answers to our inquiries, in the consideration of this Mystery. The newness of the Sepulchre typifies that purity of heart, which is so necessary in the receiving of the Sacred Body of Jesus Christ, under the sacramental species.—The sweet spices represent humility, recollection, holy desires, tender piety, and all other virtues that our Lord wishes to find sending forth their perfume, in the hearts He visits,—which perfume is again a symbol of that edification which the Spouses of Jesus should give, after being nourished with the Sacred Food of His Body and Blood. Descend into the Sepulchre of our renewed hearts, prepared to receive Thee, O Lord:—by Thy Presence there, make the practice of every virtue to become easy, and enrich our souls with the treasures of Thy grace. Come to our poor hearts: never, never leave us.

Colloquy.

O my Divine Redeemer, as I see Thy Inanimate Body taken down from the Cross, placed in the arms of Thy holy Mother, and then carried to the Sepulchre by Thy faithful Disciples, I experience in myself a desire to follow Thee in death, as in life.—Give me grace to learn each day how to die, by the practice of mortification; and to lie buried with Thee in the solitude and silence of a hidden life; so that I may be able to say: *My life is hid with Christ in God.*

Resolution.

To bury myself spiritually with Jesus in profound silence and true recollectedness; adoring Him as He rests within my heart.

Thought for the Day.

My life is hid with Christ in God.

Prayer.

Take, O Lord, and receive.

Easter Sunday.

The Resurrection of our Lord.

Behold there was a great earthquake: For an Angel of the Lord descended from Heaven: and coming rolled back the stone, and sat upon it: And his countenance was as lightning, and his raiment white as snow: And for fear of him the guards were struck with terror, and became as dead men. —S. MATT. XXVIII.

I. PRELUDE.

Let us represent to ourselves the garden, and the Holy Sepulchre, resplendent with light.

II. PRELUDE.

O Triumphant Lord, deign to fill us with holy joy, and grant that we may receive the fruits of thy Resurrection.

I. POINT.

The mysterious change that took place as regards the Sacred Humanity of Jesus, at the moment of His Resurrection.

To-day the Church calls us to look upon a scene, very different from that of yesterday. It seems scarcely like the same earth this morning, on it so great a change has come to pass. Instead of the humiliation and suffering and Death of our Divine Saviour, we gaze upon His glorious Resurrection. He leaves the tomb miraculously—re-invested with divine attributes—freed from the laws which affect humanity

—and clothed with glory. His Sacred Wounds are sources of light, which shed abroad a dazzling brightness. The eternal Diadem has taken the place of the Crown of Thorns; Jesus is the Conqueror of Death, and His Sepulchre is made glorious. What a marvellous change! From a state of lifelessness within the earth, He has risen to a condition of impassibility and immortality;—from weakness and infirmity to power immense;—from the depths of humiliation, to the height of glory! *He Who was as a worm and no man, the reproach of men, and the outcast of the people,* becomes, as Man, the Sovereign of the universe, the Judge of the living and the dead:—it is He before Whom the Heavens bow, and Who shall receive for ever, the homage due to the Divinity. What joy does not His triumph give us! To-day as Vanquisher of His enemies, and full of majesty, He invites us to share in His Victory, and to receive the fruits of it. Let us, the Spouses of Jesus, put away the garb of mourning, wherewith we have been clothed in the day of His suffering, and rejoice in His Triumph (is it not ours also?) and be glad—for is not His Resurrection a pledge of our own? We participate this Day (called so well the Queen of Festivals), in the joy of Jesus Himself, and in that of the blessed Inhabitants of Heaven: with the whole Church we sing her song of triumph: *This is the Day which the Lord hath made, let us be glad and rejoice therein.*

II. Point.

Jesus is a mighty Conqueror.

What glorious victories have earthly conquerors won! how splendid have been their triumphs! and yet all human glory, all earthly splendour fades into insignificance, and becomes a mere shadow of greatness, when compared with the Triumph—the Victory—of the God-Man over the powers of Death and Hell. *Thou art worthy, O Lord, because Thou wast slain, and hast redeemed us to God in Thy Blood, to receive power and divinity, and wisdom and strength and honour, and glory and benediction. Heaven and earth unite in proclaiming: The Lord reigneth, He is clothed with beauty; the Lord is clothed with strength. O Death, where is thy victory? O grave, where is thy sting?* Our Saviour hath risen gloriously; we shall rise gloriously likewise:—our Redeemer liveth, and we ourselves shall see Him as He is. This hope dwells within our hearts. Jesus risen, effaces all the ignominy of His passion and renders it honourable. O Mystery of consolation and of joy!—the Resurrection is the foundation of all our hope and of our love. The end of suffering, endured for Jesus, is the beginning of glory.

Colloquy.

Thy Victory is complete, O my Jesus, for Thou hast triumphed over the powers of Death and Hell. How greatly do I rejoice for the glory Thou hast attained, and I celebrate with gladness this high Festival. But, I beseech Thee, deign to finish in me the work of Thy grace, by making me to become more fully a partaker in the glorious Life Thou didst begin in this Mystery: grant that seeing Thee rise, I may rise also, to a more fervent and saintly life,—to a life of fidelity and love.

Resolution.

To spend this day in much spiritual joy, and begin to strive to live the risen Life of our Lord more perfectly.

THOUGHT FOR THE DAY.

Christ is risen from the dead, the First-fruits of them that slept.

PRAYER.

Take, O Lord, and receive.

Easter Week.—Monday.

The Resurrection of Jesus Christ is the Figure of our spiritual resurrection.

JESUS CHRIST rose again for our justification.—ROMANS VIII.

I. PRELUDE.

Let us represent to ourselves anew the glory of the Sepulchre of Jesus.

II. PRELUDE.

Adorable Lord, bestow on us grace to rise spiritually, by leaving the tomb of indifference, to lead a life of fervour.

I. POINT.

The consideration of the Resurrection of Jesus makes us see more clearly that our spiritual resurrection should resemble it.—His Sacred Body was perfectly agile.

At Easter we recal the words God spoke to Moses concerning the Paschal solemnity: *For it is the Phase—that is the Passage—of the Lord.* Now we celebrate the Passage of our Lord from Death to Life; and think upon our own passage from a life of tepidity to one of fervour,—from an imperfect to a holy life. Jesus, in leaving the Tomb, disengaged Himself from the winding-sheet, wherein His Sacred Body had been enwrapped; this should make us understand that we must extricate ourselves from the imperfections and bad habits, which for so long a time have kept our souls bound and motionless for good. If we rise with Jesus, and set ourselves free from the paralysed state in which our evil inclinations have retained us, they will infallibly disappear. Our Risen Lord was clothed with the power of agility, to teach us to despise all resistance of nature, to pass quickly out of its reach; to triumph over every obstacle; and that our souls should tend upwards to Him alone. *If we are indeed risen with Christ we shall seek the things that are above;* and our whole being will be spiritualised, responding with agility to the promptings, not of nature, but of grace. May we be enabled fully to enter into the Mystery of the Resurrection-Life of Jesus, and to receive the plenitude of His favours, offered to us at this time especially.

II. Point.

The lucidity and impassibility of the glorified Body of Jesus.

Jesus, in rising from the Sepulchre, clothed in light, wills that we should understand what is the beauty of a soul disengaged from the ties of nature, and renewed in the spiritual life. The soul, like Jesus, becomes luminous: the

Holy Spirit enlightens it interiorly, by filling it with the knowledge of divine things; it is possessed of a lustrous beauty, and its virtues shine visibly, contributing to the edification of others. By the impassibility of the Body of Jesus, we comprehend that grace raises the soul, by means of holy courage, above temptations; it renders it invulnerable against the darts of the enemies of its salvation, and gives it the power of mastering its downward tendencies. Such are the happy privileges granted to His faithful ones, who lovingly enter into the spirit of the Mystery of Easter. Sufferings indeed we must still endure, for we are still on this side of the grave; but if they serve only to raise us near to Jesus, we may be said to share already in the effects of His impassibility. We range ourselves therefore around Him, to rejoice at the sight of the glory He received in His Resurrection, and to honour the marvellous capabilities of His Adorable Body, by rendering ourselves worthy, by our fervour, to participate in them spiritually.

Colloquy.

O my Saviour, I thank Thee for the favour Thou dost accord me, in permitting me to partake in the glorious privileges of the new life Thou didst begin, as at this time. Make me to be entirely *renewed in the spirit of my mind*, so that, freed from the servitude of sense and natural affections, I may rise constantly towards Thee, with a pure and generous heart.

Resolution.

Aided by the grace Jesus bestows, I will endeavour to reproduce spiritually in myself, the capabilities observable in His Sacred Humanity after the Resurrection.

THOUGHT FOR THE DAY.

If, by the Spirit, you mortify the deeds of the flesh, you shall live.

PRAYER.

O Jesus, living in Mary.

Easter Week.—Tuesday.

On the Spiritual Resurrection of the Children of God.

If you be risen with Christ, mind the things that are above, not the things that are upon the earth.—COL. III.

I. PRELUDE.

Let us represent to ourselves Jesus Christ, rising glorious from the Sepulchre.

II. PRELUDE.

O Divine Redeemer, give us strength to destroy completely all that may be in opposition to that perfect life to which we resolve to attain :—reproduce in us Thy risen Life.

I. POINT.

The Resurrection of Jesus Christ was real :—there must be reality in ours also.

The Lord is risen indeed. Jesus Himself again assured His Disciples of the reality of His Resurrection when He appeared to them, and perceived them to be affrighted—*supposing that they saw a spirit. It is I,* He said, *fear not; see My Hands and Feet that it is I myself.* It was to confirm the truth of this Mystery that He told them to touch His Sacred Body; that He eat and drank with them. Such should our spiritual resurrection also be, not merely an appearance—a phantom; but our whole being should rise with Christ: our inner life should be renewed, our own spirit should be changed into His spirit, our natural affections into holy affections, our defects into virtues:—these changes being effected, our resurrection will be a reality. Such a signal favour we may and we ought to expect from the charity of our Saviour, since He has merited it for us by His victory over sin and hell: indeed, He offers it to us at this holy season, tenderly soliciting us to embrace that life of perfection to which He calls us. It is a matter of great importance that we should correspond to this inestimable grace, by henceforth doing the works of Jesus,—acting with Him and for Him.

II. Point.

Our spiritual resurrection should be entire—complete.

The new Life of our Adorable Master was instantaneously perfected. There was nothing in it that death hereafter could touch; He could never again experience the trials and humiliations of poverty, of an obscure life, nor the shame and anguish of the Passion. It is one of the most dangerous errors into which we can fall, that of wishing to be only half converted,—of thinking to rise in part only.—We sometimes seem to imagine that we may still retain certain cherished inclinations,—allow ourselves in certain favourite gratifications. No, the spiritual life cannot ally itself with any mere natural attachment; nor the love of God with any disorderly love of creatures, or of one's self. If God is to occupy our heart, He must find it disengaged from all that is opposed to His Will. Further, in order to enjoy the heavenly delights which are granted to those whose hearts are free from all earthly affections, we must desire only one thing—that is God—and to be united to Him by a pure and ardent love. This is a faint outline of the risen life, for words cannot picture it. O Precious Mystery of the Resurrection! A profitable consideration of it draws souls away from the service of God's foes, and frees them from the hindrances which prevent their rising towards God, and living the Life of Jesus. Do we not desire in all sincerity to be *delivered from the servitude of corruption, into the liberty of the glory of the children of God?*

Colloquy.

How good art Thou, O my Heavenly Father, thus to have given me, in Thy Divine Son, a perfect Model of the life to which Thou hast called me. Thanks to the light afforded by the Mystery of His glorious Resurrection, thanks to my Risen Saviour, I sincerely desire to renew my life in Him, so that my spiritual resurrection may be real—entire—perfect.

Resolution.

To strive from this moment to put away absolutely that defect, which prevents the reality of my own spiritual resurrection.

THOUGHT FOR THE DAY.

The Lord is risen indeed.

PRAYER.

Take, O Lord, and receive.

Easter Week.—Wednesday.

The difficulties to be overcome in order to rise spiritually.

As Christ is risen from the dead by the glory of the Father, so we also may walk in newness of life.—ROMANS VI.

I. PRELUDE.

Let us again form a picture of the wonderful change that took place in the Sacred Person of the Son of God, as He rose from the dead.

II. PRELUDE.

Fortify us, by Thy grace, O Lord Jesus, so that, allowing ourselves to be hindered by no obstacle, we may constantly persevere in the practice of the life of perfection, which we have resolved to embrace.

I. POINT.

What the difficulties are in the way of rising with Jesus.

Our Divine Saviour, in His Resurrection, indicates these difficulties, and how we can triumph over them. As He freed Himself from the linen cloths which were wound about His Sacred Body, so we must break away from all that may displease our Lord;—human respect, selfishness, attachment to earthly things, sensuality. These bind the soul down to the world and to self.—Again, the Body of Jesus was enclosed in the Tomb, a large stone being placed against the entrance. We must exert ourselves to put aside the heavy stone of habitual cowardice and sloth, if we would rise with Jesus,—and His grace will aid us to roll it away.—Around the Body of Jesus His enemies formed a guard, to prevent His friends from taking It away. The enemies of our perfection and salvation surround us incessantly, to intercept if possible, the gracious assistance of divine inspirations. But as our Lord was, notwithstanding all the obstacles which seemed to stand in the way of His Resurrection, faithful to the promise He had made to His Apostles that He would rise again, so must we be faithful to the promise we have made to rise spiritually with Him, and to lead a truly religious life.

II. Point.

There must be constancy in our risen life.

This poor human nature of ours is perpetually encountering one enormous difficulty—that of persevering in good. We consent to undertake the work of perfecting ourselves, we begin it with vigour; but how often it happens that we grow weary of the efforts we have to make, of the sacrifices we have to impose on ourselves. In order that our fervour may be sustained in the service of God, we should keep our minds lifted up towards our Divine Master, and our hearts united to Him; but frequently we fall back again, because we prefer to occupy both mind and heart with self, and the things of earth. If we only really knew how far the enjoyment of divine things surpasses that which this world offers, we should not hesitate about sacrificing the trifles which pre-occupy our mind and hinder us from thinking of God, and of all that leads to Him. We should rid our heart of the nothingness which fills it, we should empty it of self, so that Jesus might have room to enter there. To establish ourselves solidly in a truly religious life, to ensure the bestowal of God's great gift of final perseverance, let us follow the wise counsel of the Apostle: *Seek the things that are above, where Christ sitteth at the right Hand of God.*

Colloquy.

O Divine Jesus, I beseech Thee to crown the benefits Thou hast bestowed on me. To raise my soul from its state of languor, wilt Thou not use that same almighty power which raised Thee from the Tomb?—Thou desirest that I should bear a part in my own resurrection to a spiritual life, by generous efforts; I therefore promise Thee to neglect nothing to procure the accomplishment of Thy holy Will in my regard. Sustain me, by Thy grace, O my Well-beloved, so shall I be sure to vanquish all difficulties, and to persevere in living Thy Life.

Resolution.

To renounce any affection which may be placing an obstacle between my soul and Jesus.

Thought for the Day.

Thanks be to God, Who giveth us the victory through our Lord Jesus Christ.

Prayer.

Take, O Lord, and receive.

Easter Week.—Thursday.

The Resurrection of Jesus Christ is a pledge of our own.

I know that my Redeemer liveth, and in the last day I shall rise out of the earth:—And in my flesh I shall see my God.—JOB XIX.

I. PRELUDE.

Let us represent to ourselves the surpassing beauty, and the many glorious prerogatives of the resuscitated Body of Jesus.

II. PRELUDE.

Divine Redeemer, grant that having the hope of our glorious resurrection strengthened by the consideration of Thy rising from the Grave, we may think only of how to live more holily, and to render ourselves worthy of our high destiny.

I. POINT.

Jesus our Head, rose gloriously: by what means may we hope to participate in His resurrection of glory?

If we lead, with Jesus, a humble, mortified life, if we die to ourselves in order to live an angelic life, at the Last Day our bodies will rise from the grave, resplendent with glory, and clothed with immortality, to enter the Abode of eternal happiness. Then will our sorrows be changed into joy, our afflictions into celestial delight. With this hope before us, we may say with holy Job: *I know that my Redeemer liveth, and in my flesh I shall see my God.* Yes!

in this same body—now subject to so many miseries, but which will then participate, as a living member of our Risen Saviour, in the glory and beatitude of our Divine Head. He, during his mortal Life on earth, to be like in all things unto us, willed to be dependent on His creatures for its support. But when His sacred Humanity assumed the garb of immortality, It was freed from this state of dependence; and from the sufferings to which It was liable —subjected for love of us—in consequence of the permissive power that creatures had over It. We must seek to deliver ourselves as much as possible from the bondage of creatures, so that they may not trouble the peace of our soul,—desiring most earnestly to be in a condition of holy liberty. Dependent on them for the maintenance of our natural life, let us not increase this dependence by our love of luxury, nor by our sensuality, but rather diminish it by Christian mortification, self-abnegation, and holy poverty. If we are obliged to suffer pain or inconvenience, on account of others, we should bear these joyfully, and in a spirit of penance, for love of Him Who has endured far more on our account. Let us rise above our sufferings, occupying ourselves with them as little as possible, so shall we attain to the present enjoyment of freedom from much misery, and many illusions. Yet a few more moments of trial and of endurance, and we shall rise to a state of endless glory.

II. Point.

The Divine Eucharist is the pledge and cause of our glorious resurrection.

The very fact of our being members of Jesus Christ is the foundation of our hope in a glorious resurrection, and since we are His members—and have contracted a union with Him, in and through the Holy Eucharist—we comprehend that it is this august Sacrament which is the pledge and the cause of our rising hereafter, to a life of eternal bliss. It is the cause; for it is Jesus—living His glorious Life in His immortal Body—Whom we receive in Holy Communion: He unites Himself to us, to vivify, to sanctify our bodies and souls, and therein to deposit the germ of immortality. By virtue of this Sacrament we become truly the members of the Body of Jesus Christ, and at the Last Day, the Angels recognising our bodies as sacramentalised, will place us at the right Hand of our Saviour. —It is the pledge of our glorious resurrection; for Jesus Christ by the gift of Himself, confirms the promise of immortality which He has given us: *He that eateth My Flesh, and drinketh My Blood, hath everlastiny life, and I will raise him up in the Last Day.* Oh! the goodness of our Lord! He has consecrated not only His mortal Life, but His Life of glory to the promotion of our salvation. Why, O Jesus, are we not as persevering in loving Thee, as Thou art in the bestowal of Thy benefits? What an excess of love on Thy part, powerfully obliging us to correspond faithfully to it! Are we doing so?

Colloquy.

O Loving Saviour, what honour, what glory dost Thou reserve for me! After having abased Thyself even to me, in taking upon Thyself my human nature, Thou wouldst now raise me to Thyself by communicating to me Thine own divine nature. The conditions Thou layest down are, that possessing the gift of faith in Thy promises of a glorious resurrection, I may strive to render myself worthy of them by a holy life—a life of union with Thee. Thou couldst not propose terms more honourable; I accept them with all my heart, and I desire to fulfil them faithfully.

Resolution.

To remember that my present momentary afflictions are not to be compared to the endlessness of glory which awaits me.

Thought for the Day.

I am the Bread of Life. He that eateth this Bread shall live for ever.

Prayer.

Soul of Christ.

Easter Week.—Friday.

The Sacred Wounds are visible in our Lord's Glorified Body.

See My Hands and Feet that it is I Myself.—S. Luke xxiv.

I. Prelude.

Let us count the Precious Wounds, as we see them in the glorified Body of Jesus.

II. Prelude.

O Loving Saviour, give us grace to think often upon the signification of Thy Wounds, and consider why Thou dost still bear them on Thy Divine Person in Heaven.

I. Point.

The Sacred Wounds speak of combat.

The Life of the God-Man upon earth was truly a warfare; He came into this world to fight against His enemies. War was declared by the Prince of Peace against sin and death and hell, for they had to be conquered ere His reign of peace could be established. The deadliest combat was reserved for Calvary: never was there such a battle-field! never apparently, more unequal forces! and the Victor triumphed by means of a seeming defeat! A week has now passed away since that day of mortal strife, when the Person of our King was wounded, and through *His Death He destroyed him who had the empire of death.* To-day as we see Jesus crowned with glory and honour, in answer to the inquiry: *Who is this Beautiful One in His Robe, walking in the greatness of His Strength? Why is His apparel red?* He, our Saviour makes answer: *I have trampled on My enemies in My indignation, their blood is sprinkled upon My garments. The Year of My Redemption is come:*—I will bear for ever, as a sign of My triumph over Death, the tokens of My love for you, whom I have rescued from destruction; and of My sufferings on your behalf. In the sight of the Angels, I will ascend to the Throne of My Father; there will these Wounds plead with Him for you; through them you shall receive power to overcome and to pass, as I have done, through great tribulation, into the possession of eternal peace.

II. Point.

The effect which the contemplation of the Glorious Wounds of Jesus should have on us.

If we look upon the sacred Wounds, as Jesus hangs upon the Cross, we are filled with grief and compassion; grief at the remembrance of what we have ourselves done to wound Him,—compassion on account of His acute suffering. We are thus drawn to desire to share in His conflict, to bear, according to His Will, *the marks of the Lord Jesus*, so that we may resemble Him. If we gaze upon the Adorable Person of the Son of God after His Resurrection we perceive how bright, how beautiful are those very scars.—Each has become a centre of radiant light; Blood no longer flows from them, for It *has* washed us from our sins, and saved mankind; but rays of grace stream forth to enlighten, to console, to strengthen,—to animate our souls with hope, and to perfect our confidence.—Oh! with what joy shall we one day recognise our Lord! seeing the Wounds which have so often proved to be our safest refuge, as they have been also the dearest object of our veneration, we shall exclaim: *This is our God, we have waited for Him, and He will save us.*

Colloquy.

So lately have I witnessed the cruelty with which Thy Hands and Feet and Side were pierced, for love of me, O my Saviour.—Now that Thou hast risen, I behold the glorious scars of Thy Five Wounds enhancing the wondrous beauty of Thy Person; and I beseech Thee, by their most precious merits, that I too may win the victory, through suffering, over the enemies of my salvation; and rise gloriously on that Resurrection Day, *when this mortal must put on immortality.*

Resolution.

Often to press to my heart and lips the Five Wounds of the Crucifix.

THOUGHT FOR THE DAY.

See My Hands and Feet: And He shewed them His Side.

PRAYER.

Soul of Christ.

Easter Week—Saturday.

The Holy Women at the Sepulchre.

And when the Sabbath was past, Mary Magdalene, and Mary the mother of James, and Salome, brought sweet spices, that coming they might anoint JESUS: And very early in the morning the first day of the week, they come to the Sepulchre, the sun being now risen: And they said one to another: Who shall roll us back the stone from the door of the Sepulchre?—S. MARK XVI.

I. PRELUDE.

Let us see the holy Women, bearing the sweet spices, going early in the morning to the Sepulchre where the Body of Jesus had been laid.

II. PRELUDE.

O God of love, communicate to us somewhat of that love which prompted the holy Women to visit the Sepulchre, so that it may make us also strong and generous in the accomplishment of our duties.

I. Point.

The effects of true love for Jesus.

We may contemplate in these pious Women, who went to the Holy Sepulchre, the ardent love which led them there, and admire its results. We observe their activity, and how they anticipate the daylight, in setting forth from their homes to render to their Lord the homage of their zeal and charity. If we loved Jesus after this manner, how much in earnest should we be in seeking Him. Even during the hours of repose we should say with the Spouse in the Canticles: *I sleep, and my heart watcheth,* and the moment when we might go into His Very Presence, to render Him our homage, would be anticipated by our ardent longing for it. The holy Women were not ignorant of the fact that Nicodemus and Joseph of Arimathea had bound the Body of Jesus *in linen cloths with the spices*, for we are told that they *had seen how It was laid.* They, nevertheless, themselves prepared aromatic perfumes wherewith to anoint Jesus, and satisfy their loving devotion. True love can never do enough for Him; if we possess it, we shall not forego the delight of fulfilling in person the duties we owe to our Lord. Far from limiting the manifesting of our devotion to what is strictly prescribed—to what is of obligation—we shall go beyond this, and follow the counsels of evangelical perfection in order to glorify our Beloved to the utmost.

II. Point.

Love is courageous, and *hopeth all things.*

Who shall roll us back the stone from the door of the

Sepulchre? said the holy women on their way to it. Here we find a fresh characteristic of love! what courage it inspires, even in persons naturally weak and timorous! They did not pause to consider their own inability to move the stone, nor the difficulties they might meet with in the execution of their project; but continued their walk towards the place where our Saviour had been laid. Such is the courage which divine love gives,—nothing alarms it, nothing discourages it; it is capable of great deeds for God, because its fervour counts nothing as impossible; and God being the Object of such love, will undoubtedly, by His grace, smooth down all difficulties. Did He not send His Angel to roll back the stone? and to put to flight the guard of soldiers? If animated by this divine love, which is communicated by God to fervent souls, we shall be carried forward by its supernatural ardour, so that nothing can prevent our approach to Him. Neither the force of natural inclinations, nor the multitude of defects to be combated—nor suffering—nor humiliations—nothing can separate true lovers of Jesus from Him: it is His own imparted love which makes them courageous, hopeful, trustful, triumphant.

Colloquy.

O my God, would that I had courage like that of the holy Women! and love as ardent and as generous! Love that would render me fervent in Thy service! love which would make me forget myself, and think only of Thee! love which would fear neither sacrifices, nor trouble; but which would be nourished—kept alive—by the doing of Thy holy Will perfectly.

RESOLUTION.

When duty necessitates some sacrifice, I will seek to please Jesus by making it gladly for His Sake.

THOUGHT FOR THE DAY.

Love is strong as Death.

PRAYER.

Take, O Lord, and receive.

Easter Week—Sunday.

The Angel speaking to the Holy Women.

The Angel said: Fear not you: for I know that you seek JESUS, *Who was crucified: He is not here, for He is risen, as He said.*—S. MATT. XXVIII.

I. PRELUDE.

We represent to ourselves the Angel of the Lord descending from Heaven :—His raiment is shining, and as white as snow :—he rolls back the stone, and sits upon it.

II. PRELUDE.

O God, Who dost recompense so largely the little that is done for Thee, inspire us with perfect confidence in Thy goodness.

I. Point.

The goodness of Jesus towards souls that seek Him.

Let us consider how worthy of all love our Lord is, and how He blesses the efforts of those who seek Him in earnest. The good offices performed by the Angel, on behalf of the holy Women, are a proof of this. For them it was that he was commanded to descend from Heaven, and that he rolled away the heavy stone. For their instruction he remained to prepare them to meet their Saviour—giving them something to do for Him. *Fear you not.* What indeed has a soul to fear, that is really seeking Jesus? To seek is to find; and He is its strength, its light, its joy. He is all-sufficient in our every need, and holds the place of all that could fill our hearts. Souls led to seek our Lord, are not all animated by the same feelings. Some desire to see Him, and stay near Him, in the midst of consolations on Mount Thabor:—others seek Him amid the brightness of His glorious Life; there they would wish always to remain in contemplation:—and a few, like the three Marys, seek Jesus Crucified, actuated by purest love, and contented to be guided by the light of simple faith in Him. It is this purest and most generous love which gives strength to suffer afflictions and crosses patiently, thankfully.

II. Point.

To seek Jesus Crucified is a proof of our desire to love Him unselfishly.

This love, which does not seek her own, keeps the soul in contemplation beneath the celestial Tree, of which the Spouse in the Canticles speaks; and asks for the nourishing fruits it produces, that she may feed thereon,—labours—tribulations—contempt—persecutions. In these, souls that desire to be made in all things conformable to our Divine Lord, find strength and comfort; and take pleasure in participating, in some degree, in His suffering Life. What consolation may not such find in the words: *Under this Tree I raised Thee up.* It was in seeking Jesus Crucified—by honouring Him in His humiliations—that the holy Women merited to see Him, risen and glorified. From beneath the shadow of the Cross they were raised up in heart and soul, by beholding Jesus, face to face. They had sought Him purely for Himself, and received a most signal favour in recompense. Their devotion to Him could not brook delay; by the faint light of the early dawn, it directed their steps on their beautiful mission of love. There can be no danger of illusion, no fear of self-deception if we are willing to be deprived of sensible graces and benefits; and to go straight forward, in obedience to the dictates of love, and gratitude, and humility, without being troubled or discouraged by the appearance of present, or the apprehension of future, difficulties.

COLLOQUY.

Adorable Saviour, Thou knowest that I have, with heart and mind, often sought Thee.—Now I desire to seek Thee in a more sure way, in imitation of the pious Women, whose loving fidelity Thou wast pleased to recompense, by appearing to them after Thy glorious Resurrection. I will follow the attractions of Thy grace: do Thou, O Lord, grant that they may more powerfully influence me; so that, loving Thee on account of Thy infinite goodness, I may quite forget myself and seek Thee; solely that I may have the happiness of devoting my whole being to Thy service.

RESOLUTION.

I will purify my love for God, by disengaging it from the love of myself.

THOUGHT FOR THE DAY.

Fear ye not, I know that you seek Jesus, Who was crucified.

PRAYER.

O loving Jesus.

First Week after Easter.—Monday.

The Angel invites us to look into the Holy Sepulchre.

Come and see the place where the Lord was laid.—S. MATT. XXVIII.

I. PRELUDE.

Let us attend to the words of invitation spoken by the Angel, and with mingled sentiments of reverence and joy, enter the place where the Sacred Body of Jesus had been deposited.

II. PRELUDE.

O God, grant that within the religious solitude into which Thou hast led us, we may find grace to destroy, by death to self, all that may be an obstacle to the attainment of eternal glory.

I. Point.

The religious life is a spiritual tomb.

It is well to enter the Holy Sepulchre in compliance with the Angel's invitation, and ask ourselves if we have indeed died with Jesus, and been buried with Him. *Are we dead with Christ from the elements of this world*, or *do we yet decree as living in the world?* Hidden within their graves, the dead care nothing for the goods of this world, nor for its honours; they are indifferent to praise and to blame—to flattery and to disdain,—insensible to pleasure and to sorrow.—A truly religious person is equally dead, living only in the spirit, having mortified absolutely the will of the flesh, and the will of their own minds. Can we not strive to live as if our bodies were already laid in the tomb? Are we beginning in earnest to live a purely spiritual life? Are we still impatient when contradicted? sensitive, when slighted? jealous, when others are preferred? attached to own will and judgment? If so we are alive still with the old life of nature; it is not yet dead and buried. How then can we expect to rise with Jesus, if not dead and buried with Him? As we look into His Sepulchre, let us renew our promises no longer to neglect the graces we find in holy Religion, so that from it, and through it we may rise to a life of glory.

II. Point.

In the tomb of Religion, we should lead a life hidden in God, with Jesus.

The most effectual means of producing in ourselves this mystic death, is to contemplate continually the love of the

Divine Heart of Jesus; for it is love and love alone which will give us courage to immolate ourselves—to die to ourselves. It was love which perfected the sacrifice of our Redeemer, and it is love which will perfect ours. The mystery of the Holy Sepulchre speaks to us of solitude, of recollection, of hiddenness. Within it there is separation from the world—the links that bound us to it are broken—every sound is hushed there, save the soft echo of the first pulsation of the Sacred Heart, as life came back to the Body of our Lord and it passed out in an instant, beyond the region of death. That echo sanctifies for ever the tomb of the religious life; if our hearts have died to the world, they beat in unison with the Divine Heart, because He has communicated to them His Life and His love. *Therefore as we have borne the image of the earthly, let us bear also the image of the heavenly.* As we gaze within *the place where the Lord was laid*, let us question ourselves in the words of Saint Paul: *Do we reckon ourselves to be dead indeed to sin, but alive unto God, in Christ Jesus our Lord?*

Colloquy.

Holy Saviour, Thou dost call me to Thy Sepulchre, so that I may die more entirely to myself and be buried with Thee in the recollectedness and solitude of a hidden life. I fear that I have not yet learned the deep lessons which the Angel's words convey to faithful hearts;—the mystic death and burial of self is not yet consummated, but do Thou give me grace to mortify that which is merely natural, and to remain hidden in God, with Thee.

Resolution.

In order to rise with Jesus, I will avoid daily negligences, especially those which are most displeasing to Him.

THOUGHT FOR THE DAY.

Is my Life hidden in God, with Jesus Christ?

PRAYER.

Take, O Lord, and receive.

First Week after Easter.—Tuesday.

Saint Peter and Saint John hasten to the Sepulchre.

Peter went out and that other Disciple, and they came to the Sepulchre: And they both ran together, and that other Disciple did outrun Peter, and came first to the Sepulchre: but yet he went not in.—S. JOHN XX.

I. PRELUDE.

First we see Saint Mary Magdalene hastening to bring some tidings of their Master to the two Apostles;—and then the promptitude with which they go to assure themselves of His having left the Tomb.

II. PRELUDE.

O Jesus, grant that imitating the fervour of these Disciples, we may please Thee; and may merit to receive a renewed assurance of the fidelity of Thy promises.

I. Point.

Saint Peter and Saint John afford us an example of holy fervour.

Saint Augustine, in considering the two Disciples running thus quickly to the Sepulchre, says: that it was joy which gave them so much activity. They did not stay to grieve with Mary Magdalene, who feared that the Body of Jesus had been taken away; but entertaining the hope that their Master might have risen from the dead, they started forth without a moment's delay. We see the effects of faith in, and love for Jesus Christ exemplified by these two Disciples. They who are possessed of them are filled with joy and contentment: they run—they fly—they are free—no earthly affection can stay them. They feel nothing to be a trouble; love lessens the fatigue of their labours, they make sacrifices without knowing it.—Do we possess the faith and love which sent the two Disciples onwards in their path of loving duty, without stopping to consider what others were doing? Are we accomplishing all that God demands of each one of us in particular?—and unquestioningly? Do we show our love for Jesus by our eagerness in obeying the impulsion of His grace? There are, alas! many tepid, pusillanimous, indifferent souls, who go lingeringly to holy exercises of piety, who are weighed down by every little cross, and are devoid of courage; they not only cease to run in the way of perfection, but will not even take one step forward. That we may not be of this number, give us, O Lord, lively faith and ardent charity.

II. Point.

We see a holy emulation unconsciously displayed, by Saint Peter and Saint John.

We, who are bound together in the unity of the Church, by the ties of religion, and of holy affection, should provoke one another to emulation in running the way of salvation. We should encourage, counsel, and pray for one another. Those who are strong and in advance, may draw others on to quicken their pace, by their good example; but none need be slow in manifesting fervour and sincerity in the service of God, and a consistent desire to make progress in humility and devotion. We admire the self-control, and thoughtful attention of the beloved Apostle; although he reached the Sepulchre first, yet he would not enter it before Saint Peter; by which we are given to understand that we should reserve for those who have been advanced by God to any dignity, the special honour which may be their due, and which accompanies their office. Saint John courteously awaited the arrival of Saint Peter, that he might enter the Sepulchre before him; for he remembered that, although our Lord had lavished on himself so many marks of His affection, He had appointed Saint Peter to be primate of His Church; and Saint John saw in him the representative of His Divine Master. We do well to follow this example of respect and courtesy,—not being led away by impetuosity, nor betrayed by want of recollection, into any forgetfulness of the honour due to others.

Colloquy.

What an example of fervour dost Thou give us, O Lord, in the persons of Thy Disciples, on whose faith and love I have been meditating! I perceive with what ardour I should press forward in Thy service. O Thou, Who art the Light of my understanding and the Strength of my will, enkindle in my heart also the fire of Thy Love, so that I may run, not only in the way of Thy precepts, but also in that of the counsels of perfection.

RESOLUTION.

Not to be content with admiring the virtues I see in others, but to strive to copy them.

THOUGHT FOR THE DAY.

I have run the way of Thy commandments, when Thou didst enlarge my heart.

PRAYER.

Our Father, and Hail Mary.

First Week after Easter.—Wednesday.

Jesus Christ appears to Mary Magdalene.

Mary Magdalene stood at the Sepulchre without, weeping.—S. JOHN XX.

I. PRELUDE.

We may picture to ourselves Saint Mary Magdalene seeking for her Saviour, and weeping because she could not find him.

II. PRELUDE.

O Jesus, grant that while we consider the love of Saint Mary Magdalene, we may also be penetrated with a deep feeling of affection for Thy Divine Person.

I. Point.

Mary, not finding at first Him for Whom she sought, persevered nevertheless in her search.

Let us consider why the happy privilege of seeing Jesus was accorded to this holy penitent. We may well believe that it was the fervour of her desires, her tears of sorrow, and her perseverance in seeking Him which merited for her the happiness of seeing Him so soon after His Resurrection. She had conceived a great wish to go to the Sepulchre, to carry there her offerings of aromatic spices; remembering no doubt the day when she had been permitted to anoint the Feet of her Saviour, and He had shielded her from the reproaches of Judas. But not finding His Sacred Body in the Tomb, she begins to seek for It, thinking that It had been removed; she did not lose the hope of discovering where It had been placed, so bent was she on paying to It a last tribute of her devoted love. This wish manifested, no doubt, the weakness of her belief in the Resurrection of our Lord; but it sprang from the depths of purest charity within her heart: Jesus accepted the perfection of her good-will, and overlooked the imperfection of her faith. Excite in our hearts, O Lord, ardent desires of possessing Thee, of loving Thee as Saint Mary Magdalene did: may we feel it impossible to live without Thee, and give ourselves no repose until we find Thee, O Life of our souls.

II. Point.

Jesus rewarded the ardent love of Saint Mary Magdalene by appearing to her.

Her tears, joined to the sincerity of her desires, touched

the Heart of Jesus: already her tears of compunction had obtained for her the remission of her sins: to-day her tears of love procure her the privilege of seeing her Risen Lord. The other holy Women, and afterwards the Disciples, not having found Him, had withdrawn from the Sepulchre; but Mary Magdalene remained near it, absorbed in her one thought of how and where she could seek for His Body. Again and again she looked within.—In answering the Angel's question: *Why weepest thou?* she speaks only of the one cause of her grief. Insensible to all except her loss, she forgets all—herself even—and as the moments pass, her longing to find her Well-beloved becomes more intense. Can we compare our poor desires with hers? Are we as constant? Do we sincerely ask Jesus to give us the fervour and perseverance of the Magdalene? Souls truly solicitous of gaining His love, and of enjoying the happiness of His Presence, will ask and seek the means of succeeding in their holy purpose. As the loving penitent said to Jesus, not knowing that it was He, *Tell me where thou hast laid Him, and I will take Him away*, so we may say: tell me how to act—what I can do—and I will seek to take effectual measures for serving Thee better, and for proving my love. Jesus makes Himself known to all faithful souls, He will call us by our name, and by the accents of His love we shall recognise that it is indeed our Good Master Who speaks.

COLLOQUY.

Why can I not love Thee, O Jesus, better? and merit the grace of seeing Thee and hearing Thy Voice? Is it not because my perception of Thy Presence is deadened, by reason of my want of spirituality? and the feebleness of my desires after true holiness? I have not been as faithful as

Saint Mary Magdalene: she had been beside Thee on Calvary, and had shared in Thy Sufferings; while I have shrunk back from the ignominy of the Cross, although it was Thou, O Son of God, Who hung upon It. Make me a truer lover of the Cross:—may I perseveringly seek Thee in the Sepulchre of death to the world, and to self, so that I may find Thee risen and glorified.

RESOLUTION.

To do all my actions out of love for our Lord.

THOUGHT FOR THE DAY.

Jesus saith to her—Mary; She turning saith to Him—Master.

PRAYER.

O Loving Jesus.

First Week after Easter.—Thursday.

Jesus appeared to the Holy Women.

And behold JESUS met them, saying: All hail: They came up and took hold of His feet, and adored Him.—S. MATT. XXVII.

I. PRELUDE.

Let us picture to ourselves the holy Women prostrate at the Feet of their Risen Lord, and admire the gentleness with which He addressed them.

II. Prelude.

Divine Jesus, give us the grace to know more and more Thy goodness and meekness, so that we may glorify Thee by loving Thee better, and trusting in Thee more entirely.

I. Point.

The kindness with which our Saviour presented Himself before the holy women, and saluted them.

As we consider the graciousness displayed by the Son of God towards the two Marys, who were on their way to obey the injunction of the Angel, we are led to think of the kindness He manifests every day towards those who love Him. He meets us with a benediction of health, both for body and soul. He presents us with many graces, and extends to us His tender care. In how many ways He comes before us, saying: *All hail.* Saint Chrysostom, in alluding to this Apparition of our Lord, observes that when we go with alacrity where duty calls us, Jesus appears to bless our labours,—when we can go with fervour to our prayers, grace assists us to practise faithfully our exercises of piety,—when holy thoughts come—and sincere desires to mortify ourselves—and to do some act of virtue, it is Jesus who is honouring us with His Presence. Sometimes as our Lord, He comes to govern us; sometimes as our Father, to console us; sometimes as our Master, to instruct us; and again as our Friend, to encourage us, and to strengthen us in His love. His words of salutation are still: *All hail,—Fear not.* With how great eagerness ought we to welcome these daily apparitions of Jesus, from Whom we may expect to receive light, and succour and protection. Every thought, every sentiment which may tend to discouragement, to anxiety, or to a diminution of the confidence that we should have in our Saviour, can never come from Him, but from the spirit of darkness, or our own imagination. Jesus always brings Peace.

II. Point.

Jesus permits the holy Women to show Him proofs of personal attachment. We here perceive that Jesus does not deal with all souls alike; but He takes into consideration their different characteristics and capabilities. Saint Mary Magdalene was possessed of a strong and generous love for Him; she was able to bear trials, to make sacrifices, and thereby to acquire new merits. He would not allow her to kiss His Feet, but saying: *Do not touch Me*, at once gave her something to do for Him, so that she might have the merit of repressing a too natural inclination, and of showing her love and obedience at the same time, in the mission on which He sent her.—But He permitted the other Marys to touch Him, and to remain near Him for a while, so that they might satisfy their devotion, by adoring Him. Yes! Thou, O Saviour, didst thus quickly verify, after Thy Resurrection, Thy own words: *I know My sheep.* Thou knowest perfectly each separate soul, its needs and its powers. Thou canst best decide whether we need to be encouraged by consolation, or braced up to meet conflict and suffering by the withdrawal of sensible help. *Strong meat is for the perfect.* Unto Thy care, O All-wise, Omniscient God, may we safely commend ourselves.

Colloquy.

Make me, O Lord, to be thankful for all Thou dost in my regard; whether Thou givest, or whether Thou takest away those comforts which refresh the soul, may I always say: *Blessed is the Name of the Lord.* Thou knowest what is best for me. If Thou forbiddest me not, I will stay in Thy Presence and kiss Thy Sacred Feet; but shouldst Thou say—Go, and do what I command thee, in the midst of aridity and desolation,—may I promptly and uncomplainingly obey, assured that though unseen—unfelt, Thou art ever near me.

RESOLUTION.

To remember, at all times, that God knows what is best for me.

THOUGHT FOR THE DAY.

It is I:—Fear not.

PRAYER.

O Jesus, living in Mary.

First Week after Easter.—Friday.

Jesus appears to Saint Peter.

The Lord is risen indeed, and hath appeared to Simon.—S. LUKE XXIV.

I. PRELUDE.

Let us imagine what the joy of the Apostles must have been, when they heard of the Resurrection of their Master; and that He had been seen by Simon Peter.

II. Prelude.

O Lord, as we see Thee appearing to Saint Peter, give us race to understand how great is Thy tender mercy towards penitent sinners; and give us true repentance.

I. Point.

The readiness and kindness with which Jesus forgave His repentant Disciple.

Three days scarcely had passed since the threefold denial of Peter, when His Dear Master favoured him with a special Apparition. He appeared to him to console him, to restore peace to his soul, and to uphold his authority after having chosen him to be the visible Head of His Church. How striking are the considerations connected with this first interview between the Divine Master and His chief Apostle. How great must have been the consolation, the joy, and the contrition of Saint Peter! We may well imagine the kindness of the words in which Jesus addressed him, and think we hear His salutary warnings. Good Shepherd! what care Thou hast for Thy flock, and when any of Thy straying sheep return, Thou dost meet them with words of hope and love. God can bring good out of evil, and will He not do so for those who have given themselves unreservedly to Him? From their very falls He often lifts them up, through penitence, to higher graces. Witness the case of holy David, of Saint Peter, of Saint Mary Magdalene. —God may permit us to be cast to the ground, like Saint Paul, but He wills that we should rise again, and gain strength and experience as a consequence of our fall. His goodness inspires us with confidence on this point; should we ever unhappily offend Him, let us never for a moment doubt His mercy; but, recalling the subject of our present meditation, rise, and with lively contrition throw ourselves into the arms of His charity.

II. Point.

In granting forgiveness to Saint Peter, Jesus bestowed on Him further graces.

When our Adorable Saviour pardons, He does not do so by halves. By His Prophet He thus speaks of His willingness to forgive: *God delights in mercy: He will turn again, and have mercy on us: He will put away our iniquities: He will cast our sins into the bottom of the sea.* And again: *If your sins be as scarlet, they shall be made white as snow.* We see in effect, how these words were verified to the letter, in Saint Peter:—he had turned again—had been converted, and his soul was so purified by repentance, that Jesus did not account him unworthy of a most signal favour. He had already caused special mention to be made of him in the message with which the Angel charged the holy Women: *Go tell His Disciples and Peter.* Doubtless Saint Peter never forgot that sad denial of his Master, but the sorrow caused by the remembrance ever increased the ardour and piety of His love. The dearly-bought experience he had made of his own weakness, cured him of all presumption, and confirmed him in humility. It is in this way that true repentance may glorify God, by leading us to walk more safely in the paths of humility. Saint Peter, in his epistle, seems to make known his own resolution after the interview with his Master on that first Easter Day: *Be sober and watch.*—In the humility, gravity, dauntlessness, and vigilance which marked his after-life, we see the practical results of his repentance, and the powerful effects of our Lord's Resurrection.

Colloquy.

O Saint Peter, ask our Divine Master to make Himself known to me, as He did to thee, as a God Who delighteth in forgiving iniquities. I too have denied Him, and that more than once, through indifference, false shame, or human respect. Obtain for me a spirit of penitence, which shall be livelong; but whilst I sorrow for my many sins, may I, like thee, rise to newness of life; *having been regenerated unto a lively hope by the Resurrection of Jesus Christ from the dead.*

Resolution.

To banish all useless regret from my mind. If I fall, to rise again; and go to God for pardon, with all confidence.

Thought for the Day.

He hath not rewarded us according to our iniquities.

Prayer.

Take, O Lord, and receive.

First Week after Easter.—Saturday.

Jesus appeared to Saint James the Less.

He was seen by Cephas, and after that by the eleven; then by more than five hundred brethren at once: After that He was seen by James; then by all the Apostles.—I Cor. xv.

I. Prelude.

Let us represent to ourselves the profound sorrow in which Saint James was plunged after the Death of his Master.

II. Prelude.

O Jesus, grant us the spirit of recollectedness, and the gift of prayer with which Thou didst endow this Apostle.

I. Point.

Our Lord is pleased, even in this life, to manifest His love for those who love Him.

It was to the eminent sanctity of the Apostle Saint James, to his spirit of prayer, his life of love—so hidden in God, that the Fathers of the Church attribute the particular grace he received from his Beloved Master: that of seeing Him alone, and so soon after His glorious Resurrection. We are told that Saint James had been inconsolable, after the Death of his Lord; and that he would have died too, had not the faint hope of His Return to Life upheld him. Such is the love of a truly spiritual person; to whom God is All in all. His infinite perfections so captivate the heart, that nothing created can diminish the grief of losing the Presence of our Well-beloved: peace and joy are only recovered together with the Treasure which has been lost. If we do not feel this legitimate sorrow in times of spiritual dryness, we should lament over our tepidity; and strive to re-awaken our love by means of Holy Communion, and earnest prayer,—asking Jesus to enkindle in us that sacred fire of love, which has animated all the Saints. Let us open our hearts, that Jesus may find an entrance there, and converse, with His own sweet and incomprehensible familiarity, with us.

II. Point.

We should keep secret the favours we receive from Heaven.

The silence which Saint James kept about the particular privilege bestowed on him by our Risen Lord affords valuable instruction for those whom God favours with special graces. Saint Paul alludes to this Apparition of our Lord, many years after, when Saint James was Bishop of Jerusalem; the secret having been (as is supposed) imparted by himself to the Apostle of the Gentiles. Full of gratitude for a favour of which he deemed himself unworthy, he kept the precious remembrance of it hidden in his own breast. The knowledge of how to enjoy the interviews Jesus accords to spiritual souls, is most useful, most valuable. They will not dissipate the effects of these interviews, by confiding the whisperings of His love to any creature, without great discernment. These are so holy, so incomprehensible, so ineffable, that they who know by experience what they are, desire to keep them hidden in their hearts beneath the veil of secrecy. Earnestly should we long to enter into the enjoyment of a sweet familiarity with Jesus: to see Him and Him alone, to speak with Him, and with Him alone, to be absorbed in Him so as to be unconscious of the presence of aught besides. And all this is not incompatible with active zeal, and energy of purpose; as is proved by the whole tenor of Saint James's catholic epistle. He teaches us therein how to be wisely silent—truly religious, and to manifest our faith by our works. Let us ask Jesus to favour us with an interview.

Colloquy.

My Saviour, there are no true joys out of Thy Presence; no means of being happy without Thee. Pure enjoyment is to be found in Thee alone, and real delight in conversing with Thee. The precious gifts which Thou bringest would be preserved in my soul, if I possessed the true spirit of silence and recollection; and if I avoided all useless conversation. Attract me exceedingly towards a life of union with Thee: let me draw nigh to Thee, and do Thou draw nigh to me, O my God.

Resolution.

To seek to possess the spirit of prayer by the practice of recollectedness, and silence.

Thought for the Day.

Besides Thee, what do I desire in Heaven or upon earth?

Prayer.

O Jesus, living in Mary.

FESTIVALS.

Saint Matthias.

On Fidelity to our Vocation.

The lot fell upon Matthias, and he was numbered with the eleven Apostles.—ACTS I.

I. PRELUDE.

Let us represent to ourselves the Disciples in prayer, asking their Risen and Ascended Lord to bless their choice of a new Apostle.

II. PRELUDE.

O Lord, Who triest the reins and hearts, Thou hast chosen us from all eternity, for Thine own : make us faithful to the grace of our vocation.

I. POINT.

The circumstances connected with the election of Saint Matthias ought to inspire us with a holy fear about our vocation, whatever that vocation may be.

We see that this Apostle did not offer himself for the sacerdotal office. The whole Church was united in prayer, to ask of God to make known whom He had chosen to take the place of Judas. Doubtless on the occasion of this election to the first vacant bishopric, a certain fear possessed the hearts of the Apostles, who (having lost their Divine Head) were now, under the guidance of Saint Peter, to proceed to the appointment of another to the Apostleship. Therefore for their assurance and consolation, God ordained to manifest His Will miraculously, and the lot fell on Matthias. After a different manner, but none the less really, He still points out the special vocation of each of us :—though His designs are hidden for a long time, as it may seem, yet in the end they will be revealed, and He will show us what we have to do.—The Church is ever praying in the same spirit for Her children, as on the day when they numbered only one hundred and twenty. God will direct them in answer to Her prayers according to His all-wise purposes :—saying to each : *This is the way, walk ye in it.* We do well to inquire if we have been careful to know the will of God in our regard.—What have been our motives in adopting our particular state of life? have our intentions been pure? Have they been free from ambition? worldly interest?—Alas! lower motives may sway the minds of such even as resolve to enter Religion. They should also remember that God respectively calls each of them to a certain, a definite degree of sanctity in their holy estate; thus there is a vocation within a vocation. *With fear and trembling work out your salvation.*

II. Point.

The two motives which should prompt us to respond to the vocation in which we are called are: the honour of God—and the consolation of the Church.

It is doing God an injury to enter into the Religious

state without being called to it; it is a still greater injury to be unfaithful to so high a vocation. If a soul that He has called, and crowned with special graces, becomes untrue to her Spouse, what a betrayal is this! what a sad forgetfulness of God's honour! We can imagine we hear our Saviour renewing the complaint which the treason of Judas drew forth from His Heart: *If My enemy had reviled Me, I would verily have borne with it;—but thou!*—What a wrong is done to a king, if a general in his army be a traitor. Let our vocation lead us on more and more, to be true to the King of kings.—The fidelity of the successor of Judas rejoiced the Church. Judas had rejected all, even the throne in Heaven His Master had offered him: the graces he refused were bestowed on Saint Matthias, and he was elected to witness in the Church to the Resurrection of Jesus. We too are chosen to bear witness, by faithfulness in our vocation, to this same Mystery; and to our being risen with Him ourselves:—so, with the Saint of to-day, we may honour God, and be the joy of our holy Mother the Church.

Colloquy.

O Divine Saviour, Thou Who givest special graces to such as truly correspond to the grace of their vocation, preserve me from my own frailty, which causes me to fear all sorts of perils. Defend me from the malice of that enemy, who compassed the downfall of Thy faithless disciple. May Saint Matthias pray for me to-day, that by Thy grace, I may never fall away from Thee.

Resolution.

To be faithful to all the duties of my vocation; above all to my exercises of piety.

THOUGHT FOR THE DAY.

You have not chosen Me ; but I have chosen you.

PRAYER.

Take, O Lord, and receive.

Saint Joseph.

Saint Joseph living at home with Jesus.

Joseph, the Husband of Mary, was a just man.—S. MATT. I.

I. PRELUDE.

We can represent to ourselves the House at Nazareth, where Saint Joseph continually enjoyed the society of Jesus and Mary.

II. PRELUDE.

Great Saint ! whom we honour to-day, and to whom Jesus did Himself impart the method of the spiritual life, do thou discover to us the wonderful secrets of His love, and lead us nearer to Him.

I. POINT.

The great privileges with which the Lord honoured Saint Joseph.

God having destined Saint Joseph for the most sublime

functions on earth, and exceeding glory in Heaven, honoured him in this life with the very highest prerogatives. Being the depositary of the secrets of the Most High, he was initiated into the ineffable Mysteries of the love of God towards mankind. United to the purest, the holiest, the most perfect of creatures, he was chosen, by a special favour, to be the adopted Father of Jesus Christ; and His Preceptor. How often did he carry in his arms the Beautiful Child—the Saviour of the world; how often must he have pressed Him to his heart, and lavished on Him the tenderest care. He was admitted to the enjoyment of a sacred intercourse with Jesus and Mary; and during the space of nearly thirty years conversed daily with his God. How well must Saint Joseph have understood what real prayer is, and the power it has over the Heart of Jesus!—how numerous must have been the graces he received from It, how pure must have been the love which was enkindled in his own heart! Let us honour and venerate him on account of the extraordinary privileges with which God was pleased to favour his representative in the household at Nazareth: so will our love be augmented for the hidden life, the excellence of which, as exemplified by Saint Joseph, has drawn so many souls to ascend the heights of religious perfection. Yes! to know Jesus—to be united to Jesus by sweet intercourse—to possess Jesus—here is the secret of the spiritual life, here is the source of those numberless graces, which flow from a participation in that secret. Thou hast, O privileged Guardian of the Holy Child, so often controlled His Will.—He was subject to thee;—place Him now in our hearts.

II. Point.

Saint Joseph is our teacher in the spiritual life.

Saint Joseph did not content himself with merely enjoying the Presence of Jesus, but he set himself to follow His example. It was from reading, so constantly, the Sacred Heart that he learned the grand science of humility—of self abnegation; and gained that unspeakable knowledge to which, in fact, the formation of the inner life is due. It was in the school of Jesus that he studied the spirit of prayer and of recollection.—It was in Jesus that he acquired ability in maintaining a close union with his Creator, which no exterior occupation could diminish;—and Jesus taught him the practice of that pure love, which regulates the action of the pious soul. The example brought before our minds to-day for imitation, as we contemplate the character of Saint Joseph, is this: his forgetfulness of the world—of himself—for all his thoughts were centred on Jesus,—all his faculties were wholly employed in His service. And how lovingly, how largely has Jesus recompensed his fidelity!—*Because thou hast been faithful over a few things, I will place thee over many things.* Therefore holy Church sings Her antiphon in honour of him to-day: *God made him lord over His household, and the ruler of all His possessions.*

Colloquy.

O holy Protector, Friend and Counsellor of our Saviour, deign to protect, befriend, and counsel me. Speak to Jesus on my behalf, and obtain for me also the intercession of thy pure Spouse Mary; so that, on this thy Festival, I may receive an increase of those graces which rendered thee worthy to live in the company of the Son of God, and to die in His Arms. May I too live and die in His favour and love.

RESOLUTION.

Like Saint Joseph, I will place all my happiness in remaining constantly in the Presence of Jesus.

THOUGHT FOR THE DAY.

Go to Joseph.

PRAYER.

O Loving Jesus.

The Annunciation of the Blessed Virgin Mary.

Mary is the Queen of Virgins.

Mary having heard, was troubled at the saying of the Angel; and thought with herself what manner of salutation this should be.—S. LUKE I.

I. PRELUDE.

We gaze in spirit upon Mary; that humble and holy Virgin to whom the Angel is speaking. He had found her in her oratory, on her knees, praying in solitude—profoundly recollected.

II. PRELUDE.

O, our Lady! Virgin of all virgins, we lovingly admire thy sweet modesty, which forms the beautiful ornament that adorns thee to-day. May we be adorned in like manner.

I. Point.

Mary was troubled—why?—Because of her perfect purity.

The fear which arose in Mary's soul, at the apparition of the Angel Gabriel, had its source in the purity of her heart. She was troubled at finding herself thus suddenly in the presence of one who wore the appearance of a youth; and she became more anxious, when he made known to her the marvellous message with which he was charged. She had made a vow of perpetual virginity; and now she hears the words: *Thou shalt bring forth a Son.* Be not alarmed, O most pure Maiden! for thou art indeed to become the Mother of God, only thou wilt not cease to be a Virgin; for of a chaste Virgin, the Redeemer is to be born.—We, who carry in a very fragile vase the precious treasure of chastity, do well to share in Mary's carefulness, lest the lily of holy purity should fade:—so delicate a flower is it, that a single word or look, a breath of evil, may cause it to wither.—This is why they who possess great purity of soul, delight in being alone with God,—why they avoid needless intercourse, useless conversations:—they are, as it were, taken out of their element when obliged, by some exigency, to quit the solitude they love so well.—Let us see if we employ our solitary moments as Mary did.—Do we turn them to good account, by speaking to God, and praising His goodness? Can we not ask Him to send us also some announcement of joy and peace by those angelic Messengers *that minister for them who shall receive the inheritance of salvation*?

II. Point.

The humility and prudence with which Mary spoke to the Angel.

The Angel Gabriel proclaims to that lowly Maiden, in her simple home, the greatness of Him of Whom she is miraculously to become the mother. Her downcast eyes, her humble attitude, the anxious questions that her love of chastity awakens in her mind, and which she tremblingly puts into words, are indicative of her innate modesty,—yet she loses not her self-possession, and makes no further inquiries when the Angel re-assures her by the marvellous announcement: *The Holy Ghost shall come upon thee, and the power of the Most High shall overshadow thee: And therefore that Holy which shall be born of thee, shall be called the Son of God.*—Four thousand years before a fallen angel in disguise had spoken with a woman in the garden of Eden, she was the fairest creature amongst all the perfected works of God's Hand; but the serpent stung her with his lying tongue,—the poison of pride entered into her soul, and its lovely purity was gone in a moment. Sin and death were the outcome of Eve's first proud thought;—it provoked her to rebellion against her Creator.—As on this day, nearly two thousand years ago, a good Angel spoke with our Lady. We place these two visits side by side, and mark their different results with regard to those who received them, and their effects upon the human race. In the one, pride led to imprudence, curiosity, disobedience,—death. In the other, humility produced prudence, modesty, obedience,—life. Do we follow the example of Eve or of the Blessed Virgin? Are we gaining more self-control? or have we still to accuse ourselves of a want of religious gravity, modesty, humility, and holy restraint in our words?

Colloquy.

O my dearest Mother, how much the remembrance of this day's events draws out my love and veneration for thee. After the interview with the Archangel, the most astounding of all Mysteries was produced in thee, and thou didst become the Mother of God—the Saviour.—May I learn from thee to love solitude, therein to take a special delight, and hear the Voice of my Divine Spouse. Make me to avoid vanity and idle curiosity, which serve only to fill my mind with the spirit of the world.

RESOLUTION.

To preserve within myself holy purity, I will watch carefully over my heart and my senses.

THOUGHT FOR THE DAY.

Behold the handmaid of the Lord; be it done unto me according to thy word.

PRAYER.

We fly to thy patronage.

Holy Thursday.

Institution of the Holy Eucharist.

Whilst they were at supper, JESUS took bread, and blessed, and broke: and gave to His Disciples, and said: Take ye and eat: This is My Body: And taking the chalice He gave thanks, and gave to them, saying: Drink ye all of this: For this is My Blood of the new testament which shall be shed for many unto the remission of sins.—S. MATT. XXVI.

I. Prelude.

Let us enter with reverence into the Refectory where the Last Supper has been prepared. Jesus is now at table with His Apostles.

II. Prelude.

Divine Saviour, deign to admit us into this Guest-chamber with Thy privileged Disciples, to witness the Institution of the Adorable Sacrament, which is to us a proof of the excess of Thy love.

I. Point.

This is My Body Which is given for you.

Jesus perceived the hour approaching when His Sacrifice of Himself must be consummated. Like a good and tender Father He made His last testament, the same night in which He was betrayed,—and with love, unexampled, unparalleled, He leaves a legacy to His Church of His Adorable Person. He instituted the most August Sacrament, whereby, concealed beneath the sacred species of bread and wine, He wills to enter the hearts of His children, even after His Death and Ascension, until the end of time. Let us admire the excess of our Saviour's charity, and grasp more completely the thought of our peculiar happiness, in whose favour His testament of love has been made. He has given us Himself, with all His perfections—all His virtues—His merits—His graces. What an immense heritage! what a rich treasure! what a noble patrimony!—In very fact, He has not left us orphans: He said He would not. He has ascended into Heaven, and yet He has left Himself in His Church.—*Behold I am with you all days.* What more could this

Good Father in His love have done? How could our Generous Saviour have further provided for us? Could He have given anything more precious than Himself? O Charity! O Love Divine! enkindle in us Thy flame, so that we may be ourselves consumed with love for Him Who has loved us so much. *This is My Body—This is My Blood.*

II. Point.

Do this for a commemoration of Me.

These were the words with which our Lord closed His Testament. They only ask of us one thing,—that we will keep in mind the remembrance of the Death He endured for us; especially when we approach the Sacrament which perpetuates Its memory. It is for this that He comes into our hearts in Holy Communion, therein to engrave the remembrance of His Wounds and Sufferings. Not by the hand of a Seraph does He imprint them, as on the body of Saint Francis; but on our very hearts He Himself places the Seal of union with Himself; of which Seal we must never lose the impress. We receive therefore our Divine Spouse to-day, gratefully participating with Him in His Sorrows, and thanking Him if He permit us to be deeply marked with His Cross, so that we may resemble Him in His Life, and in His Death. A generous soul rejoices to suffer for the God she loves; and the Cross consoles and delights her, since it renders her more conformable to our Crucified Lord, Jesus Christ. Our motto should be this: To suffer, or to die.

Colloquy.

O my Saviour, before Thy Death Thou didst leave to me a legacy of all that is most precious in Heaven and earth—

Thy Own Self: on my part I would give to Thee, all that I have, all that I am. I make over to Thee my heart, my will, my understanding, my memory, my body and my soul: so that all my powers may be offered as a holocaust—sacrificed to Thy glory and spent in Thy service.

Resolution.

Always to draw near to the Eucharistic Feast with great love, and a sincere desire to pourtray in myself the Life of Jesus Crucified.

Thought for the Day.

He that eateth Me, the same also shall live by Me.

Prayer.

Soul of Christ.

Saint Philip and Saint James.

To know Jesus Christ is to know God the Father also.

If you had known Me, you would without doubt have known my Father also: and from henceforth you shall know Him, and you have seen Him. Philip said to Him: Lord, show us the Father, and it is enough for us. Jesus saith: Philip, he that seeth Me, seeth the Father also.—S. John xiv.

I. Prelude.

Let us represent to ourselves Jesus conversing with His

Apostles after the Last Supper. We find some of them asking Him certain questions.

II. Prelude.

Give us, O Divine Spouse of our souls, a knowledge of Thyself; of Thy goodness, Thy love, Thy perfections; and in knowing Thee may we learn to know and love Thy Father and ours.

I. Point.

The knowledge of God.

There are two ways of knowing God. The mere belief in Him, and in His revelation of Himself to man may be sterile, yielding no fruits of charity, and in the end serving only to bring about a more severe judgment on them who hold such a belief.—The other is a knowledge productive of true love—proving itself by the keeping of God's commandments, —and a sincerity of purpose, to please Him by so doing. This is the highest science to which we can attain. We find Saint James repeating the lesson taught by the Divine Master, in his Epistle: *What shall it profit, if a man say he hath faith but hath not works? Shall faith be able to save Him? Thou believest that there is one God. Thou dost well: the devils also believe and tremble.* Which knowledge of God is ours? Do we *shew our faith by our works?*—works of charity, works of obedience, works of patience, works of constancy? It would be doing our Lord an injury to ask Him if it be easy to gain this right knowledge of Himself: —to know Him, is to love Him. We are the disciples of Jesus, and yet it behoves us to examine ourselves as to whether our love springs from knowing Him; whether our knowledge of Him sustains and increases our love.—

Do we by faith, often contemplate the God-Man, and His Oneness with God the Father? *He that seeth Me seeth my Father also.*

II. Point.

God alone suffices.

On hearing our Lord say that: *No man cometh to the Father but by Him,* Saint Philip said to Jesus: *Shew us the Father and it is enough for us.* And we may say the same, for He should be the Object of all our desires,—and to see Him will be the ending of all our afflictions—of our exile.—Our life is but a time of waiting to see God; and the best and happiest way of spending this time, is in beginning to form an intimate friendship with Him, *Whom to know is eternal Life.*—Let us free our hearts from all other attachments, and let God draw them wholly to Himself. *God is enough for us,* let Him therefore take possession of our whole being: *God is enough for us,* in Him we live, from the moment of our Baptism—throughout eternity. What need have we of all those things which will leave us at the end of this mortal life? and even during its course, on what, in what, can we place any reliance, save in God?—How must the assurance that their Lord would indeed shew them the Father—that they would see Him Face to face—have sustained the Apostles, Saint Philip and Saint James, in the arduous labours of their Apostolate, and in the hour of their martyrdom. Do we sometimes think of the meeting of Jesus with those whom He had loved on earth? whom He had personally trained for Heaven? Knowing Him, they loved Him and suffered for Him, that they might again see Him, and His Father *Whom having not seen they loved.*

the conquerors of the world put together; for what can be more glorious than to share in the blood-bought Victory of the Son of God. Jesus has besides made His Cross to be the Tree producing all manner of spiritual good; It yields unfailing consolation—and remedies all our ills:—we may cling to It for support in our weakness. It gives promise of the unfading flowers which bloom in the realms of glory and eternal beatitude. It bears fruit which they are entitled to gather who love the Cross, are fastened to It with Jesus, remain there with Jesus, and die on It with Jesus. The Divine Master found nothing on earth more precious to Him than this; He preferred it to all the riches of the world.—To such as He desires to honour with His special friendship, and to raise to a high degree of sanctity, He sends this gift; that they may be wholly crucified with Him in heart, and body, and soul; rejoicing to share in His sufferings, whilst waiting for the joys which are eternal. O holy Cross! most precious token of the love of Jesus, I desire no other glory than thy ignominy, no other riches than thy poverty, no other enjoyment than that which thou dost afford.

II. Point.

The true disciples of Jesus Christ ought to take pleasure in the Cross.

God forbid, says the Apostle, *that I should glory save in the Cross of our Lord Jesus Christ.* Such should be the sentiments of all the disciples of our Saviour; but especially of religious persons, who make profession to love and imitate Jesus Christ Crucified; to carry, more perfectly, His doctrine into daily practice. And of what does His doctrine speak, if not of the crosses of affliction?—of the crucifixion of nature?—of the death of self? The holy Church recalls constantly to our minds the excellence of the Cross, and teaches Her children to revere It, from the day when they are marked with the sign of It in Holy Baptism until, when passing out of this world, the Crucifix is held before their closing eyes.—This sacred Symbol of our Faith is found in our homes to remind us of the Death of our Divine Lord; It is as an open book to enlighten us; It indicates the right road towards Heaven, our Home. We carry it on our breasts, as a witness of the gratitude we feel towards Him Who was crucified for love of us;—and in our hearts as a spiritual weapon, to repulse, and defend ourselves against the enemies of our salvation. Let us respectfully and lovingly salute the Cross when It meets our eyes,—press It to our lips in moments of joy or sorrow. Jesus, the Celestial Spouse of our souls, chose the Cross for His portion; and then bequeathed It to us as the pledge of His tender love, and the link which unites our suffering with His. We should embrace It with confidence, as well as with courage; for It is crimsoned with the Precious Blood of Him Who is our Strength: we should embrace It with joy, for Its dread appearance is changed into a reality of delight, in the hearts of the true lovers of Him Who died within Its arms. Since Jesus has sanctified It by His embrace, His elect have ever cherished and revered It.—It was but a dry and sterile branch, of a dishonoured stem, and yet no tree ever produced more leaves and flowers and fruit; for by compunction—confidence—and love, man is lifted up to God. Is not the Cross a happy Discovery of the Wisdom of God? Is it not a skilful Invention of His Love?

COLLOQUY.

O Jesus, I thank Thee that Thou didst crown with

success the pious labours of Thy Servant Helena in her search for the True Cross, to which Thou wast nailed; and that Its all but living presence in the Church, is a source of so many graces and blessings.—May I love and reverence every image of Jesus on His Cross:—beneath the Standard of the Cross—may I prove a faithful soldier and win my eternal crown.

Resolution.

To accept with love all that may be crucifying to nature, and thus unite myself, through suffering, to Jesus on His Cross.

Thought for the Day.

God forbid that I should glory, save in the Cross of our Lord Jesus Christ.

Prayer.

Soul of Christ.

MEDITATIONS.

THE FIRST THURSDAYS IN EACH MONTH.

First Thursday in March.

The sacrificial aspect of the Holy Eucharist.

In every place there is Sacrifice, and there is offered to Thy Name a clean Oblation.—Malachias i.

I. Prelude.

We consider the fact that Jesus Christ is being offered upon the Altars of the One Church, throughout all the world, at every instant of our day and night.

II. Prelude.

O Jesus, fill us with sentiments of lively faith, and deep gratitude, as we meditate upon the Adorable Sacrifice of the Altar.

I. Point.

The Eucharist reveals to us a marvel of wisdom, most profound.

It was requisite that there should exist in the Holy

Church—Altars, and a Sacrifice to be offered upon them. She could not be devoid of that which is the essential point of every religion in the world. The only true and perfect religion must necessarily comprise the law of Sacrifice, and it was Jesus Christ Who was to be the Victim—the clean Oblation.—After the Sacrifice of Calvary, the blood of animals, and similar offerings became valueless. No oblation, but that of the God-Man deserved the name of Sacrifice, and Heaven would not accept any other victim. But this Divine Sacrifice, in its perpetual renewal, must be lifted up without the shedding of blood; for the Redeemer having become, after His Resurrection, Immutable—Impassible—Immortal, could not again permit the effusion of His Precious Blood. Humanly speaking, seeming impossibilities were about to arise with regard to the accomplishing of the law of Sacrifice; but the Eucharist being instituted, all impossibilities vanish—the difficult is met—the needs of the Church are satisfied. The blood of animals flows no longer on the Altars of the living God; to Him Jesus Christ is the only Victim that is offered:—He is immolated, but not betrayed—not abandoned:—He is immolated, but not condemned—not crucified.—O Holy Church! none can rob Thee of thy daily Sacrifice; the One—the True—the Divine—the Lamb of God—offered in His own Temples, by His own Priests.—It is a Sacrifice worthy of thee, and of thy destinies, O Church of God!—It is a Sacrifice of infinite value; for it fully satisfies the requirements of eternal justice. The effects of it are immense.—It rejoices Heaven,—gives peace to earth,—sanctifies man,—and brings relief to the holy dead, by delivering them from the fires of expiation. Even they, who acknowledge not its efficacy, are benefited thereby. The Sacrifice of the Altar is mystical, as befits the religion which is founded on the mysteries of the unseen world.—How vast, how wonderful, are the counsels of eternal Wisdom! If we plunge deeply into the contemplation of them, we still find that an unfathomable ocean still lies before us unexplored!

II. Point.

The holy act of Sacrifice.

We see an Altar: on it is about to be lifted up the pure Oblation, *which is offered from the rising of the sun, even to the going down.* But where are the outward appearances of the Sacrifice? where are the victims? where is the fire? *Is the Lord to be appeased, and the High God magnified with hécatombs?*—Most simple are the surroundings of the Christian Sacrifice! We perceive upon the Altar a little Bread, and within the Chalice a little Wine:—nothing more is externally needed for the most holy, the most pure Oblation, of which the grandeur and the riches surpass the understanding of any created intelligence. The Flesh and the Blood of the Incarnate God will form the Substance of the Sacrifice, for the all-powerful word has been spoken once and for ever by our High Priest: *This is My Body:—This is My Blood.* By His almighty word He hath made all things, and it still accomplishes all that He desires in Heaven and on earth.—When His words are repeated by His ambassadors, in accordance with His command, *This do ye,* it is as if we could hear the Voice of God; and their effect is the same, as when they were originally pronounced by Jesus in the Supper-room.—*Can He also give Bread, and provide a Table for His people?* We believe in God, and trust in His Salvation.

COLLOQUY.

Lamb of God, at every moment Thou art offered in sacrifice—Thou dost offer Thyself—to appease the justice of God the Father, and to bring down upon Thy holy Church the benediction of His mercy. Cause the light of sacramental truth to shine abroad in all the world, and win hearts to Thyself by letting them know and feel Thy love, and Thy power. Speak to them, O Sweet Jesus, from the Tabernacle; *only say the word and they shall live.*

RESOLUTION.

To assist each day, with lively sentiments of faith, at the Holy Sacrifice of the Mass.

THOUGHT FOR THE DAY.

Showing forth the Death of the Lord till He come.

PRAYER.

Soul of Christ.

First Thursday in April.

Jesus Christ, in the Most Holy Sacrament, teaches us how to live according to the spirit of the Gospel.

The Word was made Flesh, and dwelt among us.—S. JOHN I.

I. PRELUDE.

Let us listen to our Lord speaking from the Tabernacle,

and saying: *Learn of Me, because I am meek, and humble of heart.*

II. Prelude.

Holy Jesus, grant to us the grace to make fervent and holy Communions, that Thou mayst dwell in us, and that we may practise the virtues of which Thou dost give us a perfect example.

I. Point.

Jesus Christ, under the Sacramental species, teaches us humility.

Jesus, within the Tabernacle, lives for, and negotiates with man; He dwells amongst sinners, His Life is all-pure,—the contagion of vice cannot touch Him. His Life is noble—excellent—divine; and yet nothing can be more simple than the appearance beneath which it is concealed.—We too must dwell in this world; but our lives should resemble the sun's rays, which, emanating from their centre, pass unsullied through the tainted air. If united to God, we may pass along our way unaffected by the vitiated atmosphere around us:—we shall draw from Him our strength—and our virtues, and learn from Jesus how to hide these, beneath the veil of humility. How much have we to meditate upon, if we consider how He, in the Blessed Sacrament, teaches us to preserve the purity of our soul, and the spirit of humility. God, in His Incarnate Life, came amongst men to redeem them; and through humility He was obedient unto the death of the Cross.—In His Sacramental Life we find Him still, in all humility, willing to be daily offered up upon our Altars, that the Sacrifice of Calvary may be perpetuated, even to the consummation of the world.

II. POINT.

The Life of Jesus Christ, in the most Holy Sacrament, places before us a model of the holy life we should lead—guided by true wisdom.

The true wisdom displayed by our Lord, is that which descends from above. He and His Father are One. His wisdom is infinite, and in the Eucharist He teaches us what its true spirit is, and whither it should lead us.—It should lead us to the adoption of a life of solitude and self-forgetfulness,—such solitude as leaves the heart tranquil and silent, holding wordless intercourse with the Eternal Father, —such self-forgetfulness as causes the soul to have no aims of self-interest. It places before it two grand motives,—the glory of God, and the salvation of souls:—on these it teaches us to expend our fervour. It admits no other intention than that of fulfilling the good pleasure of God.—*Christ, the power of God and the wisdom of God*, thus dwelling within the Tabernacle in solitude, attracting souls to glorify His Father, confounds the strong and the wise, by means of things, weak, and foolish, and contemptible in themselves. If we were thoroughly impressed with this thought, how little should we judge by appearances only;—how slow we should be to condemn what seems mean, and even despicable in the eyes of the world. Before God, what we deem little, is often great; and what we deem great, is nothing.

COLLOQUY.

O my Saviour, I adore Thee, because Thou dost make evident to us Thy divine wisdom, in chosing the solitary and narrow Tabernacle for Thy Dwelling-place. May I understand the holy lessons of wisdom Thou wouldst hereby teach me.—Grant me the spirit of recollection, of prayer, and of humility; so that I may imitate Thy hidden Life, and have a part in that mystical union which, through the Blessed Sacrament, is contracted with Thee; and with Thy Saints in Heaven, and on earth.

Resolution.

To make frequent acts of Spiritual Communion.

Thought for the Day.

The Word was made Flesh, and dwelt among us.

Prayer.

Take, O Lord, and receive.

First Thursday in May.

The Eucharist is the master-piece of the Love of Jesus Christ for men.

Jesus having loved His own who were in the world, He loved them unto the end.—S. John xiii.

I. Prelude.

Let us represent to ourselves the Cenacle, and our Lord seated at the table, with His Disciples.

II. Prelude.

Discover, O Divine Saviour, the immensity of Thy love for us in the Holy Eucharist; and grant us grace to love Thee with all our hearts.

I. Point.

The Eucharist is a proof of infinite love.

Jesus Christ loved His chosen followers up to the end of His Life on earth, and He loved them infinitely. *God is Charity*, as is manifested in all His works; but it is especially in those inspired by His divine charity, that He is pleased to display the wonders of His power. Of all the gifts that He has bestowed on man, that of the Eucharist is the most beautiful; and the most capable of insuring our happiness, of enkindling our love, and of exciting our gratitude. Yes! for Jesus, before leaving this world to ascend to His Father, makes the gift of Himself to us, in the Sacrament of the Altar. Earth will have no cause to envy Heaven, for it too is to possess its God and Saviour until the end of time. Jesus would appear to have forgotten Himself in His thought for the exile—man. In the mystery of the Incarnation *He debased Himself, being made in the likeness of men;* in the mystery of the Eucharist, hidden under the veil of the sacramental species, the appearance even of His Humanity is lost, and the only definable marks of His Presence are the sweet effects of love, which fill the pure heart, and the contrite soul.—What a new prodigy of mercy and power is thus brought about by our Lord, in order to perpetuate His Presence in the midst of the children of men; and to render Himself accessible to all. He veils Himself in mystery, and gives to His faithful ones the consolation of approaching Him, without fear. He knew to what outrages this additional invention of His love would expose Him; yet none would dare to approach, if His glory were unveiled, and Jesus desires to communicate Himself to all. Who can measure the depth and breadth of His great charity? it is an abyss in which our thoughts lose themselves:—but do we try to respond to it, even so far as we might? What a contrast exists between the Heart of Jesus and our own! between His generous love, which is carried to excess, and our love—so poor—so cowardly in facing combat, toil, or sacrifices! Why is it, that it is only in what concerns Thee, O Jesus, that we are so wanting in courage and generosity?

II. Point.

The Eucharist is the complemental work of God.

Let us gather up all our powers, and withdrawing within the sanctuary of His Abode, consider the mysteries of the God-Man Who dwells amongst us, beneath the Eucharist Veils: these let us admire—interrogate—and in the silence of contemplation, gain instruction from them. The marvels of which they speak to us are without number; and not less worthy of our admiration than those of the Creation,—and of the Redemption. In the beginning God spoke, and and as He did so, creatures awoke from nothingness—were clothed with their respective forms—and took the place appointed for them, in the universe. In the production of the mystery of the Eucharist, God speaks;—the pre-existent substances are gone—lost; wholly changed into other Substances: Jesus again descends to earth.—Instead of, as at the first, perishable creatures arising out of nothing, now

I see by faith, the Infinite—All-powerful—Eternal God—appear upon our Altars; He receives a mystic Existence there, and the Sanctuary thus consecrated by His Presence, becomes another Bethlehem.—God showed His triumphant power, in the Redemption, over sin and death.—God suffered and died, but He rose again. In the Sacrifice of the Altar, the triumph—the victory of the God-Man is lost sight of. He permits the Sacrifice of the Cross to be renewed,—not once again merely, nor in one place, but throughout the world, and in every age. O Love of Jesus! who can sufficiently comprehend it, or admire it? The heart of man is incapable of making Thee a just return. Thine is a jealous, yet patient love; watchful—generous—constant.—Thou dost ask us to give Thee ours, in return. Lord, what can we say when we contemplate Thy sacramental Love but this:—Thou art the Master of our hearts, do Thou Thyself inspire us with greater love and thankfulness?

Colloquy.

O Divine Jesus, O God of Love, grant that I may think of—desire—seek—and find Thee,—and Thee alone. I wish to consecrate myself to Thee again to-day, unreservedly:—my soul—my will—my liberty—my whole being. Would that I might die for love of Thee, since Thou didst die for love of me; would that I might be found worthy of being sacrificed as a victim, for Thy greater glory!

Resolution.

With magnanimity to sacrifice to Jesus whatever prevents His love from reigning in my heart.

Thought for the Day.

Having loved His own who were in the world, Jesus loved them unto the end.

Prayer.

Take, O Lord, and receive.

MEDITATIONS.

THE FIRST FRIDAYS IN EACH MONTH.

First Friday in March.

The Heart of Jesus is that of a most tender Father.

I will arise, and will go to my Father.—S. Luke xv.

I. Prelude.

Let us represent to ourselves Jesus, opening His Arms and His Heart, like the father of the Prodigal Son, and inviting us to avail ourselves of His mercy.

II. Prelude.

Heart of Jesus—Heart of the most tender, and the most indulgent of all Fathers, we beseech Thee to fill our hearts with feelings of that respect, love, and confidence, which are so justly Thy due.

I. Point.

The Heart of Jesus has for us a truly paternal love.

Our Saviour has given to us the supernatural life of grace: He has prepared for us the blessed life of glory: it is to His love that we are indebted for the one and the other. His Divine Heart has for us the same feelings, the same loving inclinations which that of the best of fathers has for a cherished child. We are sure of finding in It compassion—indulgence—goodness—and inexhaustible love, which even our many defects cannot weaken. He provides for all the wants of our souls.—He nourishes us with the corn of the elect,—He enlightens us and instructs us by an interior voice,—and strengthens and encourages us by the sweet action of His grace. If we fall (did not the Prodigal Son?) He kindly lifts us up again,—if we grow weary, He animates us to fresh exertions,—sometimes by a caress, which may take indeed the form of punishment, but is none the less a caress.—His love is ever tempering the severity of His justice.—*When Thou art angry Thou wilt remember mercy.*—How is it possible not to love so good a Father? how could it be that we should fail in confidence? or not obey Him out of that intuitive sense of gratitude which love inspires in the hearts of His true children?

II. Point.

Towards His most guilty children even, the fatherly Heart of Jesus is gentle and merciful.

The touching parable of the Prodigal Son presents to us, after all, but a faint picture of the sentiments of the Heart of Jesus towards ourselves, and towards all sinners. We indeed see therein pourtrayed the manner in which He not only watches for the return of the wanderer, but comes out to meet him with open Arms, and upholds him in His embrace. But besides this, He may be seen going after the lost sheep until He find them; sending His Ministers with full power to act for Him; and to tell those, who are wandering from the fold, that their Saviour is longing to pardon them. He causes solemn warnings to reach them by means of His messengers, as also his promises to restore all their former rights and privileges as His children (lost through sin) if they will only come back to their Father's House. Our past estrangements, the numberless instances of our ingratitude have not dried up the Fountain of grace. —Has He not, over and over again, accepted the expression of our regret? the sincerity of our repentance? But while thankful at the remembrance of our own pardon, let us not selfishly forget, or be indifferent to, the blindness of those who obstinately walk on towards the precipice of utter ruin; who approach it, in going further from their Saviour, Whose Sacred Heart they pierce anew. Hear us, O Father, listen to the prayers we address to Thee on behalf of Thy guilty children; touch their hard hearts, and triumph, by the strength of Thy grace, over the resistance they offer. Grant that, reunited in the One True Fold, we may together celebrate Thy paternal goodness, with cleansed and faithful hearts.

Colloquy.

I offer to Thee, O Divine Saviour, my homage of love and confidence; beseeching of Thee, at the same time, to pardon all my ingratitude and my offences,—and to give me the graces necessary to purify me from the stains of all my past sins.—And, my Father, recall to-day some wanderers from the paths of sin, that they may be numbered amongst Thy faithful children, and console Thy Sacred Heart.

Resolution.

To pray much, to suffer if it be God's Will, for the conversion of sinners.

THOUGHT FOR THE DAY.

I will arise and will go to my Father.

PRAYER.

O loving Jesus.

First Friday in April.

The Heart of Jesus is the Heart of our Heavenly King.

Rejoice greatly, O daughter of Sion: Behold thy King will come to thee,—the Just and Saviour.—ZACHARIAS IX.

I. PRELUDE.

Let us represent to ourselves Jesus Christ under the circumstances which distinguished His triumph on the day of His entrance into Jerusalem. We see in Him both gentle dignity, and the majesty of truth.

II. PRELUDE.

O Jesus, Divine King of our hearts, reign Thou in them unto life everlasting.

I. POINT.

Jesus is the rightful Monarch over us.

Jesus is our King, we belong to Him, for were we not

made by Him? and for Himself? But sin having withdrawn us from the easy yoke of His legitimate authority, He has had to reconquer His lost possession from the power of Satan, at the price of a deadly combat; in which *He laid down His Life that He might take it again.* This conquest was not necessary to His glory: He being essentially great—holy—perfect—has no need of us, nor of any creature to enchance the splendour of His Majesty; but His Heart inclined Him to make His lost creatures happy; and He, the Prince of Peace, came amongst men and bestowed true peace on them, by fighting against and overthrowing their enemies. He has dictated to us His law of love, and He wills to reign in our hearts now by His grace, so that one day, we may reign with Him in His glory. Can we refuse to our King the tribute of love which He claims? He offers His Heart as a place of refuge, wherein ours may be protected from the attacks of our foe; and at the same time, He discovers to us the treasures hidden there, which we may make our own. Are we carefully observing the law Jesus has laid down for us, His subjects? are we zealous for His glory? devoted to His cause and His interests?

II. Point.

Jesus desires to reconquer the hearts of all men.

Although our Divine King gave His Life to vanquish the devil and conquer the world, yet the empire of sin is so firmly rooted in the hearts of many, that Jesus cannot yet fully establish His kingdom.—Still the cry goes forth from the world's votaries: *We will not have this Man to reign over us.* Therefore our Lord, full of pity for the multitudes who are hastening blindly to destruction, calls upon His faithful subjects to gather together beneath His Standard, and form a holy league to war against His enemies, and deliver souls from their grasp. He promises these combatants that He will cover them with the impenetrable buckler of His protection, He arms them with the power of the Cross, and sends them forth to fight, with the weapons of prayer—good example—and such others as an ingenious zeal may furnish, against the scandals of the world, and the obstinacy of sinners. Do we fear to enter the lists? to engage in so noble an undertaking? The Heart of Jesus asks of us only good will, courage and generosity; we are sure of His help, and we are promised success in proportion to our efforts and our fidelity.

Colloquy.

O Sacred Heart of Jesus, make me to love and practise Thy law of love; may I be so devoted to Thy cause, that I may manfully fight against the enemies of those for whom Thou wast pierced by the soldier's lance.—Jesus, come Thou and reign over me, so that in fighting I may be fighting for my King.

Resolution.

To profit by every opportunity for the extension of the knowledge and love of Jesus.

Thought for the Day.

And the Lord shall be King over all the earth: in that day there shall be One Lord.

Prayer.

O loving Jesus.

First Friday in May.

The Heart of Jesus is that of the Good Shepherd.

I am the Good Shepherd, the Good Shepherd giveth His Life for His sheep.—S. John x.

I. Prelude.

We see Jesus under the form of a Shepherd, carrying on His Shoulders a sheep, which He is bringing back to the fold.

II. Prelude.

May we, O Saviour, meditate worthily upon the benefits Thou hast conferred on man; and grieve over the ingratitude shewn to Thy Sacred Heart, even by those who should console It.

I. Point.

The blessings which emanate from the Heart of our Lord; and how little they are esteemed by mankind in general.

Jesus has given His Life for us.—The Good Shepherd has delivered Himself up to the fury of the wolves, that cause such havoc amongst His sheep: He made Himself the Victim of their rage, and saved His flock by His own Death. To this proof of infinite love, He still ceases not to add a multitude of daily-renewed benefits. He covers His sheep with His protection; He sets them in a place of pasture; He allays their thirst with the waters of His refreshing grace, which have their source in His Divine Heart. What thankfulness and love has He not a right to expect from us? and yet He is but too often repaid with the blackest ingratitude. His sheep remain at a distance, and hear not His voice; the impious, like ravening wolves, pillage the Fold. His Heart is afflicted: in vain He pursues the faithless wanderers with warnings, and invitations to return; but too frequently they harden their hearts, and despise the advances so tenderly made. Can we *who are the people of His pasture and the sheep of His Hand* be insensible to such outrages, and not share the deep grief of our Good Shepherd?

II. Point.

Jesus expects that hearts devoted to Him will make reparation for the injuries His Heart receives.

The Good Shepherd, after all that He has done and is still doing for His flock, being nevertheless unknown—or insulted—or deserted, seeks for consolation from those who are still faithful. He fixes His Eyes on us, from us He looks for acts of reparation. What can we do to alleviate the grief of the Sacred Heart?—First we must recognise the Voice of Jesus, and follow it unresistingly.—If He lead us in green pastures, and near the waters of refreshment,—or over steep and rugged heights, and thirsty deserts, we must be equally submissive: perhaps He may despoil us of the fleece of sensible consolation, still let us trust Him.—By unfailing confidence, docility, and abandonment of ourselves into His Hands; by habitually seeking to please—to follow—to imitate Him; by the exercise of those interior virtues of which the Divine Heart is the centre and model:—by these means we may assuredly compensate, in some degree at least, for the rebellion, coldness and ingratitude of those who offend our Lord and Master. Are we able to ask Him to let us become victims of His love? are we ready to be sacrificed on the altar of reparation? to be consumed by the flames of expiatory charity?

Colloquy.

Jesus, I desire to thank Thee for having placed me, and for having kept me, near to Thyself in the Fold of Thy Church; never let me wander away from Thy side; and if I dare ask so high a grace, let my life be one of sacrifice; so that, contrite for my own faults, and suffering with Thee for those who are going astray, I may offer worthy acts of reparation, and console Thy Loving Heart.

Resolution.

To follow Jesus as closely as I can; and to offer myself as a victim of reparation.

Thought for the Day.

I will fear no evil, for Thou art with me.

Prayer.

O loving Jesus.

MEDITATIONS.

SATURDAYS.

Saturday after Septuagesima.

Mary is our example in the practice of lesser duties.

Fear not, Mary, for thou hast found grace with God.—S. Luke ii.

I. Prelude.

Let us represent to ourselves the perfect manner in which Mary always performed the ordinary duties of her daily life.

II. Prelude.

Grant, O God, that as she, whom thou didst choose to be Thy beloved Daughter, pleased Thee and found grace in Thy Sight, so we may learn from her how to fulfil the duties which our condition in life imposes on us.

I. Point.

Mary found grace with God, in the seclusion of her early life.

Our lives are made up of a daily round of duties, and

so was the life of our Lady. During the years which she passed within the precincts of the Temple, she spent her time in the alternate duties of work and prayer, with the other Jewish maidens who were her companions. We can imagine the spirit of obedience and submission with which she must have listened to the instructions and commands given her; the gentleness of her manner, the ingenuousness of her character surely won the affection of all with whom she came in contact. No one supposed that she would be called to so high a destiny; this was a secret known only in Heaven: unconsciously to herself and others, God was preparing her to be the saintly Spouse of the Holy Spirit. So should we pass our lives, with perfect simplicity going from one duty to another, having one thought in view—that of pleasing God. Can there be a better thought? can there be a more lofty aspiration? Our Creator may, or may not have created us to do some apparently great work for Him, but of this we are sure:—He desires us all to find grace in His Sight, and places means of doing so in our power, every hour of our lives. We should not rest content with endeavouring to please God from the secondary motive of escaping His anger, nor even of winning the eternal recompense of dwelling in His House for ever, but simply as Mary did, out of pure love and reverence for her All-good, All-wise Creator.

II. Point.

Mary found yet further grace with God, as the Mother of His Son.

The message sent by God to our Lady increased her humility, and this very spirit of humility was to be further nourished by the many humiliations she would have to share with her Son.—Is it in any degree thus with ourselves? When we receive some special favour from God, do we abase ourselves? and become so really, so sincerely conscious of our unworthiness, that we have in consequence some trial—some humiliation given us as a proof that God can trust us to bear it for His Sake? Alongside of the trial there will, in such a case, assuredly be some consolation. He will put under our care perhaps some virtue to cultivate in ourselves or others, and will bless our endeavours:—or He will give us some definite work to do for Him in the world. How full of sorrows was our Lady's life after the Incarnation; but she had special helps for special trials, and these united to prepare her more perfectly for the close companionship of Jesus, both in suffering and in glory. Thus it is that God deals with His Saints, where He finds willing hearts who trust Him entirely, *He giveth greater grace*, but often through the channel of tribulation.

COLLOQUY.

O God, may I find grace with Thee, by serving Thee in all my actions.—Give me Mary's pure intention, her willingness to fill any position in which Thou wouldst place her. If Thou wilt send me any special token of Thy favour, dare I ask that it may be marked with the sign of the Cross?—I desire to resemble in some little degree, the Mother of Thy Son; whom, having found grace with Thee, Thou didst cause to pass through much tribulation, since it is Thy Will *that they who are holy must still be sanctified*, and that by means of affliction. Let each day's duties be done by me in view of pleasing Thee, O God: each day's trials be welcomed.

RESOLUTION.

To be more careful in making the good intention, several times during the day.

THOUGHT FOR THE DAY.

Thou art My servant; I have chosen thee.

PRAYER.

O God, Who by the Immaculate Conception.

Saturday after Sexagesima.

Mary is the light of souls that are devoted to her Divine Son.

What wilt thou that I should do to thee? Lord, that I may see: And Jesus said to him: Receive thy sight: thy faith hath made thee whole.—S. LUKE XVIII.

I. PRELUDE.

We see Mary in the midst of the Apostles, of whom she was the light, after the resurrection of Jesus.

II. PRELUDE.

O Mary, thou knowest the darkness which surrounds us during the night of this mortal life; be thou our light: the guiding star of our existence.

I. POINT.

Mary desires to enlighten pious souls.

The blind man asked neither for gold, nor silver, but only for light; and his prayer was granted, because he addressed the Light of light, *Which enlighteneth every man that cometh into this world.* And Mary is herself, after her Divine Son, a true, though lesser light.—A Saint has said, that she is the light of our hearts; that she illuminates the universe; and the Holy Scriptures speak of her as being clothed with the sun—the source of light.—How happy must Mary be to communicate somewhat of her celestial radiancy to holy souls—the souls of the elect; they again will shed their light on others, and extend to them the knowledge of the glories of our Lady; so that through her they may love her Son. May God say of us approvingly: *You are the light of the world*—the reflected light, emanating from those bright orbs of purest brilliancy—Jesus and Mary.

II. POINT.

By Mary's intercession the darkness of human passion and of sin are dispelled.

The Son of God cured the blind man. He had confidence in the Heavenly Physician, and by faith was made whole. We read that Jesus commanded him to be called; He would arouse the sympathy of the bystanders and make them ministers of His mercy. May we not therefore infer how Mary ministering for Him, loves to anticipate His wishes, by encouraging us to ask for the cure of our spiritual blindness.—She says to those who cannot see clearly how to walk in the paths of virtue—how to follow in the Footsteps of her Son: *Be of better comfort; arise, He calleth thee.* By the sweet allurements of her graces she attracts us into His Presence.—Enfeebled sight—the eyes of a soul which are bedimmed by sins and defects—may be able to look at the Morning Star, but not to bear the searching rays of the Sun of Justice. Let us go to Jesus, through Mary. Let us ask her to discover to us the artifices of the devil—to dispel the shades of ignorance—to rejoice and strengthen the eyes of those who have already (through the Mother's all-powerful intercession with her Son) heard the gracious words: *Receive thy sight.*

Colloquy.

O Mary, enlighten me who am now crossing the stormy sea of this world, in the midst often of darkness and peril; I look up to Thee for light and guidance. How many dangers I have to encounter: may I steer my way, by the shining light of Thy mercy, safely into the port of Eternity.

Resolution.

In times of darkness and difficulty I will look up to the "Star of the Sea".

Thought for the Day.

If the winds of temptation arise, and you are running on the rocks of trouble, look at the Star—call on Mary.

Prayer.

We fly to Thy patronage.

THE MEDITATIONS FOR THE SATURDAYS DURING LENT ARE GIVEN AMONGST THE GENERAL MEDITATIONS.

Saturday in Easter Week.

The Joys produced in the Mother of Jesus by His Resurrection.

According to the multitude of my sorrows in my heart, Thy comforts have given joy to my soul.—PSALM XCIII.

I. PRELUDE.

Let us represent to ourselves the transports of delight experienced by the august Virgin, as she beheld her Son in His resuscitated and glorified Body.

II. PRELUDE.

Rejoice, O divine Mother! and let us share in those feelings of incomprehensible happiness, with which the Mystery of the Resurrection of Jesus filled thy heart.

I. POINT.

The joy of our Lady concerning the Mystery of the Resurrection teaches us to find our joy in Jesus only.

As Saint John tells us, *there are many other things which Jesus did*, not recorded by himself nor the other Evangelists; and the appearing of our Lord to His Mother is one of those *other things* which we find omitted by them. Silence on this point need not astonish us; tradition supplies the fact that it was to her, Jesus first appeared, in the stillness of the early morning, but Mary again *kept all this in her heart;* there she silently stored the memory and the joy of that meeting after three days' separation, as she had done once before, when she found her Son at the end of three days' absence from Him. It is easy to understand how impossible it would have been for Him Who had said: *Honour thy parents*, not to have honoured His Mother by appearing to her immediately after His Resurrection. She had been the first to see Him when He miraculously left her chaste womb, in the hour of His Birth to a Life of mortality; now she must be the first to see Him when He miraculously leaves the Sepulchre, and begins His Life of immortality. *Rejoice then, O Queen of Heaven*, we repeat with the whole Church to-day, *for He Whom thou didst deserve to bear has risen.* What joys can be put in comparison with that of her who gave us our Saviour? May we so live as to merit to be consoled by God, and may we refuse all other consolation which does not come from Him.

II. Point.

The joy of Mary relative to the Resurrection, teaches us to place great faith in the promises of Jesus.

The narration of our Lord's Apparitions after His Resurrection was written *for our learning.* He desired in the first place that His Apostles should believe in it; and He reproached them for their incredulity. He convinced them by numerous arguments, of the reality of this striking miracle: but He wished also to confirm our faith. The Blessed Virgin never doubted for a moment the reality of this wonderful prodigy, before it was accomplished: if we compare her faith with that of the Disciples, we see at once how great it was—how unchangeable. It gives us a striking example of that lively faith which cannot be deceived; which, soaring above the evidence of our senses, grasps those things which are invisible, extends itself beyond the limits of human reason and experience, and lifts itself above the ordinary laws of nature. —God has said—He has spoken—He has promised;—that is enough to enable faith to wing its flight into the region of eternal truth. Let us beg of Mary that we may have grace from her Son to preserve, to augment, and to perfect this faith in our souls.

Colloquy.

O Mary, powerful Mother of God, by the ineffable joy and consolation which filled thy soul at the Resurrection of Jesus, obtain for me an entire detachment from all those affections which may hinder my union with Him, and the perfect accomplishment of the duties of my vocation. Ask for me such a lively faith, that it may be a source of peace, of merit, and of happiness.

Resolution.

To live by faith, so that my most ordinary actions may be thereby spiritualised.

Thought for the Day.

Queen of Heaven, rejoice! Alleluia.

Prayer.

We fly to thy patronage.

Saturday in the First Week after Easter.

The devotion which should be given to Mary, under the title of our Mother of Good Counsel.

He that is Mighty hath done great things to me.—S. Luke i.

I. Prelude.

Let us pay due homage to our Lady as the Oracle of the universal Church;—we represent her to ourselves in the midst of the Apostles, whom she directed by her wise advice.

II. Prelude.

O Mary, Mother of Good Counsel, in the midst of the darkness which surrounds us, deign to direct our steps in the way of salvation and perfection.

I. Point.

We should honour Mary as our Mother of Good Counsel.

By a divine and extraordinary counsel of God, the Holy Spirit overshadowed her, and made her the Mother of the Word. In her was wrought the grandest Counsel of God, that is, the Incarnation; by her came into the world "the Counsellor"—Jesus, the Instructor of all nations; Jesus—the Divine Legislator of the new Law. Mary is the Mother of Good Counsel because she was filled with the Holy Ghost, Who shed into her soul His gift of counsel in all its plenitude; and, guided by the light this gift imparted to her, she ever chose the better part. Still by her example, her words, and the favours she obtains for us; she offers us continual counsel; hence she has been styled: "the universal counsellor," whose direct or indirect advice we may have in all our necessities. To her therefore let us have recourse, in every doubt or perplexity; let us honour her by manifesting confidence in her power and willingness to assist us; and by inducing others to avail themselves of her aid and her counsel.

II. Point.

We should invoke Mary as our Mother of Good Counsel.

The Blessed Virgin had indeed reason to say: *He that is Mighty had done great things to me.* God did great things in her, in order to render her the noble and illustrious Mother, not only of His Divine Son, but also of all His children. Amongst the children of God, those who have entered the religious life are in particular need of counsel. They are peculiarly exposed to frequent attacks on the part of the enemy of their salvation, in consequence of the envy of the fallen angels towards those who are specially destined to take the places in Heaven which they have lost. It is required of them that they reach a very high degree of perfection, which shall correspond with the sublimity of their vocation. Again, they, on their part, must direct souls entrusted to them, practise works of mercy, give advice sometimes to such as may turn to them in their doubts. They therefore, for many reasons, are particularly in need of the assistance of Mary. If we had always invoked her, how much more advanced should we be in true wisdom, how much more helpful we should have been to others! Well had it been if we had followed the injunction of Saint Bernard, "In all cases of doubtfulness, think of Mary, invoke Mary, and you will never be deceived".

Colloquy.

O Mother of Good Counsel, thou who hast preserved me in so many dangers, and hast made me to know the Will of thy Divine Son by calling me to the religious life—to a life of union with Him—be thou my light, my guide, my adviser in all the doubts and difficulties of this life. Influence me in all I say and do, I would owe my own advancement, I would owe my success in helping others, to thee; for thou art able to obtain all necessary graces from the Fountain of grace, for me thy child, and to counsel me how to make a right use of God's blessings.

Resolution.

To ask counsel from our Lady, in times of doubtfulness.

Thought for the Day.

O Lady of Good Counsel, pray for me who have recourse to thee.

Prayer.

We fly to thy patronage.

MEDITATIONS.

SUNDAYS.

Septuagesima Sunday.

The Parable of the Labourers in the Vineyard.

The Kingdom of Heaven is like to a householder, who went out early in the morning to hire labourers into his vineyard.—S. Matt. xx.

I. Prelude.

Let us imagine that we see and hear the master of the vineyard speaking to the labourers, whom he sent there from hour to hour, during the day.

II. Prelude.

Grant, O God, that my heart may be attentive to Thy Voice, at every instant of my life.

I. Point.

We ought, from our youth, to serve God perfectly.

Our life is but as a day that passes rapidly. In the morning, that is to say, during our earliest years, God presents

Himself to each one, and says:—*Go into My vineyard;* attracting us lovingly into His service. Our own soul is the vineyard which we are charged to cultivate, so that it may bring forth the fruit of justice and perfection. It is an inestimable grace, to which it is important we should correspond throughout our whole life, that of being permitted and enabled to work in this vineyard. It is well to look back, and see if we have really consecrated the best years of our life to the holy career which God has opened out before us: how we have cultivated our hearts at a time when they were fittest to receive impressions of virtue?—It is in youth that they incline most readily towards what is good; that they are more easily subjugated beneath the yoke of obedience, and that both our thoughts and senses are best trained to the practice of continual mortification. Have we refused to God the first-fruits of the vineyard under our care? Is the longest life of labour too long to work, in order to gain Heaven? It is only as one day of toil, compared with the eternal repose in which we shall enjoy God, if we are faithful in His service here.

II. Point.

God ceases not to draw us by His love, until we cease to live.

And the householder going out about the third hour, saw others standing in the market-place idle: He said to them: Go you also into my vineyard: And he went out again about the sixth and ninth and eleventh hour, and found others standing idle: He saith to them: Go you also into my vineyard. Alas! there are slothful souls in the Church of God. They idly depend on His goodness, and take no trouble to expiate their past sins by penance, nor to work out their salvation by the practice of Christian virtues. Unfaithful to the first advances of grace, they let their precious time pass by, without doing anything towards the cultivation of their souls. Yet, notwithstanding this unfaithfulness which has so grieved the Heart of God, He still waits for them: He still goes in search of them. He calls them a second—a third—a hundredth time perchance;—to the end of their lives He puts before them means of conversion and of amendment. Are we refusing to give our hearts to God? Similar ingratitude towards creatures would be considered unpardonable: how ought we not then to reproach ourselves for the perpetual resistance offered to the best and most long-suffering of friends! Whatever hour of the day it now is for us, it behoves us to see whether we are really at work:—and if so, how much we have done? Have we destroyed the noxious weeds of human passion, and cleared the ground of evil propensities? Have we eradicated our dominant fault? Have we watched over the growth of those virtues which God expects us to cultivate? each one according to his capabilities and advantages. Let us put our hand to the work with better courage, so that we may amply repair our losses, and deserve to receive at the close of the day, the reward of good and faithful servants. Our Master calls us to greater diligence: the last hour may soon strike!

Colloquy.

My God, I will not wait until near the end of my life to serve Thee truly. From this moment I will devote all my time to do the work Thou hast given me to do: without further delay, I yield to Thy gracious invitation, and will begin to lead a more laborious and mortified life. How many years have I lost, how many privileges have I neglected, how little work have I done! Help me, by Thy grace, to make up for these past losses and negligences by greater diligence, and never again to be unfaithful to the sacred charge of working in Thy vineyard.

Resolution.

To labour to eradicate my dominant fault.

Thought for the Day.

Go and work in My vineyard.

Prayer.

Our Father, and Hail Mary.

Sexagesima Sunday.

The Parable of the Sower.

Jesus spoke this parable unto the people: The sower went out to sow his seed: And as he sowed some fell by the wayside, and it was trodden down, and the fowls of the air devoured it: And other some fell upon a rock; and as soon as it was sprung up, it withered away, because it had no moisture: And other some fell among thorns, and the thorns growing up with it, choked it: And other some fell upon good ground; and being sprung up, yielded fruit a hundred-fold. —S. Luke viii.

I. Prelude.

Let us join the multitude who are gathering together unto Jesus. He goes up into a boat on the shore,—and thence speaks to the people many things in parables.

II. Prelude.

Fill our minds, O God, with true esteem and respect for Thy divine Word: may we receive it into well-prepared hearts.

I. Point.

God has sown His divine Word in our hearts.

According to the explanation which Jesus Himself gives of this parable, the Seed is the Word of God. This divine Seed is of infinite value, and possessed of extraordinary productive force, when it falls on fertile soil. The Heavenly Sower is perpetually sowing this Seed; for when is it that He is not speaking to us?—In the first place God speaks to us, as we view the wonders of Creation: *The heavens shew forth the glory of God, and the firmament declareth the work of His Hands.*—Secondly, He speaks to us by the holy Scriptures; making us to understand the truths they contain.—Thirdly, we are listening to His Word, when we hear the Voice of His Spirit, interiorly teaching and directing us.—Lastly, in another admirable manner God speaks to us in the Mystery of the Incarnation of the Word-made-Flesh; —that mystery of love by which He discovers to man the way of salvation, and the paths that lead to the very heights of perfection. Happy is he who is attentive to the Voice of God in such a manner, that it enters both heart and soul; and fructifying, yields a plenteous harvest of virtues. Word of God! make known to us His adorable Will, and produce in us grace to accomplish It.

II. Point.

What the obstacles are which hinder us from profiting by the Word of God.

The principal obstacles are pointed out to us by our Divine Master.—They are levity—inconstancy—and the cares of this life. One who is shallow-hearted, and trifles with the things of God, Jesus compares to the hardened wayside, into which the seed enters not;—there is much coming and going of human passions, and in the midst of the unrest Satan snatches it away. Where there is no perseverance, our Lord likens the soul to a rock, wherein the seed cannot germinate nor throw out roots; so beneath the scorching sun of difficulty or opposition it soon withers away. How dangerous is this inconstancy, in how many souls are its effects fatal, since it prevents all real spiritual progress.—The cares of this life form the thorns among which good seed may also fall; but here it is again rendered fruitless, being choked by worldliness, and the deceitfulness of riches.—Do either of these obstacles affect the growth of the Divine Seed in ourselves? Do our souls lie open only to the holy influences of the sunshine of God's love? and the dew of His grace? Can we feel sure that the Seed which is the Word of the Lord, is springing up vigorously and yielding fruit? either thirty, sixty, or a hundredfold? God grant that the Seed may not have been sown in our hearts in vain.

Colloquy.

Eternal Word of the Father! Thou art the source of all

holiness.—May my heart and soul be ever prepared to give heed to Thy teaching, and receiving it with profound attention, may it take deep root, and bear the fruits of piety—constancy—recollectedness—patience; and that not in a lesser degree, but a hundredfold.—By the power of Thy Word, and for Thy Sake, O God, make me holy, so that I may be numbered hereafter among Thy Saints.

RESOLUTION.

To prepare by silence and recollection to receive the Word of God.

THOUGHT FOR THE DAY.

Be ye doers of the Word and not hearers only.

PRAYER.

Our Father, and Hail Mary.

Quinquagesima Sunday.

Jesus predicts His Passion and Death to His Disciples.

And taking the twelve Apostles, JESUS began to tell them the things that would befall Him: saying: Behold, we go up to Jerusalem, and the Son of Man shall be betrayed to the chief-priests, and to the scribes and ancients; and they shall condemn Him to death, and shall deliver Him to the Gentiles: And they shall mock Him, and spit on Him, and scourge Him, and kill Him.—S. MARK x.

I. Prelude.

Let us see Jesus on the road which led to Jerusalem, where our Divine Saviour was going, to sacrifice Himself for us.

II. Prelude.

Grant, O Lord, that our love for Thee may render us prompt and generous, in executing all that Thou demandest of us.

I. Point.

Jesus manifested His love by delivering Himself up to death for us: it is by suffering in His cause that we manifest ours for Him.

It came to pass when the days of His Assumption were accomplishing, that He steadfastly set His Face to go to Jerusalem. Our Saviour was not ignorant of the conspiracy that the chief-priests and the pharisees had formed against His Person; He knew too what the result would be. He foresaw the hour of His Death approaching, and could number the dreadful torments which would precede it. Nevertheless, He went up to Jerusalem of His own accord, though it was to be the scene to Him of disgrace and suffering.—Why did He go?—To prove to what a degree He loved us, He willed to face the enemies of our salvation, to go forth to war against them; knowing that His apparent defeat would issue in a glorious triumph for us.—What should this teach us, but that we ought, with promptitude and generosity to make any sacrifice God asks of us, suffer ing patiently any sorrow—sickness—humiliation which He permits us to pass through. The triumph they assure to us is as certain as was the triumph which followed the humiliation and sufferings of our Master. *If we be dead with Him, we shall also live with Him : if we suffer, we shall also reign with Him.* Let us reflect upon the manner in which we prepare ourselves for trials and difficulties : do we turn aside from the path of duty and go into the bye-ways of self-will and cowardice? *Our Lord steadfastly set His Face to go to Jerusalem;* do we say to Him, when trouble is at hand : *I will follow Thee whithersoever Thou goest?*

II. Point.

It is to our eternal interest to be generous in the service of our Master.

God will not allow Himself to be outdone in generosity; of this we are certainly convinced, but we often forget it. If we follow Him closely, we shall ever find ourselves under the immediate influence of His beneficence and His bounty. From His Hand we shall receive a hundredfold, even in this life, in return for any efforts or sacrifices made on our part, out of love for Him. Jesus seems to speak to us, as He did to the Apostles, and to put before us a choice,—either to go with Him up to Jerusalem and share in His sufferings, or to follow some other road.—He lets us know beforehand what to expect if we accompany Him : we go forward to meet contempt, derision, humiliation, and the Cross,—but by the eye of faith, we see the open Sepulchre beyond, and that the enemies' three short days of exultation are quickly at an end. Can we hesitate about taking the same road as Jesus did? if we have gone aside, or loitered, or even turned back, let us not lose a moment in useless regrets; but remembering our first choice, renew in ourselves our first fervour, and set ourselves more steadfastly to follow in the Footsteps of our Lord.

Colloquy.

O Jesus, I hear Thee explaining the difficulties Thou didst expect to encounter, as Thou didst set out on the road indicated by Thy Heavenly Father, and yet Thou saidst to Thy Disciples: *Follow Me.* Thou dost ask me to bear Thee company, even up to Calvary.—Can I refuse? If my frailty suggest the question: Is there no cause of apprehension, that I perish in the midst of so many dangers? at least give me courage to reply: No! *though I should walk in the midst of the shadow of death I will fear no evils, for Thou art with me.*

Resolution.

I will follow Thee whithersoever Thou goest.

Thought for the Day.

I will fear no evils, for Thou art with me.

Prayer.

Take, O Lord, and receive.

First Sunday in Lent.

Jesus was tempted in the Desert.

Jesus was led by the Spirit into the desert to be tempted by the devil.—S. Matt. iv.

I. Prelude.

Let us represent to ourselves Jesus in the middle of the desert, where He had been alone, and fasting, for forty days and forty nights. The devil approached Him in human form.

II. Prelude.

For us, O Lord, it was that Thou didst suffer the prince of darkness to tempt Thee to sin; by Thy victory over him Thou dost instruct and encourage us.

I. Point.

The temptation of our Lord was threefold;—relative to the *concupiscence of the flesh, the concupiscence of the eyes, and the pride of life.*

It is recorded in the holy Gospel that after our Blessed Lord's long Fast, He was hungry. Satan adapts himself to circumstances; it was the moment, he thought, to tempt Jesus to a sin of sensuality. *If Thou be the Son of God, command that these stones be made bread,*—so to satisfy the demands of nature before the hour when His Heavenly Father should direct the Angels to minister to His necessity.

If tempted in like manner to gratify our appetite unduly, or out of time, we must remember the words of our Lord: *Not in bread alone doth man live*, and with these rebuke the tempter.—He was next permitted to exercise an extraordinary power over the Body of our Lord :—*the devil took Him up into the holy city and set Him on a pinnacle of the Temple ;* and this time He himself quotes the words of Holy Writ, to make the temptation of vain-glory all the more plausible. *Cast Thyself down*, he said—to prove the truth of God's Word—*for He hath given His Angels charge over Thee, that in their hands they shall bear Thee up ;* but Jesus shows us, by His reply—*Thou shalt not tempt the Lord Thy God*—that we must not tempt God by running into danger either of body or soul. His Angels' care over us extends only so far as we are conforming ourselves to His manifest Will. All that might be done which appears great or useful, merely out of vanity, boastfulness, or to attract attention to ourselves, is most reprehensible. We cannot ask God's blessing or assistance about an act of vain-glory, however cleverly disguised it may be as a virtue.—Although again defeated by Jesus, Satan returns to the charge ; and to carry out his plan of assault, places our Lord on the top of a high mountain, whence could be seen *all the kingdoms of the world and the glory of them.*—He, the prince of this world, claims his right as such, and is as ambitious still, as on the day when he was driven out of Heaven : he again seeks to usurp the divine prerogatives of God, and dares to offer a bribe to Jesus, to induce Him to fall down and adore Him. —It behoves us to beware of the temptation of ambition.—We see what it is—in Satan. From Jesus we learn how to repel it.—*The Lord thy God shalt thou adore, and Him only shalt thou serve.*

II. Point.

All meet with temptations; they prove, indeed, that we are striving after perfection.

Jesus was tempted:—who then can expect or hope to be free from temptation? The perfect Life of our Lord excited the malice of the devil, and he brought into action all his most subtle artifices to make the temptations, as he vainly supposed—irresistible. No degree of holiness can exempt us from similar trials; how often has God permitted His Saints to be proved by them, so that their fidelity and the power of His grace in them, might together be manifested. The most advanced in spirituality are the most careful in avoiding occasions of sin; they guard most vigilantly the outposts of the soul—the senses; they are quickly alive to the first suggestions of evil; they know by experience—sometimes dearly won—the necessity of calmness and recollection in the midst of temptation. By our Lord we are instructed how to meet temptations of every kind; how in humility, but with great confidence, to resist them; so that the arch-deceiver himself will take flight, before the good Angels whom God will send to minister to us, and to strengthen us. *Begone, Satan!* it is written:—*When we have been proved, we shall receive the crown of life.*

Colloquy.

Jesus, I beseech Thee, by Thy victory in the desert, aid me in all times of temptation. And if by the power of Thy grace, I escape from the assaults of the enemy, may I never feel secure from further attacks, but increase in prayerfulness and watchfulness,—in distrust of myself, and confidence in Thee,—to Whom be everlasting thanks for every victory gained!

RESOLUTION.

In times of apparent security to watch and pray, lest I fall into temptation.

THOUGHT FOR THE DAY.

Blessed is the man that endureth temptation.

PRAYER.

Our Father, and Hail Mary.

Second Sunday in Lent.

The Transfiguration of our Lord.

JESUS taketh unto Him Peter, and James, and John his brother, and bringeth them up into a high mountain apart: And He was transfigured before them: And His Face did shine as the sun: And His garments became white as the snow: And behold there appeared to them Moses and Elias, talking with Him: And Peter said to JESUS: Lord, it is good for us to be here: if Thou wilt, let us make here three tabernacles, one for Thee, and one for Moses, and one for Elias: And as He was yet speaking, behold a bright cloud overshadowed them: And lo, a voice out of the cloud, saying: This is My Beloved Son, in Whom I am well pleased: hear ye Him.—S. MATT. XVII.

I. Prelude.

We represent to ourselves Mount Thabor: on it we see our Lord in glory.—We see the three Apostles who accompanied Him.

II. Prelude.

Give us, O Saviour, to remember that from Thabor Thou didst pass to Calvary:—all the joys of this world are transitory, the glory which fadeth not is ours after death.

I. Point.

Jesus selected three Disciples to witness His Transfiguration. They represent those who are called to the Religious Life.

Our Divine Master chose Peter and James and John as His companions on this occasion, from amongst the twelve Apostles. Why was this preference shown?—Because these three loved Him the most.—It is thus that God acts towards souls that are worthy of His special favours: He communicates Himself to them, and calls them apart to enjoy tokens of His peculiar friendship. Generally these chosen souls are recipients of God's greater favours, on account of their past fidelity to His lesser ones,—to encourage them to be more faithful still,—and to evince His love towards them. Some are called apart from the rest of the world, and led by Jesus up the heights of the Thabor of Religion, where He imparts to them divine secrets which are hidden from others. There He instructs them practically concerning the Mystery of His Cross—His sufferings and theirs. O Sweet Saviour, deign to increase our love for Thee, so that we may courageously enter into the spirit of Thy sorrowful Mysteries, even in the midst of spiritual joy, such as the Apostles experienced when beholding their Master clothed in heavenly light. What happiness we feel when our Lord appears to us, adorned with the beautiful attractiveness of His love; and shows us His divine charms, so that our hearts may be captivated, our love may become all His—and remain His alone, when all sensible consolation shall have passed away.

II. Point.

Jesus speaks of His approaching Death.

Our Lord conversed with Moses and Elias. He spoke to them of the suffering and ignominy He would have to endure, and of His Death. In the midst of His glory, He thinks of His Passion, and to His friends He mentions it. His love for all mankind is so great, so absorbing, that at all times He has the thought before Him, that He is our Saviour. He appeared only once on Mount Thabor, and there, spoke only of the proof He was about to give of His love —of the laying down of His Life for man's salvation. Once He appeared in glory: but throughout His Life He carried the Cross—all the way from the Stable to Golgotha. Saint Peter would detain his Master there, where he beheld Him thus clothed in light, and exclaimed: *Lord, it is good for us to be here*:—he forgot, or did not yet fully understand, that no sensible joy is durable in this life. The spiritual delights which Jesus causes His elect to experience, do not always last.—A further privilege awaited the Apostles ere they returned to the toil of their daily life: they were permitted to hear the Voice of God the Father, proclaiming the Divinity of their Lord; and this made so deep an impression on their minds that, thirty-five years afterwards, Saint Peter refers to it, and repeats the words heard from Heaven on Mount Thabor: *This is My Beloved Son: hear ye Him.* May they make a like impression on our hearts and minds.—After the Transfiguration *they saw no one any more, but only Jesus.*—So it should be with us also, as we meditate on that which we have seen and heard, on the holy Mount.

Colloquy.

It was to Thy greatness, Thy majesty, Thy holiness, O my Jesus, that the Voice from Heaven witnessed in so wonderful a manner:—*Thou art the Everlasting Son of the Father.*—I rejoice with the Apostles, and offer Thee the homage of my affection; being ready to prove its sincerity, by accompanying Thee to Calvary, and enduring all the trials Thou mayst please to give me to bear.

Resolution.

To be more grateful to Jesus for taking me apart with Him,—that I may *see Him only*, and *hear Him.*

Thought for the Day.

They saw no one any more, but only Jesus.

Prayer.

Soul of Christ.

Third Sunday in Lent.

Our Lord casts out a devil which possessed a dumb man.

They brought to Jesus a dumb man, possessed with a devil. —S. Matt. ix.

I. Prelude.

Let us see this man in the Presence of Jesus: he cannot speak to Him, but others ask our Lord to restore to him the use of speech.

II. Prelude.

Preserve us from a yet more dangerous evil, O Almighty God, that of spiritual dumbness, of which this demoniac is a figure.

I. Point.

The characteristics of spiritual dumbness.

The spirit of darkness, who had deprived this unfortunate man of the power of speech, exercises a still more tyrannical influence upon souls over which he has gained the mastery. Sometimes he paralyses spiritual force, and prevents souls from speaking to God, either about the faults which may prove their destruction, or the virtues of which they stand in need; or they have no voice to praise His goodness, nor to publish His glory. Sometimes the evil spirit puts a restraint upon the heart, and inspires persons with a fear of opening theirs to those in whom they ought to confide. To a devoted friend, an able director, a good superior—

capable of recalling them to their religious and moral duties by means of good advice—they will not make known their failings, nor the dangers they are incurring : for them alone they have no words at command.—In other cases, the devil deprives persons of that zeal for God, which formerly rendered them so eloquent in persuading others to enter the paths of virtue; now they have nothing to say on God's behalf; or if they attempt it, their language is devoid of life, it finds no echo in the hearts of others.—Lastly, in the minds of some, the spirit of darkness produces heavy clouds of sadness, so that they maintain a morose silence; melancholy renders virtue repulsive to their imagination, and they are plunged in the depths of discouragement and despair. We should understand how dangerous these different forms of Satan's power are; if we are so unhappy as to be under his influence in any way, no time must be lost in seeking Jesus and asking Him to heal our souls.

II. Point.

What the remedies are which we should employ against spiritual dumbness.

Evidently the different characteristics of this malady necessitate different forms of treatment, and the application of a fitting remedy in each particular case. But it may safely be affirmed that in whatever way a soul be affected by spiritual muteness, it should be, like the dumb man in the Gospel, presented to Jesus—directed to Him. If during the time of prayer and other exercises of piety, the soul can find nothing to say to the All-powerful Physician, let it remain humbly in His Presence, think upon its great need of help, its dependence on His mercy, and of all that Jesus has done to ensure its salvation. As a consequence of these considerations it becomes easier to ask Jesus for the use of our spiritual faculties; and that we may be re-animated, by His grace, in the spirit of fervour and of divine love. Doubtless He will have pity on us, and deliver us from the power that the devil seeks to assert. It is plain that the renunciation of all self-will, and confidence in a wise and faithful counsellor, are two indispensable things in going to Jesus to be cured of this disease of the soul. They are proofs of humility; consequently we shall be more likely to obtain from Him deliverance from spiritual dumbness, and grace to make a good use of the gift of speech. So shall we be enabled to sanctify ourselves, by a renewed intercourse with God; and by our intercourse with others, to promote their sanctification also.

Colloquy.

I thank Thee, O Jesus, that in considering this manifestation of Thy power in casting out devils, my soul is enlightened concerning the dangers to which I am exposed. —May this consideration produce in me more circumspection in avoiding the snares which the dumb spirit may lay for me; and more fidelity in following the spiritual advice given by those who direct me. Preserve me from becoming the slave of my own inclinations, which may lead me to maintain a dangerous silence of heart and soul: may I never lose the power of speaking to Thee, O my Jesus—of telling Thee all my needs, and assuring Thee of my love.

Resolution.

Never to give way to sadness, or moroseness; remembering that through these I may lose the power of conversing with God.

THOUGHT FOR THE DAY.

My mouth shall speak the praise of the Lord.

PRAYER.

Take, O Lord, and receive.

Fourth Sunday in Lent.

The Miracle of the Multiplying of the Loaves.

JESUS saw the great multitude, and He had compassion on them, and began to teach them many things: And when the day was now far spent, His Disciples came to Him, saying: This is a desert place, and the hour is now past: Send them away, that going into the next villages and towns, they may buy themselves meat to eat: And He answering said to them: Give you them to eat. And JESUS took five loaves and two fishes, and gave to His Disciples to set before the five thousand: And they all did eat.—S. MARK VI.

I. PRELUDE.

Let us go in spirit into the desert, where Jesus is about to feed miraculously the multitude who have followed Him there.

II. PRELUDE.

Give us grace, O Lord, to understand with what merciful goodness Thou dost come to the help of those who forget themselves in attending to Thy holy teaching.

I. Point.

Jesus shews His compassion towards the multitude:—the reason of this.

Let us first contemplate Jesus, our Divine Master, as He stands in the midst of His hearers.—His outward appearance betokens His goodness—His gentleness; we observe the calm dignity of His bearing. Far from being wearied by the presence of this crowd of persons, who had remained with Him throughout the day, He will not suffer them to depart: His Heart is moved with compassion, and He tells His Disciples that they must not send them away fasting. It is ever thus with Jesus!—His Heart is touched where He finds true fidelity in those fervent souls, who cannot withdraw themselves from His Presence; and even forget themselves in their enjoyment of the delights they find in it. We see the Apostles pre-occupied and disquieted; they ask their Master promptly to dismiss the people.—But to such a prayer as this Jesus does not listen. When our requests are dictated by self-interest and impatience, we must not expect an answer favourable to our wishes. We should rather, in considering those who were concerned in this miracle, prefer to follow the example of the multitude; who, entirely occupied with Jesus, forgot all else, even the necessity of taking food. O Jesus, may we have only eyes to see Thee, only ears to listen to Thee, hearts to love Thee, and eagerness to seek Thee; so shall we win Thy favour; and Thou wilt feed us with spiritual food, and, if needs be, wilt wonderfully provide bodily sustenance also.

II. Point.

Jesus cares for our bodies as well as our souls.

Let us admire the goodness of our Lord. The people were lost in wonder as they received His divine instructions; but He Whose power equals His goodness, observed their wearied condition of body, and as God, He would provide miraculously for their wants. Ordering the Apostles to make them sit down, and taking in His Hands the five loaves and the two fishes, He lifted His Eyes to Heaven, and blessed them, and commanded the Apostles to distribute them to the assembled people;—upwards of five thousand ate and were fully satisfied. Yes! to our Heavenly Father let us give humble thanks for His goodness in taking care of the multitude of His creatures that are on the earth: but above all we should praise Him for His mercy, which causes Him to multiply the Precious Food of His Body and Blood, in every place, for the nourishing of our souls. Whilst thus adoring our Lord—All-powerful and All-good—we shall learn to confide more in His Providence, and lay down at His Feet all fear and anxiety concerning the wants and necessities of both body and soul.

Colloquy.

O my God, when I think of the numberless graces which Thou hast granted me, I must condemn the disquietude and distrust about the future, which sometimes arises within me. My daily bread will not fail—neither that which is necessary for my body, nor for my soul. Both belong to Thee, and Thou wilt take care of what is Thine. Help me never again to be solicitous for my own life in any way; but to leave all that concerns it in Thy Hands, O my Father, Who knowest so well of what I have need.

Resolution.

To look to Jesus for all,—whether in temporal or spiritual matters.

Godhead, and invited mankind to listen to His teaching. At His Death, as He was expiring in the midst of every circumstance of ignominy, all nature declared the fact of His Divinity, and reproached the Jews with the Deicide they had committed. His own words were verified in His own case, and they are still verified in our daily life. *Whosoever shall exalt himself shall be humbled: And he that shall humble himself shall be exalted.*—True glory shall be the portion of the lowly-minded, whilst the proud shall be despised. For instance, God often manifestly blesses the humble labours of one who possesses no brilliant talents, nor deep learning; and renders fruitful, modest, patient zeal; so that good works, done for God's glory alone, form a halo of benediction even in this world, and an unfading crown of glory in the next. In a contrary case, there is often a great display of knowledge and skill in the employment of means to effect a good purpose; but because human pride is directing the undertaking, hopes are deceived; —God renders proud designs barren and ineffectual. Carefully, then, must we avoid seeking any glory apart from that glory which it appertains to God alone to bestow.

Colloquy.

To Thee only, O my God, be honour and glory, and to me contempt and disdain; I can pretend to nothing more. And, by Thy grace, I will render myself conformable to Thy Divine Son; and retain as my due, no vestige of honour. May I never be ashamed to repeat in word and action: *If I glorify myself, my glory is nothing:*—may I also put this truth so deeply into my heart, that it may destroy the very root of all false pride and vain-glory. In Thine own good time do Thou permit me, O Jesus, to share in Thy exaltation.

He had become the admiration of the people; nevertheless He carried humility so far, as to proclaim aloud, before His enemies—the scribes and pharisees: *If I glorify Myself, My glory is nothing;* adding that He had no other glory than that which came from His Father. It is our divine Model Who makes use of this language, and by it strongly urges us to refer to God alone all the good which we may be enabled to do. Can we ever glorify ourselves with regard to our good deeds, when we remember that if others honour us in consequence of them, it is because we are acting for Jesus and by His grace? and it is His delegated power which is acknowledged in us. Can we be ambitious of glory, when Jesus, to Whom it is so justly due, would take none to Himself on earth? but entirely referred the honour offered Him by men, to His Father. Never should we render ourselves guilty of such an injustice; but rather acknowledge that humiliation and contempt ought to be our portion. Do we not desire to share the lot of the God-Man, and to practise the doctrine of humility which He taught by word and example?

II. Point.

God takes care to exalt such as are truly humble.

This truth is proved in all those Mysteries of our Saviour's Life, which peculiarly evince His wonderful humility. At His Birth, when veiled beneath the weakness of infancy, and the externals of poverty, Angels appeared and published His glory.—At His Baptism, the heavens were opened, and a divine Voice announced Him to be the Beloved Son of God.—When speaking on Mount Thabor of the humiliations and apparent defeat He would meet with at the hands of His enemies, again the Voice from Heaven proclaimed His

I. Prelude.

Let us represent to ourselves the road strewed with palm-branches; and the crowd that is accompanying Jesus.

II. Prelude.

Divine Lord, enter triumphantly into our hearts in Holy Communion, and do not suffer us to imitate the inconstancy of those who gathered round Thee, when Thou didst, as on this day, enter Jerusalem.

I. Point.

The lessons to be learned from our Lord's entrance into Jerusalem.

The Church rejoices to-day at the remembrance of the triumphal verification of the prophecy: *Shout for joy, O Daughter of Jerusalem: Behold Thy King will come to Thee, the Just, and Saviour: He is poor.* We see Jesus, maintaining His wonted appearance of lowliness and meekness, although (as He foreknew) He was to be the Object of universal attention and applause when He entered the devoted city. The crowd believed themselves sincere in their demonstration of joy and respect,—but Jesus knew that the major part of them would, before the week had expired, be joining in shouts of mockery, and in acts of derision; and that they, who now cried out *Hosanna*, would shortly change their exclamations of welcome into: *Let Him be crucified.* All this should teach us to beware of excited feelings of piety;—they will not last, and they leave the soul hard, and cold, and exhausted. Agitation of mind and heart is not compatible with perseverance; there is but a step between mere demonstrativeness in religion, and its complete disappearance. It is not difficult to grasp the thought which Jesus would inspire us with to-day. Let us unite in singing His praises, as His faithful Disciples did: let us welcome Him as He comes to visit us, and prepare the way for Him by casting at His Feet the superfluities of undue affection for creatures, and the vaunting, hollow branches of self-esteem and vain-glory. Our symbols of triumph to-day are borne in *His* honour, *we* have not yet won the palm: we are, however, accompanying our King towards the Heavenly Jerusalem, and have begun those songs of praise here below, which shall one day swell into an eternal *Hosanna in the highest.*

II. Point.

Blessed is He that cometh in the Name of the Lord.

Jesus was on His way into the city of Jerusalèm, where a Throne and a Crown were awaiting Him. Is was meet that He should be hailed as One coming in the Name of the Lord, although they who greeted Him little knew the deep import of the words they used. The Son of David was bringing in His royal Hands, gifts of pardon, and of deliverance, and of peace; and from the Throne on which they will place Him, He will dispense these gifts until the end of time. *Blessed is He that cometh in the Name of the Lord.* God made use of the multitude to fulfil His designs; had they held their peace, the stones would have cried out, and proclaimed that their Creator was passing by. In the midst of this triumph *Jesus wept*, as He spoke of the destruction which was coming upon Jerusalem, the ingratitude and crimes of her inhabitants rendering this destruction inevitable. The contrast between the external signs of joy, and the internal reality of rebelliousness against God was so vivid—so grievous, that it moved our compassionate Saviour to tears. Let us look within ourselves and see if there be any cause for Jesus to sorrow over us ;—are we truly sincere? Do we praise and glorify our King, not with our lips only, but with faithful, loyal hearts?

Colloquy.

Give me, O Jesus, the grace of sincerest gratitude, and as I go to meet Thee to-day, and welcome Thee into my heart, I trust that Thou wilt find nothing therein to cause Thee sorrow. Amongst the joyous but inconstant throng, by whom Thou wast accompanied into Jerusalem, some few there were who remained faithful—being true of heart, and devoted to their Master. With them I would celebrate Thy praise, and rejoice greatly, with holy heartfelt joy, in singing Hosanna to our King.

Resolution.

I will glorify Jesus, not only with my lips, but in my heart.

Thought for the Day.

Blessed is He that cometh in the Name of the Lord.

Prayer.

Soul of Christ.

Easter Sunday.

The Joys of Easter.

This is the Day which the Lord hath made; let us be glad and rejoice therein.—Ps. CXVII.

I. Prelude.

We see, by faith, our Lord rising from the Sepulchre.

II. Prelude.

O Risen Lord, we beseech Thee, replenish our hearts with holy gladness, as we remember that Thy Passion and Death are past; that as Man Thou art now impassible, and that Death hath no more dominion over Thee.

I. Point.

The joy of Easter is comprehended in the words: *He is risen.*

Can we enter into the joy with which the Angels announced the fact that Jesus had risen? Never before had they had such a charge confided to them—that of keeping guard over the dead Body of Him Who is their Eternal King.—With what adoring vigilance must they have watched that lifeless Form, until they saw—what no human eye might gaze upon—the first movement of restored life; the return of the Holy Soul of Jesus to His Sacred Body, henceforth and for ever to be positively impassible and immortal. Happy Angels of the Sepulchre! how gladly did they impart to the holy women the good tidings, and recal to their memory the words our Lord had spoken to them that *the third day He would rise again.* How interested are the Angels in all that concerns our sorrows and our joys!—We are taught that our Lord's Resurrection was next made known to His Blessed Mother; not even an Angel might carry the tidings to her, He would Himself turn her mourning into gladness. Who can picture that meeting? The Son of Mary stands before her:—in the Stable of Bethlehem, and on Mount Calvary she had held Him in her arms, and shared in His humiliations and His sufferings: now she participates in His triumph, as she beholds Him the Victor over Death and Hell.—If we can only in a little degree enter into Mary's joy, it is because we have not passed through the depths of her sorrows: but our own Easter joy will surely be increased as we think of hers.

II. Point.

The words *He is risen* are a source of strength, founded on faith; and consolation founded on hope.

Who could realise what this life would be without the glorious beacon-light of the Resurrection of our Lord? *If Christ be not risen again, your faith is vain; If in this life only we have hope in Christ, we are, of all men, most miserable.* But now over the portals of the grave are written in shining characters the Angel's declaration: *He is risen*, and death is deprived of its horrors, as we see the stone rolled back from the Holy Sepulchre. Sometimes our faith is weak: hope, as it were, dies down within us, and we dread the separation of soul and body, as if they were never to be reunited:—our faith becomes strong again, our hope revives, as we stand and gaze into the forsaken Tomb in Joseph's garden. *He is not here.*—When we weep over the grave of some one dear to us, does not our sadness give way to joy, when we hear the Voice of our Risen Lord, saying: *I am the Resurrection and the Life, he that believeth in Me, although he be dead, shall live.* Let our rejoicing to-day be in union with that of the holy Angels and their Queen, as we think of them, together celebrating in Heaven the victory won on the first Easter morning.

Colloquy.

How great, O Lord Jesus, must Thy joy have been in giving such joy to the holy Angels, and to Thy dear Mother; Thou didst make them the first witnesses of Thy triumph over Death. Bestow on me the grace to rejoice with them—and with Thee; grant that my faith in the power of Thy Resurrection may never waver; that my hope in Thee, my Risen Lord, may never fail. I will look more confidently beyond the grave, knowing that my resurrection is as certain as Thine own.

Resolution.

To excite in myself more joy and thankfulness, on account of my Saviour's Resurrection.

Thought for the Day.

He is not here, He is risen.

Prayer.

Take, O Lord, and receive.

Low Sunday.

Jesus appears the second time to the assembled Disciples.

After eight days, again His Disciples were within, and Thomas with them. Jesus cometh, the doors being shut, and stood in the midst, and said: Peace be to you: Then He saith to Thomas: Put in thy finger hither, and see My Hands, and bring hither thy hand, and put it into My Side; and be not faithless, but believing. Thomas answered and said to Him: My Lord and My God.—S. John xx.

I. Prelude.

Let us see Jesus convincing Thomas of the truth of the Resurrection.

II. Prelude.

Grant, O Lord, that we may gain from this meditation a greater distrust of ourselves, and a more entire confidence in Thy goodness.

I. Point.

How necessary it is to distrust ourselves, and avoid all singularity.

Although Jesus permitted the unbelief of Saint Thomas in order to render the fact of His Resurrection more incontestable, we should not hesitate to inquire into the cause of his infidelity. Why had this Apostle separated himself from the rest, at the time when our Lord first appeared to them? Was not his absence the result of singularity? and this, the cause of that fault of incredulity into which he fell? It seems evident that if he had received the graces Jesus communicated to His Disciples on the occasion of His first Apparition, he would not have been guilty of so much pride and presumption; but by keeping aloof from their company, he won for himself the inevitable singularity of losing the benefits of that first visit of his Divine Master; and of His special gift of Peace. We may observe the continued disquietude of Thomas, while the other Apostles were glad: for *they had seen the Lord.* We learn from this how dangerous it is for members of the Holy Church,—for those who live in community life, to continue in forgetfulness of this important truth, that it is in union of prayer there is strength; and that where there is a gathering together of the faithful in our Lord's Name, He is present according to His special promise.—God generally bestows His graces more largely where they are sought by means of the common exercises of piety and devotion; therefore the commandments of the Church, and the rules of a religious Order call upon those who are bound by the obligations of the one and the other, to assemble themselves together:—*with one mind and with one mouth to glorify God.* By unity of action and of belief, in accordance with the spirit and teaching of the Church, we are preserved from the unhappy consequences of private judgment. We are united together by the holy ties of charity and mutual confidence; we may edify one another, and sustain one another in moments of weakness or of affliction.

II. Point.

The goodness and condescension of Jesus towards His erring Disciple.

For eight days Thomas remained in this condition of unbelief and hardness of heart.—Is it not the servant's place to find his master? should not the sick man seek to be cured? But in this instance, because of the Divine Master's great goodness, it is He Who goes to look for the faithless servant; the Heavenly Physician offers—unsought—to heal the soul of His unbelieving Disciple. So large is His charity, that far from punishing him for his self-sufficiency, He made use of his fall as a means of fortifying his faith, and our own; so compassionating and so ingenious is it, that He passes over the presumption evinced by the conditions which this incredulous Apostle laid down, and accepts them literally. *Put in thy finger hither, and see My Hands, and bring hither thy hand and put it into My Side; and be not faithless but believing.* Within the Wounds of Jesus he found faith, and love, and peace; and became henceforth a faithful witness, and zealous confessor of the Resurrection of His Master.—In those Sacred Wounds we too may, at all times, find a renewal of confidence and love:—they are Fountains of grace, whence flow the living waters of life and of salvation.

Colloquy.

Thou, Who knowest and understandest all hearts, and dost condescend to our wishes with so much kindness, do Thou permit me, according to my heartfelt desire to touch, by faith, Thy Hands and Feet and Side. Grant that my soul, entering those very Wounds touched by Saint Thomas, may be lost in Thee, and live by Thy Divine Life;—then like him I shall be enabled by my zeal, to make amends for past infidelities; and by the exercise of charity, to gain hearts for Thee, O Jesus.

Resolution.

To shun all attachment to my own judgment, as being a mark of a proud and obstinate spirit.

Thought for the Day.

Thomas was not with them when Jesus came.

Prayer.

Soul of Christ.

DAYS OF RETREAT.

The Day of Retreat in March.

The inestimable value of the Cross.

God forbid that I should glory, save in the Cross of our LORD JESUS CHRIST*; by Whom the world is crucified to me, and I to the world.*—GAL. VI.

I. PRELUDE.

Let us represent to ourselves the Cross of our Lord Jesus Christ.

II. PRELUDE.

Enlighten us with Thy Divine Truth, O Jesus, and discover to us the value of the Cross, and of the suffering.

I. POINT.

The advantages of the Cross.

We often look upon sufferings and afflictions as a matter of grief and sadness, simply because we are so apt—so accustomed to judge of things according to human reason only. Thus our first thoughts especially, on any point are so different from what they would be, if we were continually influenced by the spirit of faith. The evils which seem to us so hard to bear, are alarming only to nature; but grace finds in them both life and nourishment. The Cross purifies us from the stains of sin, satisfies the justice of God, enriches us with abundant merits, unites us to Jesus in this life, and prepares us for the blessedness of Heaven. What inestimable advantages! Can the pain attached to either physical or mental suffering be allowed to enter into comparison with the happiness of growing in Thy love, O Saviour, and of becoming more intimately united to Thee? Thou art the Treasure of all faithful hearts, who have made experience of Thy sweetness: is it possible that any temporary affliction, if softened by the unction of Thy grace, could alarm us? Should we not remember that in the very act of accepting it, God marks another trait of resemblance to His own Son upon our souls? May He sustain our weakness, while we gladly receive the crosses He may be pleased to lay upon us; taking them from His Hand as a pledge of His love, and desiring to carry them to our life's end.

II. Point.

We do not love the Cross enough.

Our Divine Saviour, Whose goodness is infinite, provides for each one of His Elect the cross best fitted for his sanctification. He forms it according to the needs, and proportions it according to the strength of each; and He never sends a cross without offering at the same time the grace necessary to carry it aright. Some He afflicts with bodily sufferings—others with the loss of property or friends: these with great spiritual trials—those with little vexations, often more difficult to bear than severe tribulation. He has special designs with regard to each: He would have all to participate really in the merits of His Sacrifice. O Jesus, grant that we may not misunderstand Thy divine goodness when Thou designest to favour us, by giving us a cross to bear. Thou visitest us in two ways, by joy and by tribulation: joy indeed tends to render the pain of exile less bitter, and to make our labours less wearisome; yet the effects of affliction are infinitely more precious, for Thou hast taught us that this pays our debts, and increases our resemblance to Thee. Have we learned to regard sufferings in this manner? Whatever be our trials, our troubles, let us place ourselves in God's Hands; and ask Him to give to us, as He sees fit, either consolations or crosses.—Let either be accompanied by Thy grace, O God, we need desire nothing more.

Colloquy.

Ought I not indeed to feel it to be a real honour—a true mark of God's favour—if I am permitted to carry a portion of Thy Cross, O my Jesus? Dare I ask to be made a partaker of Thy Sufferings? Thou dost reserve the dearest tokens of Thy love for such as prove themselves worthy to suffer for Thy Sake. My weakness, my want of courage, may sometimes give rise to apprehension lest the Cross should prove too heavy; but do Thou banish my fears, and remind me that Thy grace will lighten it; that in Thy strength I shall be able to bear it, and that *if I suffer, I shall also reign with Thee.*

Resolution.

Willingly to suffer, in union with my Dear Saviour, all that may appear to me painful and humiliating.

THOUGHT FOR THE DAY.

If any man will come after Me, let him deny himself, and take up his Cross and follow Me.

PRAYER.

Soul of Christ.

The Day of Retreat in March.

CONSIDERATIONS.

The heart of a truly religious person should be disengaged from all that does not lead it up to God.

Thou art the God of my heart, and the God that is my Portion for ever.—PSALM LXXII.

I. POINT.

In what true detachment consists.

Let us consider the salutary effects of religious detachment: freed from the anxieties which disturb the minds of worldlings, they who practise this detachment lose not their peace and serenity. We may be attached to three different kinds of objects: to other persons—to things—and to one's self; but the heart really consecrated to God is wholly detached from all created things. It contracts no mere natural friendships, nor attachments, fearing to deprive God of what belongs to Him alone: it forms such spiritual relationships, as may be helpful in rendering it yet more faithful to Him. These rightly maintained do not disturb the soul, but serve to unite it more closely to Jesus: but there should be a readiness to sever even these, did they become an obstacle to the perfect love which it owes to Him. They who practise detachment are far from being troubled by the withdrawal of any particular person's presence or sympathy; they are fully aware that God can and will turn to their spiritual advancement any privation of this sort, even when it would appear to entail present grave consequences. They then possess Him still more entirely, and learn to repose more completely on His loving assistance. Let us not forget that we must carefully watch over our affections, lest they betray us in our intercourse with those who possess merely natural attractions: they may so easily come between us and God, like thick clouds which arise and obstruct the clear light of the sun. It behoves us then, if we would retain a relish for heavenly things, to watch against any attachment which is not formed in God, and for God.—The want of detachment with regard to objects by which we are surrounded, may also produce undesirable results in one who aims at perfection. There may be snares lurking beneath all that which is most agreeable to our eyes, most in accordance with our taste and natural inclinations; let us be on our guard, lest even inanimate things lead our hearts away from, instead of up to, God. It is meet and right, O Jesus, that hearts made for Thee, and consecrated to Thy love, should keep themselves disengaged absolutely from all created things; and still farther, should die to all that they have renounced. Yes! they are wise and truly spiritual, who set their affections on nothing here below; but look on all, that is not for eternity, as passing vanities. Implant, O Lord, this lesson deeply in our hearts, so that no person, no thing, may hinder our affections from tending directly towards Thee. Deign to illuminate our minds with the clear light of faith, by which we shall understand that if we would enjoy real peace and glorify Thee, we must be dead to the world, *our lives being hidden with Christ in God.*

II. Point.

A heart, to be in a state of true liberty, must be detached from self.

After being delivered from attachment to exterior things, we must seek to acquire that to which it is yet more difficult to attain—detachment from self. To arrive at this, a very faithful correspondence, on our part, to the operations of the spirit of God, is necessary. But divine assistance will not fail us, and we shall certainly succeed, if we firmly purpose to do so. If there be a paradise in this world, it exists for the heart that is free from the many forms of self-love. It fears nothing, it is solicitous about nothing, it needs nothing save God, and it possesses Him :—an offence against Him is the only thing that can afflict it. Agitated though the world may be around a perfectly detached person, this affects him not; for he dwells, as it were, on the summit of the mountain, above the world's storms and tempests, in a region of perpetual calm : he is free from emotion, if persecuted or humiliated : his whole attention is directed away from all that could interrupt his communion with his Heavenly Father. If he seek intercourse with his neighbour, it is to serve him—to do him good in some way : he still enjoys profound peace, because he is wholly bent on pleasing God alone. If we think for a moment of the many links which are allowed to bind hearts to creatures and to self, we are not surprised when we find them suffering extremely in the hour of separation from them. Our own conscience condemns us perhaps on this point. Do the changes which occur, the humiliations we have to bear, the privations imposed on us, disquiet our hearts? Are we convinced that a total disengagement is most important, if we would become more perfect? Is it not especially essential for us, who through human frailty, attach ourselves so easily to objects of vanity? Let us then seriously apply ourselves to study the tendencies of our heart's affections, and have the courage to root out those which have not God for their object. From Him we should constantly be asking strength to break the chains which tie us down to earth, and courage to sever the bonds of self-love; remembering that we have been dedicated to Him—*that we may not now live to ourselves, but unto Him Who died for us, and rose again.* Though all creatures should abandon us, we lose nothing if we lose not God.

The Day of Retreat in April.

Means for acquiring the habit of recollection.

Our conversation is in Heaven.—PHIL. III.

I. PRELUDE.

Let us represent to ourselves the state of perfection to which so many Saints have attained, by means of perseverance in the exercise of repressing natural inclinations.

II. Prelude.

O God, endow us with the spirit of religious restraint, and of reticence; and thus increase in us the facility of remaining in Thy Presence, absorbed in the thought of how best to please Thee.

I. Point.

To practise recollection constantly; it is necessary to mortify the senses, exterior and interior.

The senses are the inlets of the soul; a watch must be set to guard them perpetually, for by them death may enter, and exert its fatal power. Therefore it is that the masters of the spiritual life teach us, that if we would preserve our souls pure, we should become, as it were, blind, and deaf, and dumb: for by means of the senses, dangerous impressions may be made on the soul—the imagination may be sullied—and sin invade the heart. To attain the habit of recollection, not only should we turn our eyes from vanity, but also close our ears to vain and frivolous discourse. Yet it is not enough to watch over our exterior senses and to mortify them, if we do not use the same diligence in mortifying our interior senses:—susceptibility of emotion, hasty perceptions, or uncontrolled imaginings. This costs much to nature, in the way of combats, efforts, and sacrifices. The interior senses are like *enemies within the household*, they have a secret understanding with the evil part of our nature. In vain shall we shut the gates of the soul, and close the five avenues of the senses which lead to it, if we deliver ourselves unrestrainedly into the power of foes within; they will hold the soul captive, they will on their part close the avenues of grace, and obstruct the progress of the Life of Jesus Christ in us.

II. Point.

It is an illusion for religious persons, under a pretext of zeal, to engage in useless intercourse with the world.

We sometimes see persons whom God has withdrawn from the world, and placed in a Religious Order approved by the Church, that they may lead the life of Angels upon earth—we see even these (forgetful of their supernatural vocation) seeking satisfaction in vain and useless intercourse with the world; thus misappropriating that precious time they should give to the duties of their holy estate, and to the real obligations of their rule of life. Of such it could not be said *their conversation is in Heaven.* The trifles and futilities which occupy the time and attention of so many, ought to be incapable of affording gratification to those who are consecrated to Jesus Christ by the most holy of all engagements. Our senses will deceive us if we are not very watchful; let us not abandon ourselves to them; if we do so, we abandon ourselves to illusion. The treacherousness of our own secret passions is most lamentable; the transitory illusions of sense often cause the loss of eternal blessedness. And what a loss is this!—We must expect to pass through combats in securing our own salvation; but it is these very combats which will enhance the joy of belonging to Jesus entirely; of owning Him as our Sovereign Lord. If we have once tasted what this joy really is, it will of itself produce a great disgust for all earthly vanities, which are but temptations, and tend to corruption. We shall long to be free from all the deceits by which it is so easy for us to be seduced, and earnestly beg of God to deliver us from evil.

Colloquy.

☛ How sweet are the hope and the desire of possessing Thee,

O Jesus, eternally. To ensure their realisation can I consider any warfare too prolonged, any labour too arduous? To acquire the practice of the Presence of God, I know how important it is for me to keep my thoughts—my imaginations—my own judgment—under control; to banish susceptibility, curiosity, and dissipation. Draw my heart and mind so entirely away from myself, and the things of this world, that *my conversation may be now in Heaven.* Jesus and Mary, help me to imitate your equanimity and recollectedness, by striving while *in this world*, to be *not of it.*

Resolution.

To gain more self-control as a means of increasing in spirituality.

Thought for the Day.

Seeing Him Who is Invisible.

Prayer.

O Jesus, living in Mary.

The Day of Retreat in April.

CONSIDERATIONS.

On Holy Poverty.

Blessed are the poor in spirit: for theirs is the kingdom of Heaven.—S. MATT. V.

I. POINT.

The value and excellence of holy Poverty.

We may judge of the dignity of this virtue by the choice that our Lord Jesus Christ made of it. From the moment of His entrance into the world, during the whole course of His Life, and in His Death, He made holy poverty His constant companion. And in order to imitate Him how many kings and princes, and others possessed of wealth and position, have left a life of opulence and luxury to espouse holy poverty, and to enrich themselves with its treasures. What celestial riches does it not secure to those who embrace it! With them we pay our entrance into Heaven! The thought of death, which is so bitter to a heart captivated by the pleasures of this world, is full of gladness to such as have left all to make themselves like to Jesus Christ, and to honour His poverty. They who have done so are free from those innumerable cares which torment the slaves of wealth.—Who can count their difficulties in amassing, their anxieties when in possession of, and their sorrows in losing it? Holy poverty provides the precious ornaments, which the Spouses of the Son of God will wear before the Throne of the Divine Majesty; the tokens that they have followed Jesus in all the lowliness of this virtue. It assures to them eternal happiness, for does not He declare that *there is no one who has left house, or friends, or lands for His Sake, who shall not receive an hundred times as much, now in this present time; and in the world to come, life everlasting.* They who make the vow of poverty give little and gain much;—they leave all earthly advantages, and acquire those which are eternal;—they renounce perishable goods, and find laid up for them in Heaven those which can never decay. Let us therefore bless Thee, O Jesus, our Divine Spouse, for the favour Thou hast shown us, in calling us to participate in Thy poverty. Give us grace to understand the value of this virtue still more; inspire us with a truer love for it, so that we may practise it more perfectly. When we feel how unworthy we are of the benediction bestowed by our Lord on those who are poor in spirit, we should betake ourselves to the little house at Nazareth, and emulating the examples we there find, strive to adopt, in a more practical form, the essential parts of this most practical virtue.

II. Point.

The extent of religious Poverty that we should practise.

If we would exercise ourselves unsparingly in poverty, we must not only give up possession of all temporal goods, but retrench all superfluity in such things as we are permitted to use. This use should be restricted to what is simply necessary: we should be poor in our lodging, nourishment, and clothing; have nothing superfluous in any way whatever, nothing costly, nothing unsuitable to the condition of the poor. Is it not right that this spirit of poverty be that of the Spouses of Him Who was born in a Stable, lived in extreme indigence, and died on the Cross, despoiled of all? Is it not right that, making profession of imitating His virtues, we should aspire to become perfect in that one which He loved so much? Is it not right that we should be generous in regard to the sacrifice we have made to God, in engaging ourselves so solemnly to keep the vow of poverty? May there be no robbery in our holocaust; may we not be of the number of those who pride themselves on a spirit of poverty, avoiding at the same time all that is hard and painful—entailed by poverty. Some declare themselves ready to follow Jesus in His indigence, but on condition that they find all that is necessary for their comfort and convenience. Such poverty is but a phantom. They who would imitate Him through love, make no reservation in their offer to accompany Him; they will not go back from their proposition—*Master, I will follow Thee whithersoever Thou shalt go*—although the Son of Man reply: *that He hath not where to lay His Head.* Jesus! Thou Thyself art to us all that is necessary.—Thou art our happiness; in Thee we find all, for Thou art our God. Can we say this from the bottom of our heart? Are we true disciples of Him, *Who being rich, became poor for our sakes, that through His poverty we might be rich?*

Day of Retreat in May.

Our Lady's example given us to follow.

Behold the Handmaid of the Lord. Behold Thy Mother. —S. LUKE I., S. JOHN XIX.

I. PRELUDE.

Let us listen to Mary as she says: *Behold the Handmaid of the Lord:*—let us listen to the words of Jesus as He gives her to us: *Behold thy Mother.*

II. PRELUDE.

O Mary, who wast so perfect a model of humility, and of resignation to the holy Will of God, teach us how to yield ourselves wholly to its guidance; and looking upon thee as our Mother, may we strive to imitate thy virtues as Jesus would wish us to do.

I. POINT.

We honour the Son of Mary in honouring her, and imitating her virtues.

Next to the gratification which a good prince would feel in being beloved and revered by his people, would be the pleasure of knowing that his own mother is also beloved and revered, not only for his sake, but for hers also—on account of her virtues and her goodness.—How pleasing therefore must it be to Jesus when we strive to form a resemblance between ourselves and her, who called herself *the Handmaid of the Lord*, and whom He called—*Mother*. At this time, when the Church especially desires Her children to show their love and devotion towards our Lady, we do well to think over all those virtues which shone forth in her, and made her worthy to be chosen as the Mother of Jesus. When she discovered the meaning of the message brought by the Angel Gabriel her acquiescence was given in a spirit of profound humility, arising from the deep knowledge she had of herself; and which made her understand perfectly that, by nature, she was the servant of God, and consequently under an obligation to carry out His commands. The humility of our Lady proved her to be worthy of the high position to which she was to be called; she *humbled herself in the sight of the Lord*, as His Handmaid, *and He exalted her* to be the Mother of His Son, and Queen of Heaven and earth. We too are servants of God, not only by creation, but also by the profession we have made. We dwell in thought upon the lowliness of Mary, she who was the fairest and purest, the most favoured of all God's creatures; and we place it in contrast with our own. With what result? At least this thought should have the effect of increasing it. Do we consent fully, unreservedly, to all the demands of God? are we prompt in accepting His wishes and making them ours without a murmur? do we submit to the will of superiors? looking out beyond, with the eye of faith, to Him Whose Will directs all wills for our present good and our future exaltation, if we with our Lady, sincerely say to Him: *Behold the Handmaid of the Lord.*

II. Point.

The Mother of Jesus is our Mother.

Jesus and Mary—the Mother and the Son! The words she utters, as the Eternal Word is made Flesh are: *Behold the Handmaid of the Lord:* the words Jesus utters as He is leaving her to the care of the beloved Disciple, our representative, are: *Behold thy Mother.* The links which have bound Jesus to Mary are henceforth to bind us to her: her Mother's heart is to draw to itself the love of all who love her Son, whilst she will obtain from Him everything which her children tell her they want. Can He refuse any request that she makes on our behalf, since it is He Himself Who has knit us together in this sacred relationship? We gather round her, as the dying testament of Jesus is sealed by His Blood, and there on Calvary we learn from His Lips to call her by the name of Mother. She stood there; sharing in His spirit of resignation to the Heavenly Father's Will, and commended herself, with Jesus, into His Hands. We have seen her consenting to the Mystery of the Incarnation: her humility, her submissiveness is now called to a severer test; but she acquiesces in the divine purposes of God by consenting to the Death of her Son. We cannot honour Mary more than by keeping before our minds her likeness to Jesus, and tracing out the points of resemblance between them. Let us make good use of this season of special graces; and ask our Mother, now seated in Heaven, and crowned as Queen of the Angels and Saints, to obtain for us an increase of those virtues which rendered her worthy to be exalted above all other creatures, by *Him that is Mighty.*

Colloquy.

O Mary, my dear Mother, in thee and with thee I praise God for the privileges lavished on me, as thy child. Exert on my behalf thy power over the Heart of Jesus; tell Him all that I say to thee about my many spiritual necessities; and plead, as only a Mother can plead, with Him for my forgiveness when I displease Him and thee.—Obtain for me grace to be entirely submissive, under every circumstance, to the Will of God, so that His designs may be accomplished in me; that I may one day behold thee, my Mother, face to face.

RESOLUTION.

To be a truer child of Mary.

THOUGHT FOR THE DAY.

Mother of Jesus, and my Mother, pray for me.

PRAYER.

We fly to thy patronage.

The Day of Retreat in May.

CONSIDERATIONS.

On Modesty.

Let your modesty be known to all men: The Lord is nigh. —PHIL. IV.

I. POINT.

The necessity of interior modesty.

It is not sufficient that the Spouses of Jesus Christ have the exterior appearance of modesty: there is the other, not less necessary;—interior modesty. Saint Peter, after having recommended to Christians modesty in their attire, thus continues: *Let your adorning be of the hidden man of the heart in the incorruptibility of a quiet and a meek spirit, which is rich in the sight of God.* The ornament so precious in His Eyes then, is the spirit of meekness with regard to our neighbour, and the spirit of tranquillity with regard to one's self. Without this, what is the real condition of Religious? A studied manner may draw forth the esteem of men; an acquired appearance of modesty may cause them to seem holy in their eyes, but what are they before God, Who knoweth the secrets of the heart? *They resemble whited sepulchres, which outwardly appear to men beautiful. They seem to be just, but are inwardly full of hypocrisy and iniquity.* If our spiritual life be not united to God, if the desires of our heart be not regulated according to the promptings of His holy Will, then to us may the reproach be addressed: *I know Thy works that Thou hast the name of being alive: And Thou art dead.* Exteriorly modest we must indeed be; and we must be within that which we appear to be without. *With all watchfulness*, says the Wise Man, *keep thy heart, because life issueth out from it.* If in the least degree we cease to watch over our thoughts, our desires, our actions, we give entrance to the evil spirit, who is ever watchful. We must therefore by our vigilance oppose his vigilance,—be always on our guard, and so foil his attempts to surprise us: *The God of peace will be with us.* He is on our side, let us confide in Him; but this we shall be unable to do unless we have simple hearts, and can look up into our Father's Face with childlike confidence. Are we able to do this? Do we find any hypocrisy in our words and actions? Have we to reproach ourselves with faults of this nature? While we acknowledge them, let us make a firm resolution so to order our hidden life, that we may really be interiorly what we rightly strive to appear to be in the eyes of others. Thus to sanctify ourselves in body and soul, let us study the divine modesty and calm dignity of Jesus, begging Him to clothe us with these. Let us obey the injunction of the Apostle when he says: *Whatsoever things are pure, whatsoever modest, whatsoever just, whatsoever holy, whatsoever lovely, whatsoever of good fame, if there be any virtue, if any praise of discipline, think on these things.*

II. Point.

An interior modesty is the basis of other virtues. We may well consider that it is the recollection of God's Presence within us, which gives solidity to the edifice of our perfection. If we had a real personal experience of this truth, if we felt that our own union with God was based upon the consciousness of His Spirit's abiding in us, we should not evince so much vanity in our way of speaking—so much want of gravity in our intercourse with others: we should not manifest so great susceptibility and little mortification regarding all that may wound our self-love. We perhaps reject the good counsel given us on these points: it is ineffectual, because we are not seriously considering how to acquire interior modesty, and tranquillity of soul. Are we not agitated by different passions, which dispute with God for the possession of our hearts; and if He be driven out, then will they be tyrannised over by pride, vanity, jealousy, resentment, sensuality;—and how can we expect any repose? How can the foundation of true peace be laid in the midst of chaos? Long ago these passions should have been uprooted, whereas we have perhaps been encouraging their growth ; and if we have at the same time worn the mask of apparent modesty, we have added hypocrisy to the list. God sees the depth of our hearts, and knows our most secret imaginings ; it is profound respect for His holy Presence within us, that will alone render the correspondence perfect between our exterior actions and our hidden life. It is this deep respect then that we should seek to cultivate ; it would render our whole being subservient to Jesus : He would rule supreme : consequently, such an incongruity, such an inconsistency could not then exist, as the absence of interior restraint together with the appearance of exterior modesty ; or *vice versâ.* It is Jesus alone, by the sweet power of His grace, as Master over mind, and body, and soul, Who can rectify the balance between inward reality and outward seeming. When we feel that a disparity no longer exists, then and not till then may we humbly rejoice in the assurance that our modesty is pleasing in the sight of God.

LONDON : BURNS AND OATES.

www.ingramcontent.com/pod-product-compliance
Lightning Source LLC
Chambersburg PA
CBHW021114270326
41929CB00009B/882

* 9 7 8 3 3 3 7 2 5 6 8 2 1 *